The Bay Area at Your Feet

Revised Third edition

Compiled and revised from
San Francisco *Chronicle series,
"Bay Area at Your Feet"*

The Bay Area at Your Feet

Walks with San Francisco's
Margot Patterson Doss

with photos by
John Whinham Doss, M.D.

Don't Call It Frisco Press

Copyright © 1988 by Margot Patterson Doss
Published by Don't Call It Frisco Press

First edition of *Bay Area at Your Feet*
published by Chronicle Books in 1970.
Second edition, Presidio Press, 1981

Library of Congress Cataloging in Publication Data

Doss, Margot Patterson.
The Bay Area at Your Feet.

"Compiled and revised from San Francisco chronicle
series, 'Bay Area at Your Feet'."
Includes index.
1. Walking—California—San Francisco Bay region—
Guide books. 2. San Francisco Bay region—Description
and travel—Guide-books. I. Doss, John Whinham.
II. Title.
CV199.42.C22S2693 1981   917.94'604'53   80-20540
ISBN 0-917583-12-4

Cover design by Naomi Schiff
Typesetting by BookPrep, Gilroy, California
Printing by Delta Lithograph Co., Valencia, California

Contents

I saw a multitude of men coming toward us
—I saw them coming from every direction,
filling all the roads.
St. Francis of Assisi

It is to this advancing multitude that I
dedicate this book of loving exploration.
May they treasure and protect the sweet
land that is the Bay Area. Now, before it
is too late.

Introduction

The pleasures of walking, particularly in the Bay Area, were what I planned to consider in this introduction. Ours is a more pleasurable place to walk than most metropolitan places. However, it gets less so every day. So this is my subject instead, which by extension becomes man's place in nature.

In pursuing it, I went back to read what other walkers had written in their time. One beautiful passage by George Macaulay Trevelyan in his essay "Walking" embodies the kernel of the problem in a sort of gentle prophecy.

"From out of the depth of days and nights gone by and forgotten, I have a vision not forgettable, of making the steep ascent to Volterra [read Mount Tamalpais if you will] for the first time, under the circlings of the stars, the smell of unseen almond blossom in the air; the lights of Italy far below us; ancient Tuscany just above us, where we were to sup and sleep guarded by the giant walls. Few went to Volterra then, but years have passed, and now I am glad to think that many go, *faute de mieux*, in motor cars; yet so they cannot hear the silence we heard, or smell the almond blossom we smelt, and if they did, they could not feel them as the walker can feel."

If Trevelyan were to write his essay today, I think he would no longer be glad to think that many go to Volterra in motor cars. I am not glad that motor cars go up Mount Tam. For the motor car has been revealed as a Frankenstein monster in our culture, destroying not only the silence and the smell of almond blossom, but the air, the land, and the oceans too in its hunger for fossil fuels. Indeed, the pleasures that the automobile seemed to make accessible to all, the almond orchards and the vast starry silent places, have been among its victims. Today the best favor one can do for any place is to leave it inaccessible: not to build a road to it.

For the most part, we Americans hurtle headlong at sixty miles an hour, encapsulated in our armorplate-on-wheels, alienated from our fellow man, shut off by our speed from the beautiful world we seek. In our time roads have become not only "hardened arteries"—as Brooks Atkinson, another walker-writer, once described them—but worse, freeways, dangerous roaring raging rivers of steel, great untrammeled cataracts of metal far more harmful to the terrain and communities through which they go than most of the errosive streams the U.S. Army Corps of Engineers is so busy walling up and piping underground.

Not long ago, a member of the East Bay Regional Park District arranged for me to visit Brooks Island for a walk around it. It was an enlightening experience.

"Meet me at the Channel Marina in Richmond at 9:30 A.M.," he had said. "We'll embark from there."

To reach the Channel Marina I passed through endlessly sprawling and slummy industrial lands. There were no buildings more than two stories high. What few there were were surrounded, higgledy-piggledy, with vast flat empty unused spaces. Here and there were hulks of abandoned machinery. some of these raped once-virgin marshlands had "For Sale" signs among great concrete slabs where buildings once had stood. Some few were orange with dodder that had found the weeds reasserting themselves among the rubble of foundations. I was appalled at the waste of land, at the evidence of misuse of land. Here, for sale in the Bay Area, were hundreds of filled acres of bay which had been in use by industry less than ten years ago. Now, as hideous as any city bombed out and destroyed by war, they lie idle. Industry doesn't want them anymore.

Within six minutes after we left the Channel Marina, our boat docked on Brooks Island. It was land that seemed untouched by the hideousness of the mainland we had left. It was the bright fair land that is the California dream, a paradise as yet unbesmirched. Off to the right, Canada geese were rising from a long sandspit. A twinkle of sandpipers flitted along three horseshoes of beach any child would love. Shorebirds were calling from the pickleweed marsh of a tideflat. We walked along the shore toward Brooks

Island's hill and soon came upon an Indian mound. In the layers of this kitchen-midden, archeologists were painstakingly tracing out the preexisting culture. For 4,000 years human beings had lived on Brooks Island, thriving on the cockles, mussels, oysters, on game, fish, and vegetation, without damage to the land. Now, less than a hundred years after the heavy hand of "the gringo" had touched down, one could look in any direction and just beyond the surrounding water see ugliness and devastation.

It was only the week before that I had seen a new factory set down into the precious vineyard land of Sonoma County. Despite its handsome landscaping, that factory has a doomsday feel to me. It heralds the death of the sweet land surrounding it. Factories and their acres of parking lots have long since consumed the prune and almond orchards of Santa Clara County. Now they are stalking Sonoma County in a ridiculous chase after the worker. The worker, of course, has moved to what he thought was country, trying to escape in his automobile the factory-slums of the city. This is what suburban tracts are all about: escape from industrial and commercial ugliness—until there is nowhere left to escape to, for the high-tension electrical wires of industry have even intruded into our parks and preserves.

What is it that has made us at once so greedy and so wasteful of land? Only our ignorance.

What makes us exploit nature so selfishly? Only our inability to perceive the consequences.

How can we treat this lush land that is California so dismally, so dangerously? Our selfish profit-motive, to use a more digestible euphemism than the ugly old Anglo-Saxon word, greed. Make no mistake. The great industrialists, are already threatening us in the pocketbook. They can clean up the environment, they say, but it will cost you, the consumer.

As I stood on the Brooks Island shore, I suddenly realized that here, emerging, is a new pornography. Something is being hidden under the table. As the Victorian Age made sex obscene, so the Automotive Age, our own culture, is pretending that if we do not look at man's depredations, they don't exist. I blushed with shame for my arrogant race. No Mongolian horde ever wreaked such permanent damage on the land and sky as we. No plague of locusts ever irreparably laid waste such acreage as one could see all about. The contrast between the lovely natural land underfoot and the monstrously changed unnatural shorelines beyond was shocking.

A man in a car, insulated from reality, is to busy avoiding instant danger on the freeway to have time for safe reflection, or indeed understanding of the displacement of responsibility to the environment and what it really means. He isn't about to develop an ecological appreciation (especially when lumbermen leave a 300-foot cosmetic border of trees to hide the slash and erosion), much less an ecological conscience, until he shucks his two-ton, four-wheeled insulation. It is only when a man gets out on foot to walk in intimacy with the land that the ancient tribal memories return. How long since most motorists have smelled a fresh sea breeze clean upon their faces, or sensed the instant pungency of a bay tree in the sun?

With these thoughts heavy upon me, I took a step up the hill. The climb to the top of Brooks Island, like any climb, was harder walking than the beach. But as I climbed, quail ran. A pheasant flew heavily, flashing in the sunlight. The scent of chamomile came up from the grass. A garter snake wriggled off the path. A lark called. Within another hundred yards, the shame and burden of mankind's stupidities fell from my shoulders.

Soon I felt refreshed, invigorated, for walking is a healer, too. Like sleep, it knits us up, repairs our minds, and renews our strength. By the time I got back in the boat to return, my mind was full of resolve, keen to take up the good fight again.

As we chugged back into the shore wasteland, I was reminded of Marston Bates, who said, "In defying nature, in destroying nature, in building an arrogantly selfish, man-centered artificial world, I do not see how man can gain piece, or freedom, or joy."

Like Dr. Bates, "I have faith in man's future, faith in the possibilities latent in the human experiment: but it is faith in man as part of nature, working with the forces that govern the forests and the seas; faith in man sharing life, not destroying it."

Mine is a faith in man removed from his production-line-built conquerer's chariot. The man who understands we have only this one world to live in is man standing on the land in his own skin. On his own two feet. Sensing, smelling, seeing, feeling, tasting and touching. It is natural man. The walker.

Margot Patterson Doss

North Bay

Marin County

A Walk on the Lonely Farallones

The rarest Bay Area walk of all, the walk you cannot take, and indeed, unless you are an ornithologist, research mammalogist, coast guardsman, misanthrope, murre, puffin, cormorant, sea lion, or fairly intrepid journalist, would really prefer not to take, is thirty-two miles at sea on one of those barren rocks that are the lonely Farallones.

As close as it may seem on a golden day, sitting castle-like on the blue horizon, South Farallon Island, which is the one we see from Ocean Beach in San Francisco, is less accessible than Alcatraz and not nearly so diverting. It has no dock, no church, no store. It has a derrick on which cargo or passengers are swung ashore in a canvas basket loaded from a small boat, frequently in rough sea. Until it was automated, five courageous Coast Guard families lived in old frame houses on a marine terrace under the powerful Farallon Light, to the tune of the mournful Farallon diaphone. The island also has kelp flies, sea birds, sea lions, the old foundations of a Russian otter-hunter's house, and an unbelievable eye-watering odor of putrefaction compounded of guano, dead rabbits, and broken eggs. These days the only human residents are staff members of the Point Reyes Bird Observatory.

Since the Farallones are not open to the public, take this walk with me vicariously in the comfort of your own living room. Or if you prefer a setting at once suitable to the adventure and luxurious by contrast, indulge in the fine San Franciscan tradition of Sunday breakfast at Cliff House, within sound of the sea but snug from squalls.

Presuppose that the mails have brought permission for the trip from the Twelfth Coast Guard District, which inherited the Farallon light station from the U.S. Lighthouse Service in 1939. Having reread Stoddard's "With the Egg-Pickers on the Farallones" as a primer, donned your mountain boots and sturdiest go-lightly gear, packed a sandwich, apple, small plastic bottle labelled "Survival Kit," and a copy of Peterson's *Field Guide to Western Birds*, you have made your way by 7:30 A.M. to the Yerba Buena Island Pier of the Coast Guard Cutter Magnolia.

Five hours later, having signed a liability release, enjoyed passage through San Francisco Bay in the dawn's early light, weathered the roll and pitch of the Potato Patch, watched with interest while Lt. Comdr. Richard G. Donaldson, the Maggie's skipper, put supplies, water, and men aboard the lightship *San Francisco*, you go over the side on a Jacob's ladder into a small boat, climb into the cargo hoist, and are swung up and over the frightening rocks. You walk ashore on the landing platform of South Farallon Island to be greeted by a very small boy named Michael Wheeler, who asks wistfully, "Have you ever been in a dime store?"

In one glance you can see Michael's entire desolate world, about a mile long, half a mile wide, and not more than 3½ miles around, a hostile desert mountain with two peaks, Tower Hill and Maintop, a surge channel called the "River Jordan," two trees, and a handful of houses. You have been in Cost Plus, the grown-up dime store and, thank heavens, the bookmark in your bird guide is an origami paper toy that unfolds to amuse a child who has not. "Thank you," he says shyly, but with a face like Christmas morning; "would you like to take my walk with me?"

Michael's father, Chief Engineman William J. Wheeler, must supervise the landing of supplies and water, for the cutter is his tie not only to civilization but to survival and will not come again for two weeks. His wife, Barbara, should check the lists as groceries are unloaded, as her neighbors, the Madames Pfister, McGrath, Buck, and Reis are doing. At no little sacrifice, then, she agrees to go. With three-year old Michael in the lead, we follow the hazardous zig-zag trail that begins behind his spotless house and winds up the 320-foot peak to the 500,000 candlepower light. Lighthouse keepers have crawled this walk on hands and knees in rain, sleet, hail, and torrents of birds, to check the light down through the years. It has never gone out, nor has the diaphone. Eleven ships ran aground on the treacherous rocks in the last century, although the hazard was known as long ago as 1579 when Sir Francis Drake anchored *The Golden Hind* here to take on seal meat and murre eggs. Breaker Cove, North Landing, Shubrick Point, and Maintop are all outlined like a map below the light. Six peaks, the *Farallones de los Frayles*, as Viscaino called them, or "watery mountain peaks of the friars," lie nearby: Sugar Loaf Isle, Aulone Isle, Seal Rock, Arch Rock, Finger Rock, and Sea Lion Islet, all outlined in birds or lolling sea lions. These are the South Farallones. Five miles north is another cluster, of which the most important is Noonday Rock, where the clipper *Noonday* ran aground in 1863.

Imagine Seal Rocks, just offshore from Cliff House, enlarged one hundredfold, and you can picture the Farallones, craggy, eroded with sea caves, carved by unceasing waves into archways, slick with lichens, and barely habitable.

"On a clear day," Michael says from the balcony around the light, under the eaves that turn out surprisingly to have gargoyles, the one architectural frivolity on the island, "on a clear day, we can see San Francisco."

Camp Reynolds on Angel Island

2

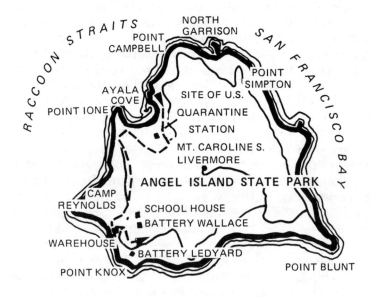

The setting is romantic. Soft lights twinkle through trees surrounding the little parade ground on three sides. A moon-path shimmers on the water fronting it where a small steamer bobs at anchor near the dock. A young officer in dress uniform and white gloves leaves the dance floor with his long-skirted lady and slips away from the veranda to seek out the "Courtship Seat" or the path called "Pop the Question." Over it all float the hearts and flowers strains of "Beautiful Ohio" or " Missouri Waltz."

The place was Camp Reynolds on Angel Island in the halcyon years between the Civil War and World War I, when the social scene there would have rivalled *Daughter of the Regiment*. It was so lively in 1880 that Headquarters of the U.S. Eighth Infantry published an Angel Island Guide, rediscovered by historian John Langellier, Ph.D., formerly of the Presidio Museum. Its price was ten cents.

Time and history have made Camp Reynolds even more romantic. If you haven't been out to Angel Island State Park, consider a walk around old Camp Reynolds, sometimes known as West Garrison. To enjoy this walk, pack a picnic, bikini, sweater, and lug-soled shoes. Then transport yourself to the island via ferry from San Francisco's Fisherman's Wharf, Pier 41. Price of the roundtrip ticket includes a park entrance fee. The boat trip was just as scenic when U.S. Commissioner George Penn Johnson, author of the California antidueling law, and State Senator William I. Ferguson rode out to settle a difference in one of the last duels in the state. Both men were injured but Ferguson died of his wounds.

Once on the island, follow the crowd toward the grass of Ayala Cove, or Hospital Cove, as this was known when it was a quarantine station. First stop, at the walk leading to park headquarters, is to read historical marker 529 and admire the tallest flagpole on the bay. From the marker, leave the sidewalk and walk along the seawall above the curving beach. Small boats can berth for the day in the cove. Sunbathers dot the sand but swim at their own risk, for there is no lifeguard. When you come to the Charles Winslow Memorial, an antique cast-iron water fountain designed to

serve a dog, horse, and man all at once, look for the wooden sidewalk that leads uphill. When it reaches a broader ledge of path, bear right. In Camp Reynolds's heyday, this was Laurel Walk. At the "Hazardous Area" sign, go left uphill. When the wooden steps reach the road, bear right. Views toward Belvedere and the Golden Gate Bridge along this stretch of trail are fronted by banks of Pride-of-Madiera, a showy echium botanists believe may have floated to the Bay Area from the Azores.

When you reach Camp Reynolds, named for Maj. Gen. John F. Reynolds, who was killed at Gettysburg in 1863, pause a moment for a look at the station hospital building. It is a mirror image of the Golden Gate National Recreation Area headquarters building at Fort Mason. Resist the trail that goes off to the right and continue past the brick building to take the gravel road that slants downhill on the right. Look for hitching rings along the wall shortly before you reach the next building, a mule barn. Then continue downhill toward the two duplex quarters. Stand between them and look downhill at the parade ground and the water beyond. Officers' quarters, among them the home of Gen. William Rufus Shafter, who weighed more than 300 pounds, are on the left; enlisted quarters, now razed, were on the right. The brick building near the water was a quartermaster's storehouse. Walk downhill on the right to reach it. Agave gardens have been rescued recently by the Youth Conservation Corps. Go around toward the water's edge to locate the dock where the steamer *General McPherson* used to bring in passengers and freight from San Francisco's Washington Street wharf. Near the dock, look south to locate Point Knox and the last remaining fog bell in the bay. Then head back up Officer's Row. When you have returned to the stables, bear right to reach the post chapel, which also served as schoolhouse. Its most famous sermonizer was the post chaplain Lt. Col. Allen Allensworth, highest ranking black officer of his time. Camp Reynolds was in use through 1946.

For a fantastic view of San Francisco, return with the trail to the main road and continue to the overlook above Battery Ledyard. Don't be tempted down, however, for there is a heavy growth of poison oak around it and erosion is cracking the battery.

When you have enjoyed the panoramic sweeps of bay and land, head back on the main road. It drops you down with a sharp left turn to park headquarters. If time is plentiful, this main trail also loops the island completely. Leave yourself time to catch the last boat home (check with the ferry boat operator).

Bonita Lighthouse

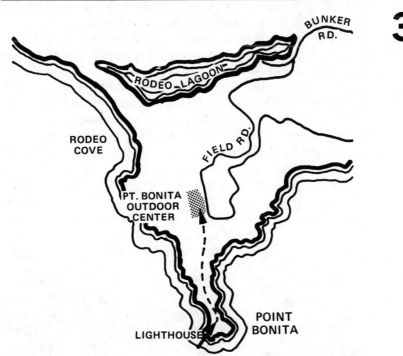

Bonita Light!

The name alone is enough to send thrills of high adventure down the spine of anyone who has walked out to it "on a windy day with the white clouds flying, and the flung spray, and the blown spume, and the seagulls crying."

For Bonita Light, romantic, snug sentimental sentinel at the Golden Gate's dangerous northeast gatepost, is not only beyond compare for the splendor of its distant vistas and the savagery of abrupt headlands meeting the relentless sea, it is also unique for its foot-trail approach.

The time to make this walk is in winter. Or on one of those blue and gold days on which early morning sunlight reveals roads etched like scars on the voluptuous bare headlands. Open for tours every weekend year-round, from 12:30 to 4:00 pm, Bonita Light also has occasional moonlight tours. (331-1540 is the number to call.) Like the Marin County itself, the best way to get to Point Bonita is through a tunnel and a suspension bridge.

Take the Alexander Avenue turnoff north of Vista Point, the overlook at the north end of the Golden Gate Bridge, then swing left at the sign indicating Forts Barry and Cronkhite. In a trice you will be waiting for the six-minute signal that admits one way traffic through the half-mile long Fort Cronkhite tunnel under Highway 101. Look uphill to see the larger Waldo tunnels plugged into the ridge.

Once through the Fort Cronkhite tunnel you are

immediately in wild wonderful rangeland, rescued from development by inclusion in the Golden Gate National Recreation Area. Drive left or west on Bunker Road, which leads through a long narrow strath along a streambank thick with willows, past military housing of many eras and a rifle range transmuted to an equestrian field. The road forks at Rodeo Lagoon. Take the uphill road south past the church and watch for a sign indicating the Point Bonita YMCA Outdoor Center.

Then drive past missile sites and other Fort Barry installations ever more southerly until a stunning panorama unfolds, with the Golden Gate Bridge in the middle distance, San Francisco behind it, and in the northerly foreground, the charming white buildings of the Coast Guard light station. You have arrived at Point Bonita, a thin gnarled finger of seaworn rock that is the southernmost point of land in Marin County, the site of the oldest manned lighthouse on the Pacific Coast, and the last to be automated.

Park and look for the trailhead. Before you reach the lighthouse, a crooked half mile away, there are eroded cliffs, sheer overhangs, the low tunnel hewn long ago supposedly by Chinese coolies working with picks and crude black powder, and the 165 foot long suspension bridge that is reputed to be a wooden counterpart of the Golden Gate Bridge.

As you walk, the boat landings below reveal a former life-boat station, scene of more than one heroic episode. None was more exciting than the time in 1915 when the steamer *Eureka*, 315 tons, fouled her propeller with a rope out in the four fathom bank of Potato Patch Shoals and drifted helplessly onto the rocks.

A surfman, Al Fisher, patrolling the frightening cliffs above Bonita Light, saw her crash and alerted the lighthouse where assistant-keeper Alex Martin let himself down in the dark to the ship on 100 feet of rope, only to find he was dangling 50 feet too high. He went back up the rope for more help and returned to save all aboard but one man who had gone back to the ship for something he'd forgotten.

A cannon, now on display at the Coast Guard base in Alameda, was the first fog signal here. Manned by a Sergeant Maloney, who found it rough going, the cannon was fired every half hour during fog. The first light replaced it in 1855. It stood higher than the present light at an elevation of 324 feet. In 1877, the light was lowered below the fog level to stand 124 feet above the water. Augustin Fresnel and his staff ground and polished the giant lens, which is made up of many separate prisms. When the "wickies", as lightkeepers were known in days of the oil lamps, manned the station, the lamps burned about seven gallons of oil each night. A counter weight system, rather like a cuckoo clock, lifted a screen that made the light blink. Now two Herntzing current makes the electric lamp blink.

The lens—8'7" tall and 4'6"" wide—cost $6,000 new. The station itself, with three-foot thick walls, cost $25,000. The contractor gave the Revenue Service, which preceded the Coast Guard in tending light stations, a one-hundred year guanrantee of his work! The present light produces 40,000 candlepower and is visible seventeen miles at sea. As many a homebound mariner can tell you, it flashes one second, eclipses two, flashes two and eclipses fifteen. The horns are in two buildings on the point and are louder than any amplified rock band. They can be heard four miles out at sea. One, a super tyfon, which has been compared to a seagull's shriek, has a two-second blast, two-second silence, two-second blast, then twenty-four seconds of silence.

Romantic as it is, the spectacular coastline is really the scene stealer. Turn away from the city view if you can and look at the seastacks ranging toward Rodeo Cove. It is as rugged, wild and seemingly remote as the Oregon Coast.

Sausalito

4

"Oh, to be in Sausalito when the herring run," the man at No Name Bar said. "Browning can have his England."

The herring run can occur at any time between December and mid-March but most frequently happens in

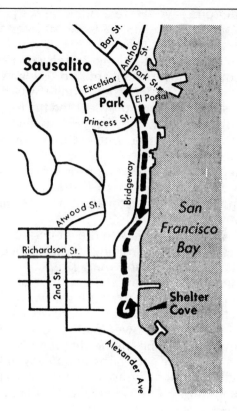

mid-January.

Sausalito is a walker's town, a sailor's town, a painter's town, a poet's town, a shopper's town, a potter's town, a browser's town and a good place to spend a weekend.

By car, take 101 north across the Golden Gate Bridge, turn right on the Alexander Avenue off-ramp and continue of the Sausalito Lateral. It soon joins Alexander. Thereafter, stay as close to the water as you can. The route goes via Second Street to Bridgeway. Stay on Bridgeway until you reach Plaza Vina del Mar, the little triangular park that is Sausalito's heart. Turn right on El Portal to reach the parking lot.

Walk over to the little park south of the ferry dock to discover the double-tiered fountain whose lower basin is surrounded with the message "Have a drink on Leland."

The upper one says "Have a drink on Sally." The fountain honors onetime mayor, madame and restaurateur Sally Stanford and her dog, Leland.

Start walking south along Bridgeway. Fifth-generation Marin County native Tom Plant said "Bridgeway was Water Street until the Golden Gate bridge was built. The city fathers renamed it when they learned the freeway wouldn't run through Sausalito. They feared Sausalito would become a ghost town. Quite the contrary. Being off the freeway is what saved Sausalito."

When you reach the Quonset hut-shaped building at Princess Street, walk east to the sea wall to discover a miniature park with a water stair, then continue south on Bridgeway.

Pass Ondine and walk to the far end of the fishing pier alongside. You are now looking at what Plant calls "the most prolific Pacific herring spawning site."

Return to Bridgeway and continue south, if the tide permits, on the lower waterside walkway, which is about eight feet below street level. Otherwise, use the sidewalk. Rocks alongside the lower path become slick with fish sperm and eggs during the herring run.

Soon you leave the shops behind. Well-kept cottages and small apartment houses facing the water enjoy the same beautiful water-level view of San Francisco that the walker sees.

All too soon you arrive at sculptor Al Sybrian's sleek sea lion statue, poised off Tiffany Beach. West of Bridgeway, the nest of Tiffany Park snuggles against a cliff rampant with flowers, like a little chunk of Mediterranea.

As soon as you reach Richardson Street, you are in what the Chamber of Commerce calls Shelter Cove. Old timers called it Hurricane Gulch. Follow Front Street, the wooden walkway that continues along the shoreline.

At the dead-end of the wooden sidewalk, you are also at The Valhalla, the restaurant Sally Stanford made famous. One block uphill is the Old Town section of Sausalito, often obscured by the fog formation that reaches down this canyon.

Turn around and return along the waterfront the way you came. If you missed the herring run try again next year. You will have seen something of Sausalito and had a pleasant walk, with or without herring.

The New Pacific Coastal Trail

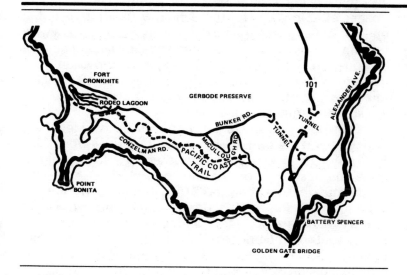

5

When the Coastal Trail in the Marin headlands of the Golden Gate National Recreation Area was sign posted and opened to walkers, the first lap provided a splendid three-mile walk through spacious sea meadows with views of San Francisco and the Golden Gate strait that had long been inaccessible to the public.

It also did rather more than that. The first lap is the southern Marin starting point of an entire network of inter-connecting trails. It links San Francisco with Tomales Point, forty miles north; each trail is routed as far as possible from the sight and sounds of traffic. Under the guidance of a citizens committee of veteran hikers and horsemen, the Pacific Coast Trail was in preparation for more than two years. Now that the system is completed it is possible for a vacationer, scout troop, wilderness class, indeed, for anyone, to begin hiking at the southern boundaries of the GGNRA (Sweeney Ridge in Pacifica or the Golden Gate Promenade at the foot of Hyde Street on the east) and finish at the tip of the Point Reyes National Seashore, sixty miles to the north. En route at the appropriate distances, overnight pioneer camps are located. Three hostels and three camps are already established. The trail also joins many shorter scenic or nature trails to create dozens of loop walks for the Sunday walker interested in one-day or half-day outings. The first lap of the trail is a walk that almost anyone sound of wind and limb should be able to complete in half a day. To enjoy it, provision your daypack with lunch and liquids, for there are no drinking fountains along the way. Lug-soled shoes and warm jackets are also prerequisites for seaside trails.

Transport yourself to the north end of Golden Gate Bridge. If you are on foot, go under the bridge from Vista Point, through the west parking lot, then up onto Conzelman Road and head west on the shoulder.

If you are on wheels, take the Alexander Avenue off-ramp from U.S. Route 101; turn left at the stop sign, as if to return to San Francisco. Once under the freeway, instead of joining southbound bridge traffic, go right and take the road uphill. This is Conzelman Road. (When Muni bus 76 is running, it is possible to be picked up at both ends of the trail on Sundays.) Seven-tenths of a mile from Battery Spencer, you will reach a right-hand turn, McCullough Road.

Ignore the turn, but at this juncture park parallel to the Golden Gate Strait.

Cross Conzelman and make a sharp left. A cable gate across an old ranch road signals the Coastal Trail head. Go around the gate, a vehicle barrier, and follow the ranch road past a fine stand of leather fern. As you walk, Capehart housing on the border between Forts Barry and Baker comes into sight on your right. Beyond is Gerbode Preserve. The raw road visible there was hacked out for Marincello, the subdivision that so outraged conservationists they fought it out of existence. Mount Tamalpais, Wolfback Ridge, and Mount Beacon come into view in quick succession. One rounds a curve and suddenly there is a Pacific Ocean, with Fort Cronkhite in the foreground and, on a fair day, the Farallones.

At the next trail marker, ignore the sharp right downhill and continue straight on. An abandoned quarry will appear on your right. At the next right, hew to the main trail. The steep downhill offshoot goes to the abandoned rifle range, once used by army and police. Immediately past the firing range, bear left uphill near four cypress trees about fifty feet short of Bunker Road, which is the main approach to Rodeo Lagoon. At the next rail sign, bear right (if you hit Conzelman Road, you have gone too far). There will be a "One Way" and a red "Do Not Enter" sign. Leave the road via the grass double-track. At the cross-trails on the top of the ridge, go straight ahead and start down toward the stables in the valley, marked by a big blimp hangar now used for an indoor riding ring. Continue downhill at the next road. Cross the parking turnaround and follow the asphalt road. New horses in the stable spend two weeks in the smaller quarantine paddock on your immediate right.

The stables are the three-mile point on the Coastal Trail. Backpackers planning to go north by the interior ridge can connect with the Miwok Trail 2/10 mile north of the stables at the footbridge over Rodeo Creek.

If instead you wish to continue to Rodeo Beach, take the next two-mile continuation of the Coastal Trail. Across from the lower sign as you come down above the stables, bear left to go up to the next hilltop. Thereafter bear right, following the fence line with the lightpoles on your right. Before you reach the eucalyptus grove, bear left, skirting the canyon around the grove. You emerge by a sign saying "Road Closed." With the church on your right, cross the asphalt toward Rodeo Lagoon but stop short of the weir that divides the two lakes, bearing left on the near shore. Follow the trails parallelling the viaduct, to come out finally at the sand dunes. The new foot-bridge across the lagoon leads to the ranger station, drinking fountain, and privies. Buses back to the city come in here. Glorious as this trail is, remember to pace yourself to your physical capacity. Five miles out is also five miles back.

From Tennessee Cove to Muir Beach

6

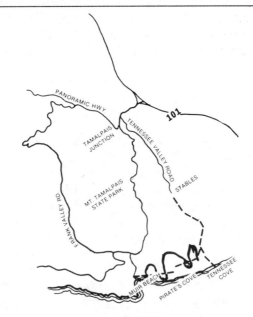

PACIFIC OCEAN

One of the few places where the California coast is not rimmed with highway is along the cliffy headlands between Tennessee Cove and Muir Beach. Fortunately for the sturdy walker, there is an excellent length of the new Pacific Coast Trail traversing it. It is steep, challenging, 4½ miles long, and only for the spry, but the views are spectacular in clear weather. Although within two miles of San Francisco as the hawk soars, Bonita Channel and the sheltering Wolf and Coyote Ridges make this walk seem remote. It is as rugged with sea stacks as the Oregon coast and silent of urban noise. In short, an ideal place for those who, like Thoreau, "love a broad margin" to their lives.

Either a two-car shuttle or Golden Gate Transit is the

ideal way to make this exploration. For the former, join
forces with your favorite trail companions and embark in
two vehicles. Head north across the Golden Gate Bridge
and take the offramp labelled Highway 1. Go to Muir Beach
parking lot and leave one car here. Then reverse your
direction and return to Tennessee Valley Road in Tamalpais
Valley. Bear right on Tennessee Valley Road and leave your
other set of wheels at the parking area here, just shy of
Miwok stables.

If you are going by bus, get off at Tamalpais Junction
and walk out Tennessee Valley Road.

All of Marin is a tinderbox in summer, so forget your
matches. Many places have been closed to the public, but
the Pacific Coast Trail will remain open as long as there are
no brush fires or extreme fire danger. Wearing vibram-soled
wafflestompers and a jacket against the capricious onshore
breeze old-timers call "the westerlies," shoulder your daypack, lunch and thermos. There is no potable water, nor are
there concessionaires along this new coastal trail.

Follow Tennessee Valley Road toward the sea as it
dwindles from asphalt to gravel to footpath. You will reach
the well-marked Coastal Trail in the meadow downhill from
what was for many years the Witter Ranch. Bear right
through the meadow to the road, left on the road, then right
uphill at the next fork. You will be walking away from the
lagoon.

At each thirty- or forty-foot rise, pause to look back at
the valley below. The trail visible across the canyon is part of
the Pacific Coast Trail leading south to Rodeo Lagoon.
When I made this walk with park planner Doug Nadeau,
Zen priest Yvonne Rand, and Ginny Baker of the Zen
Center, frog song from the lagoon became audible as we
climbed, but not when we were level with the water. Higher
yet, from a miniature mountain nose we could hear gulls
mewing and crying. At another pause, one can see that
distance protects one from a hillside thick with poison oak.
Higher still, you can see Point Lobos beyond Tennessee
Point. Oregon grape, Indian paintbrush, mimulus, lizard-
tail, and mule-ears are among the wildflowers along the trail.
From the crest of Coyote Ridge, Ocean Beach and Seal

Rocks are visible.

Bear left, hewing to the coastline at the first fork, a junction of the Coyote Ridge fire road. This is a tricky place for the Coastal Trail becomes less well-defined here and the temptation is to go with the best-beaten trail. Don't do it. Coastal Trail broadens out again in the long descent into Pirate's Cove. No one seems to know which pirates gave this rocky pocket its name, though local oral history indicates they may have been rum-runners during Prohibition. A party of walkers we met along this length of trail included Bill Kilpack of San Francisco, enjoying it for the first time in thirty years. "Last time I walked to Pirate's Cove," he said, "we took the train from Sausalito, got off at Waldo Station, and did the rest on foot."

An old jeep trail goes down the steep canyon face. Stay away from it, for headlands can crumble unexpectedly. Instead, circle down gradually on the gentler grade. Even this is steep enough to deserve the name "toe grabber." Bear right on the low road overlooking the cabin platform ruins to go to Muir Beach. It circles the canyon in a climb that is steep but exhilarating, revealing some of the most panoramic coastine in Nothern California as it rises. Over the next hump, glorious glimpses of Spindrift Point and the Muir Beach overlook appear. Sea Cape is the development of new houses in the foreground with Bolinas and Point Reyes visible beyond.

On the next crest, bear left at the fence and go through a stile, a gap in the fenceline. (If you go right, you loop back to Tennessee Cove via the Coyote Ridge Fire Road.) Descending toward Muir Beach, the trail is its own map on the land. At the foot of the hill, bear left toward Big Lagoon. The trail follows the long dragon of Green Gulch Valley snaking toward the sea. Building and gardens visible to the right are part of the Green Gulch Zen Center farm.

Short of the beach, the road crossing the valley floor takes one out to Highway 1 near the Terwilliger Monarch Butterfly Grove, the Pelican Inn and a Golden Gate Transit bus stop. Continue on to the beach instead, cross the bridge, and you have a perfect place to picnic.

Rodeo Lagoon

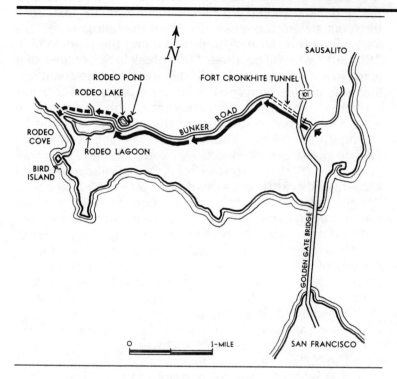

7

Rodeo Lagoon is not one, but three, secret silver blue lakes whose beauty, like that of the human face, changes from moment to moment. They lie in a hollow of land where the southernmost mountains of Marin go down to the sea. It is their happy destiny to be the important central part of the Golden Gate National Recreation Area headlands. The walk around them is interesting indeed, for few places so near the city of San Francisco have been, until now, so relatively undisturbed.

To make this walk, take the Alexander Avenue turnoff just north of the Golden Gate Bridge and Vista Point, and turn left at the Bunker Road entrance to Forts Barry and Cronkhite. In a moment you will reach the tunnel under U.S. Route 101, the main entrance to the headlands. Once through the tunnel, follow Bunker Road west as it borders the willows that hide Rodeo Creek. At Field Road, park by the little red-roofed church, near the road that goes between two of the lakes. Go down the railroad-tie steps and follow the red-rock path bordering the road. Within 100 yards, you will be abreast of a break in the willows that leads to a weir. Walk out on it, staying within the guard rail, and you are between the two uppermost lakes. The army, on whose land ninety-four percent of the lagoons were formerly situated, distinguished the middle-sized one by calling it Rodeo Lake. Rodeo Pond is the smallest, Rodeo Lagoon the largest. Rodeo Cove, Rodeo Avenue. All three lakes derive their names from Don William Antonio Richardson's cattle sales, held here after 1835, when he bought Rancho Saucalito from on of Anza's soldiers, Nicolas Galindo of Durango. Helen Van Cleave Park, a Mill Valley historian and authority on Richardson, has found a reference in which "Richardson and a party of hunters started up a band of elk, seven bear and three cubs" nearby. The Rodeo Lagoon name was well established by the time Van Dorn published his Marin County rancho map of 1860.

One used to be able to drop a line in the water of the upper lakes and catch a trout. The state Department of Fish and Game used to stock the freshwater lakes. No longer, alas. The NPS decided against it.

In early spring, look north to see a carpet of wildflowers on the beautiful hillside on the opposite shore. This is the old Silva Ranch, once proposed as the site for the controversial Marincello development. Before it became a park, bulldozers changed the upstream ecology by removing streamside willows and brush needed to sustain fish life.

After you have searched for nesting marsh-birds and raccoon pawprints, follow the bridge by the road across the dam to see screens that protect trout from wandering into the wrong body of water. Long ago steelhead came up Rodeo Creek to spawn.

Then continue around the border of the larger lagoon toward the Pacific Ocean, passing the Marine Mammal Center, Headlands Institute, and the GGNRA Energy Center, all recycling the Fort Cronkhite military housing, to reach the gravelly beach between Bird Island Point and Tennessee Point that defines Rodeo Cove. The bridge in front of the Ranger Station is a short cut. Anglers treasure Rodeo Beach for surf fishing, rock fishing and mussel gathering. Birders love it for the variety of shore-birds and water-fowl. But to the rockhound, Rodeo Beach is Mecca, for it is here that he can see gem quality carnelians, jade chalcedony and jasper pebbles washed smooth by the everlaving sea.

Whalewatching at Muir Beach Overlook

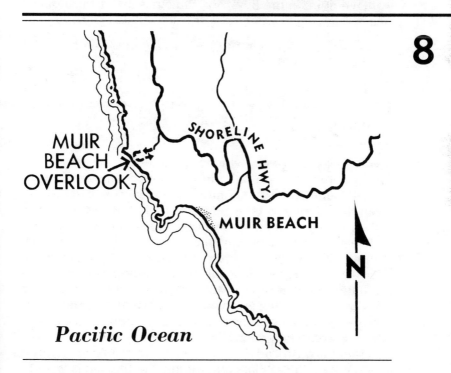

8

Twice a year in California it is whalewatching time. In January the southward wave of California gray whales en route from the Arctic oceans to the breeding grounds at Scammon's Lagoon is underway. The migrating pods, as groups of whales are called, skirt the coast as they swim south, moving about six or seven miles per hour. Every seven or eight minutes they surface and blow several twenty-foot-tall spouts of warm wet air. Dr. Carl Hubbs of the Institution of Oceanography at La Jolla reports that entire pods of whales have been observed to surface, blow, and submerge at nearly the same time. This was one of the clues that led researches to believe whales communicate with one another.

The most I've ever seen spouting at one time is nine. This was from the Chimney Rock Trail on Point Reyes Head in the national seashore, which is the best whalewatching vantage point in the Bay Area, since it is the farthest out to sea.

Second best whalewatching spot, for my money, is the Muir Beach Overlook, just off California Highway 1. It was a Marin County park. It is about 400 feet above the water, with an almost unobstructed view in all directions. Not surprisingly, it was once the site of coastal fortifications as the Frank Valley Military Reservation. Now it is part of the Golden Gate National Recreation Area.

To make this walk, which is short, easy, and suitable for the old, the very young, and for those would-be Sunday walkers who are out of condition, transport yourself north from San Francisco via Shoreline Highway to Muir Beach. When you reach the long row of mailboxes and Pelican Inn that signal the junction that is the little residential community known as Muir Beach, check your mileage gauge. In 1.4 miles you will reach a green sign that says "Vista Point." With the distraction of recently constructed seaside homes, it is easy to miss. Turn left toward the ocean as soon as you can after you spot the sign. In a moment you are in a well-arranged parking lot, complete with portable privies and trash can.

Get your binoculars out, bundle up, then walk west to the observation post for one of the gun batteries at Muir Beach Overlook, which offers rich pickings for the military archeologist as well as the whalewatcher. Military historian Dr. E. R. Lewis has listed these as Battery Wallace, Battery Hamilton, Battery Hamilton Smith, and Battery 243, a submarine mine unit. All are stations of batteries of the same name in Fort Barry and like naval destroyers, are named for heroes who died in battle.

It is the enticing little fenced walkway leading out to the cliff beyond that lures the walker however. Follow the northernly steps and trail as far as you can see, passing two half-hidden observation stations as you go. About 8½ acres of this land are level. Leading down are another fifty acres so steep only deer or antelope could play on them. As you walk down to the overlook, observe the cliff. No matter how intriguing, stay off those little paths that beckon toward the water. This is slide country. Each year some of the land crumbles away.

Notice the thriving colonies of leather ferns, the wind-sheared sage, and coyote-brush as you walk to the north view-point. Whales sometimes come fairly close inshore; possibly, because unlike other large whales, the California gray whale has lived after being stranded until the tide returned to let it swim off. Don't count on it, however. To quote poet William Rose Benet, it is only the Lord who can say, "Let Whale be! and There was Whale!"

Given a clear day, one can see north to Point Reyes, north-east to Mount Tamalpais's three peaks, and south to Point San Pedro. When you have enjoyed the first overlook, retrace your steps and bear right after you pass the group of military observation bunkers to find a second fenced over-look. It offers an unexpected glimpse of the little town of Muir Beach, of Big Lagoon, and of Zen Center's Green Gulch Ranch. Before you leave, look down to discern one of those slides that sheared away recently.

Then follow the trail toward the pines to find a hidden and sheltered picnic spot. On one of the tables a setting sun has been lovingly whittled by a master woodcarver. Climb up the embankment shy of the fence for a quick return to your wheels. Unless, of course, someone shouts, 'Thar she blows!'

Pomander Walk in Belvedere

9

Pomander Walk is a country lane that rides the crest of beautiful Belvedere. Tall hedgerows define it. Blooming vines entwine it. The linnets twitter as they flit along it.

At any moment Greer Garson, in the role of Mrs. Miniver, might come hurrying out of the swinging gate at Number 2 Pomander, bound perhaps to a fundraiser for a worthy cause.

If you have never walked around Belvedere, you've missed one of the Bay Area's most exotic experiences. This is the densley packed, Riviera-like community that launched lagoon-living, suburbia's best antidote to the unimaginative tract.

For a leisurely look at this remarkable community, begin this excursion at the juncture of Highway 130 (Tiburon Boulevard) and San Rafael Avenue.(This is also a bus stop.) Walk south-west across the Tiburon bikepath. In 1882, tracks, now gone, were built by the San Francisco and North Pacific Railroad, popularly known as the "Donahue Line" and the "Irishman's Railroad" for owner James M. Donahue, whose ferries to San Francisco raced a rival line out of Sausalito. Follow San Rafael Avenue and in a trice it is out of the trees and bordering the shoreline of Richardson

Bay, where a narrow, parklike promenade is now emerging, complete with six benches placed at intervals for bird-or-moon-watching.

Bear consistently right, or west, pausing for a look at the lagoons from the floodgage, the only viewpoint accessible to the public from this northern spit. In the 1880's, houseboat dwellers who called themselves "the Venetians of the West" and "Descendants of Noah" brought arks to winter in this sheltered cove, making a procession through a comparable floodgate in the southern spit, now Beach Road. It was then called Hilarita's Spit, for Hilarita Sanchez, whose name is commemorated in St. Hilary's church, the charming landmark uphill on the eastern ridge.

San Rafael Avenue soon turns, following the lagoon to the yacht club, Belvedere Land Company, and municipal offices, and passing, en route, the award-winning Christian Science church designed by Warren Callister. For this walk to see how Belvedere is evolving, however, continue along the water's edge and bear right on West Shore Road past new shingled houses, each architect-designed. The cliff above is known as Britton Ridge.

As you pass 8-10 West Shore Road, once a Pacific Heights mansion which was floated over from San Francisco on two barges, notice the gray and white layers in the cliff behind. This was one of the many Marin Indian shell-mounds. As you walk, notice that viewpoints, open to the water, have been left for the delight of walkers.

If you can take your eyes away from the splendor of Sausalito, its hills, and the Golden Gate Bridge, look landward across from Number 83, to see steps in the cliff. From here to the end of the road was once the site of Belvedere's lone industry, the codfishery of T.W. McCollam. Around 1875, great four-masters brought their cargo here to the Union Fish Company's long wharf and curing sheds.

Zig-zag uphill to Belvedere Avenue, then bear south to Pine, swinging back to Golden Gate to find Pomander Walk. It is hard today to envision the burly codfisherymen climbing up and over this spine of land to spend their money in the raucous bars of Sharktown, as Tiburon was then known. It's equally difficult to believe a man named

Israel Kashaw once tried to prove this was an island, but there's still a pear tree from his orchard near the corner of Laurel and San Rafael Avenues, if you care to hunt it out.

St. Hilary's Garden

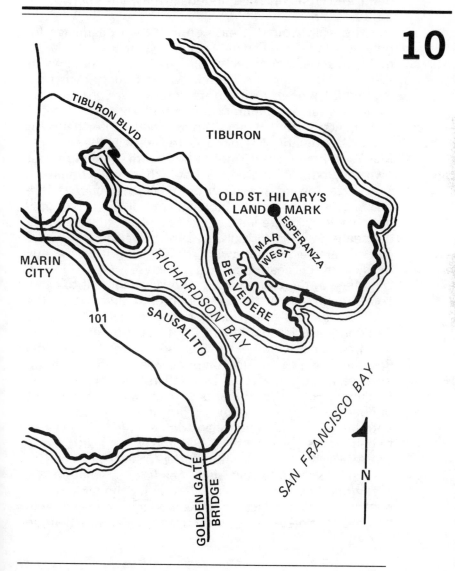

10

St. Hilary's Garden is a four-acre wildflower preserve which sustains 215 varieties of plants on a steep Tiburon hillside. Some of them exist nowhere else in the world. It also contains a small museum within a pioneer "carpenter's Gothic" church of simple classic lines, a fragment of old-rock-banked road known as "the old Spanish trail," a dedicated group of civic-minded citizens, and a network of unusual paths.

The walk around it has come to be a pilgrimage for botanists and can be an unusual outing for anyone. Plan to make this walk between 1 and 4 P.M. on Sundays or Wednesdays when the church, Marin County registered landmark 1, is open. Or if you are a music lover, go late in the summer when the summer concert series presented by the Landmarks Society is held. To reach the site, transport yourself, preferably via Golden Gate Transit, to the corner of Mar West Avenue and Tiburon Boulevard. If you use your own car, park near Reed School, then walk uphill on Esperanza toward the handsome white shiplap church building visible on its little mountain meadow. As you climb, notice the dark green "fingers" of plant growth which delineate St. Hilary's hillside springs against the dryer golden grasses. Wildflowers thrive almost constantly because of this year-round water source.

Once at the church, go in and sit a moment to catch your breath, enjoy the restful interior and locate the overdoor stained-glass window commemorating St Hilaire, The donor was Hilarita Reed Lyford, daughter of Don Juan Reed, original grantee of Rancho Corte Madera del Presidio, of which the Tiburon peninsula was the southern-most part. "For the sum of two dollars," her husband, Dr. Benjamin Lyford, gave the land for the new church. Before it opened in October, 1888, "a grand musical and literary entertainment" was held for an admission fee of fifty cents to help defray costs. Musicals here today cost a little more.

After you have examined the charmstones, thigh-bone flutes, metate and shell beads excated from the shellmound known as Marin 27, look for the table to the right of the altar, which contains wildflowers presently in bloom on the preserve. When you are familiar with them, go outside and walk down to the foot of the stone steps to find a marker dedicating the garden to John Thomas Howell, curator emeritus of botany at the California Academy of Sciences, who has dedicated his own life to wildflowers. On the occasion of his seventieth birthday, Howell, whom one young admirer described as "a young man who has lived a long time," stood on the stone looking at the garden below and commented "It's nice to see your monument while you're still alive."

A chain barricades the fragile downhill section, since visitors trampling plants below could destroy the habitat. Turn instead to your right and look down at your feet. Zygadene, yarrow, stinking hedge nettle, and mimulus were blooming when I made this walk with Phyllis Ellman, who guided school groups here by appointment. The black jewel flower and the Tiburon paintbrush, which grow nowhere else, bloom early in spring. Cross the little section of creek and in a moment you will be abreast of a bench honoring founder Beverly Bastian Meyers. Walk ten more steps and look downhill to locate a stand of the California leopard lily and, closer underfoot, the coast buckwheat. Property line of the preserve is the old stone wall which serves as embankment of the so-called Spanish Trail, never used by the Spanish. Possibly the route of Indians coming for shellfish to the shallow waters of what is now Cove Road, it later became a buggy route for churchgoers from San Rafael and San Quentin. Elsewhere on the peninsula, much of it has now been bulldozed away. As you walk, keep your eye out for the rare Tiburon buckwheat, the Marin dwarf flax, and dry leaves of the coffee fern. Across the canyon, in midsummer, tracks are left in the dry grass by youngsters who slide down the hill on cardboard cartons. Red Hill behind it has also seen some slides. Tiburon Peninsula Club is the complex of swimming pools and tennis courts.

Take a path on the right going uphill through indigenous grasses to the steps on the left and reach another welcome bench, the gift of the late Winifred Allen. Sit a moment here to enjoy a broad view of the bay with one of the Golden Gate Bridge towers to the left, Mount Tamalpais on the right. Then climb a little higher to the Caroline Livermore Vista Point marker. Hikers game for a longer walk can climb about twenty feet higher and bear left to find themselves on a country road. Landmarks members hope to acquire the creek drainage basin to which it leads.

The less active can look for a trail leading downhill on the left as you face the church. This is Dakin Lane, named for benefactors Susanna and Richard Dakin. The conical structure near its end is the bell tower, still in use. The anchor was fished out of Belvedere cove long ago. But the little white building, now a storage building was, yes, you've guessed it: formerly a two-hole "Chic Sale."

Richardson Bay Wildlife Sanctuary

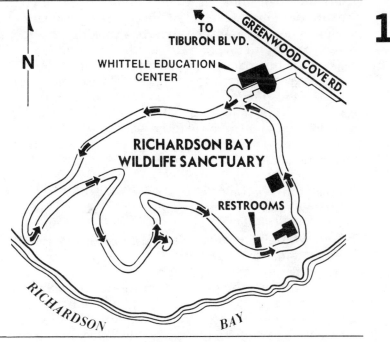

Come, fill the Cup, and in the fire of Spring
Your Winter garment of repentance fling;
The Bird of Time has but a little way
To flutter—and the Bird is on the Wing.
                                    Omar Khayyam

The National Audubon Society's Richardson Bay Wildlife Sanctuary at Tiburon will be thirty years old in 1989. Each winter, its eleven onshore acres and 900 tideland acres under water give refuge to the hundred or so beleagured harbor seals left in San Francisco Bay and feed around 350,000 birds of 200 species. If you wonder how they arrive at that number, birders with tongue in cheek often tell you, "We count all the bird legs and divide by two."

Richardson Bay Wildlife Sanctuary also offers walkers an unusual stroll that borders the bay, climbs a hill to reveal a spectacular view of San Francisco, and loops past the oldest Victorian home in Marin County. The trail coincidentally demonstrates to Johnny-come-lately apartment neighbors how pleasant it is to have a walking path, rather than a road; bordering one side of their property.

To visit this paragon of places, head north from San Francisco with vibram-soled boots, gloves and a long-sleeved windshirt to protect you from poison oak. Since birds shy off from visiting animals, leave your dog, cat, goose or ocelot at home. There are three ways to go. One is on the Golden Gate Transit bus 10. One is on the Tiburon ferry and the bicycle-and-jogging path that borders Tiburon Boulevard. If you must use your own wheels, start via U.S. Route 101 and take the Tiburon turnoff, California Highway 131, east to Greenwood Cove Road. Turn right, or south, and drive until you see the sign that says "National Audubon Society George Whittell Education Center. Open 9 A.M. to 5 P.M. Closed Monday and Tuesday." Park where you can. There is plenty of good bicycle parking.

Walk through the gate and down the steps. Soon you will be abreast of sculptor Bob La Voy's big brown metal pelican, my choice for the totem bird of fathers because it has such a large billfold. The rust on this pelican is intentional. Follow the walk into the breezeway between the Book Nest on your left and the handsome museum display cases that front the lecture hall on your right. For Audubon members, the walk around the sanctuary is free. For visitors, the fee is modest. Come along at 9 A.M. Sundays and you can connect with a regular bird walk led by the sanctuary manager, or his assistant, both experts on the resident bird-life. Weekdays, one often finds bird lover Elizabeth Terwilliger, a quail-like little naturalist, bobbing along the trail with a class of children.

The route leads past a fine stand of California poppies and across the bridge over a freshwater pond and little marsh which usually has some resident mallards. At the far end of the bridge, bear right and follow the shore. Soon you are in a corridor of willows and plum trees which screen the adjacent decks better as the season progresses. Along the trail in spring you may see hounds-tongue, Douglas iris, checkerbloom, mimulus, and other native plants that were here when Mrs. Rose Rodrigues daFonta Verrall arrived in 1886. Grass is deliberately left shaggy, the better to encourage ground-nesting birds. The path swings around a curve and soon brings you out above a shaly beach. It's strictly for the birds. Walkers are asked to follow the path through eucalyptus and wildflowers to the crest of the little hill. At the top, veer to the right to find the hidden overlook for birdwatching the beach. From it one can also see the long dredge-spoil islands where the harbor seal colony hauls out of the water to rest. This is also the spot for a good hard-edged view of San Francisco framed by water, sky, and hills.

When you have looked your fill from this aspect, follow the path downhill and soon you swing through coastal brush. The sharp-eyed may find nests through here, but everyone will notice the old nopal cactus, probably planted by Rose Verrall, better known as "The Goat Lady." Inspired by conservationist Caroline Livermore, who arranged a lifetime annuity for her in return, Rose Verrall deeded the land to Audubon on her death.

As you parallel the second beach, notice the handsome yellow and white three-story Victorian house. Although it looks totally at home here, it was actually built on Strawberry Cove, the next peninsula west. Dr. Benjamin Lyford and his wife, Hilarita, daughter of Juan Reed, the grantee of Rancho Corte Madera del Presidio, made their headquarters in it in 1876. It was barged here in 1957 to save it from demolition. Clifford Conley did the handsome restoration and furnishing of the interior. Lyford House is open for guided visits between 1 and 4 P.M. Sundays. Look for plaques on benches and by the door. Another bench near the overlook may have been the place where Rose Verrall watched San Francisco burning in 1906. She could also have seen the big Alaska codfishing deepwatermen sail into Belvedere's Union Fish Company's long wharf.

Next building along here is the Junior Center, in which fledgling Audubon members create all the displays. Especially worth looking at is a papier mâché model of the sanctuary on which the bird of the month is pinpointed.

When you have seen your fill, if you are still game for a longer walk, the trail on the old roadbed of the San Francisco and North Pacific Railroad leads into the charming village of Tiburon. Much of the trail goes through Shoreline Park, where the picnicking is pleasant indeed.

The Three Wells and Cascade Park

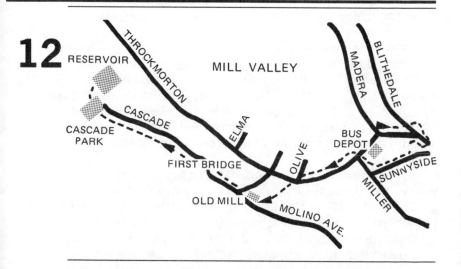

Mill Valley is a walker's town. It always has been, which may well be the primary reason it has more charm and pleasanter amenities per square foot than almost any other Bay Area community. In the golden era of the ferryboat, when trains were brought across the bay by boat, the trains disgorged their passengers at what is now the bus depot. Then, depending on their stamina, visitors took "the crookedest railroad" to the top of friendly Mount Tamalpais, or mounted the mountain burro, or hiked up. The walkers made trails over the ridges and up the canyons along the most scenic of routes. One of these, along the Three Wells Trail and up Cascade Canyon, can rank with any summer resort trail anywhere.

Small wonder. It was as a summer resort that Mill Valley really began. San Franciscans, Oaklanders and Berkeleyites all began building weekend houses here before the town was incorporated. Many of them were farsighted enough to try to protect the scenic charm through the Mill Valley Outdoor Art Club, founded in 1902. The Chamber of Commerce office at 85 Throckmorton Avenue is open weekdays and provides a trail map of the Three Wells and Cascade Park, and there in the map's list of community supporters, along with the Girl Scouts—another ecological advance guard unit—is the still-active Outdoor Art Club.

The leaflet is deceptively simple. No gaudy prose. No glamorous lithographs. But the excursion is so good, it is cherished by those who know it as one of these scenic places we all yearn to keep secret. To discover it, transport yourself miles north of San Francisco to downtown Mill Valley. From the bus depot, follow Throckmorton Avenue, the concentrated village shopping street, as it curves around Old Mill Creek until you reach Cascade Drive.

If you'd like a long, level, streamside walk through silent redwoods, past rustic houses old and new, park by the handsome Mill Valley Library, cut through Old Mill Park, past the amphitheater, cross the stream and bear right along the path that intertwines with Cascade Drive and the creek.

Look for Number 320 Cascade Drive (one of its signs has had the 3 removed). Near the concrete bridge on the wilder side of the road and about fifteen feet up a redwood should be a bullet-pocked sign saying "The Three Wells."

Walk into the redwoods toward the creek and bear consistently right, following the path alongside Old Mill

Creek. The vernal pools are clean and lovely. Frogs jump. Wildflowers bloom in the springtime, and the one house on the immediate streamside has, if anything, the character of a 400-year-old British country manor. When you reach the bridge to it, follow the trail on stepping stones to cross Old Mill Creek, if you are agile. Otherwise climb up to the road. Three Wells Trail ends in a few hundred feet. You then come out across the road from another green and white sign, again high on a tree, saying "Cascade Park Waterfall." As you face the sign, Old Mill Creek will be on your left and Cascade Creek, the smaller rivulet tumbling down, on the right. Step over the parking barrier and start uphill.

Look underfoot for redwood sorrel (which was white, rather than pink, when I saw it), trillium, milkmaids, and Solomon's seal. Redwoods, tan oaks, and bay trees filter the sunlight overhead. When the trail forks, bear right and cross Cascade Creek at the first bridge. Within a few feet, the tall waterfall that gives the canyon its name comes cascading down. A simple log bench is nearby on which the walker can rest from the climb.

When you have caught your breath, return to the trail and continue up around the waterfall past a tremendous rock on your right. Wild rose often blooms at its base. Soon you will be looking down on the cascade; then the trail leads to a second bridge. Cross it and bear left, downhill, to make a loop that will return you to the entrance. Fritillaries, Clintonia lilies, starflowers, and fairy lanterns are some of the wildflowers to watch for along this stretch of the trail.

Muir Woods Bicentennial Tree and Trail

13

"By George, you are right!" wrote Teddy Roosevelt in 1908 after Congressman William Kent had declined to have Muir Woods named for him. "It is enough to do the deed and not to desire, as you say, to 'stencil one's own name on

the benefaction.' Good for you and for the five boys who are to keep the name of Kent alive! I have four who I hope will do the same . . . ."

Appropriately enough, one day in 1976, the woods were thick with Kents—grandchildren, great grands and possibly even great great grands—in the sunlight filtering through the redwoods when a simple ceremony designated the interpretive trail on the canyon floor as The Muir Woods National Recreation Trail and, along it, The Muir Woods Bicentennial Tree.

The trail was the first of eighty-three dedicated as national recreational trails, and the tree is about as old as the nation (a mere youngster as coastal redwoods go). More than 1¼ million visitors walk through the cathedral of redwoods that is Muir Woods National Monument every year, so its interpretive nature trail certainly qualifies as national recreation. The trail makes a loop up one side of Redwood Creek and down the other. It is level and easy enough for the oldest shuffler and the youngest trudger. Tourists, awed though they may be by the regal trees, seldom venture far from the visitors center. For the native, this means the walk along the interpretive trail can be uncrowded, especially for the early starter or the lingerer. The gate opens at 8 A.M. and closes as the sun goes down.

This walk begins seventeen miles north of San Francisco via U.S. Route 101, California Highway 1, and Panoramic Highway. Take the well-marked left turn off Panoramic to Muir Woods on Sequoia Valley Road. After parking, ask for a mimeographed sheet about canyon trails. The historic Muir Inn where the celebrated photo of William Kent and John Muir was taken in 1913, burned down in 1939. Nor is picnicking permited along the six miles of trails within the canyon. These trails all tie into Ocean View, Dipsea, Bootjack, Alice Eastwood and Ben Johnson Trails, however, so the hearty hiker may choose to bring along his daypack and enjoy lunch in neighboring Tamalpais State Park, which surrounds Muir Woods.

For the newly renamed National Recreation Trail, you might want to pick up a copy of Gladys Smith's excellent *Flowers and Ferns of Muir Woods*, which has an explict map as a frontispiece and fine drawings and color plates. Cross the creek on the bridge nearest the comfort station and bear right, hewing to the creek through the deepening forest. A medallion on a post indicates the new trail designation. The Bicentennial Tree will be on your left. Go through the Bohemian Grove and pass, but do not cross, the second bridge. En route you may see the western starflower, fringecups, sweetscented bedstraw, alumroot, oxalis and thimbleberry, through these "corridors of light and shadow" where "flowers play a delicate descant to a symphony in green." Although scattered, Muir Woods flowers bloom from January to October.

One of the charms of Muir Woods is that it offers something for everyone. Toddlers especially enjoy the ladybug colonies. These clever insects change locations constantly but a perceptive youngster may still spot them around Cathedral Grove.

"All Americans who prize the natural beauties of the country and wish to see them preserved undamaged," Roosevelt wrote from the White House on January 22, 1908, in a thank you letter to William Kent, "and especially those who realize the literally unique value of the groves of giant trees must feel that you have conferred a great and lasting benefit upon the whole country."

T.R.'s vision was just as great when he told John Muir, "We are not building this country of ours for a day."

Rocky Point Trail

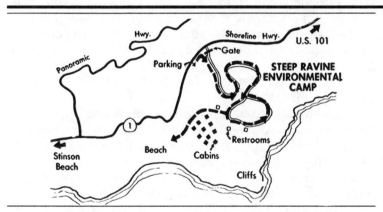

14

Rocky Point and its 10 rustic cabins may well be the most romantic spot on the coast of Marin. Seen from high above on Highway One, it looks like nothing so much as a piece of Ireland where the Mountains of Mourne go down to the sea.

There is mystery here. No motorist noticing the cabins below ever passes without puzzling about them. How did they come to be there, so simple, so stark against the landscape? And there is enchantment. The cabins cast a spell on many who see them only from afar and on everyone who ever stayed in one.

A case in point is the beautiful book "To a Cabin" by Dorothea Lange and Margaretta K. Michell. Wrote Lange, who stayed there often, "This cabin is not a summer cabin; this cabin represents something to me that is much more elemental . . ."

As Lange's co-author explains the allure of the cabin, "For some it is a hardship place. For others, like me, it stands for freedom, for space to think clearly, to kill complexities that crowd out creativity, to cut out bickering which festers in family flesh, for lessons in simplicity—survival."

Quite possibly their photo-essay book has helped preserve these 10 rustic cabins, long the source of one of Marin County's most bitter battles. Now the conflicts are resolved.

Rocky Point is the lowest part of Steep Ravine Canyon. Newly opened to the public—without modern conveniences —as the Steep Ravine Environmental Camp, the primitive cabins are nevertheless sure to be in high demand. (Reservations must be made by mail at least three weeks in advance through the Reservation Office, Department of Parks and Recreation, P.O. Box 2390, Sacramento 95811. There is a modest fee.)

One needs no reservation to enjoy the spectacular meander down to the beach. To make this walk, transport yourself north from San Francisco via the Golden Gate Bridge, Highway One and Panoramic Highway. (If you made a cabin reservation, stop en route at the Pantoll Ranger Station, 801 Panoramic Highway, to register.)

Panoramic reaches the coast at Stinson Beach. Turn left (south) on Highway One and—a mile beyond—look for a place to park along the roadside as you near the gate.

Once parked, follow the path on the safe side of the traffic bumper until you reach the campsite gate. (A sign near the hiker's entrance stile gives reservation information.) Go through the stile and start down the narrow country road that is the trail, keeping an eye out for the unlikely car. Campers are permitted one vehicle per cabin—only to transport gear in and out.

As you walk, look along the upper cliffside for wild flowers. Milkmaids, shooting stars, Indian warrior, iris, lupin, clarkia and godetia all make their appearance as the season ripens. Once you are around the cliff and on the downward track, traffic noises fade immediately.

Dorothea Lange said it a little more poetically. "Down, down the cliffs from the shore road. Fennel, lupin, sage and walls of thistles form the edge. A narrow road. Room for only those in need of sea and sky and infinity."

For a while the cabins are out of sight as you descend through the meadows. Gradually one, then another emerges as the walker draws near the compound. As Margaretta Mitchell described the sight, "Here on the rocks the cabin waits. There is little to recommend it; small, even cramped for space, you might say. Few improvements since it was built, whenever that was, out of redwood planks and whatever was on the beach. No electricity. No hot water. Only boards and battens against the wind and rain, a woodstove against the cold."

Encouraged by Pat Stebbins and other staffers of the North Central Regional Coastal Commission, the State Park system kept the spirit of the place when it renovated the cabins; the state has done an accurate historical reconstruction.

Built almost 50 years ago for members of his own family by Congressman William Kent, the cabins, at Rocky Point below Steep Ravine, were a gift to the state. Steep Ravine, drained by Webb Creek, was added to Mount Tamalpais State Park after the congressman's death in 1928.

Repeatedly delayed by prominent Bay Area citizens with considerable political clout who held long-term leases on the cabins, Rocky Point came into possession of the State Park system in 1960. Several years ago the state Legislature finally terminated the cabin leases and ordered the buildings vacated.

During 20 years of debate, the cabins grew more weathered with every storm. Should the park system tear them down? Should it allow an RV camp here? Should the cabins become hostels for hikers? Tamalpais Conservation Club once proposed a compromise that would raze the walls and leave the floorboards for tent platforms.

In the end, no one could bear to part with the cabins.

When you reach the old marine terrace on which they stand, you understand instantly why. In "To a Cabin" it says "Here is life distilled, encompassed by earth and sea; a spare sanctuary."

Go around behind the long, low building, which housed horses and buggies as well as Reos, Merry Oldsmobiles, Henry Ford's Models A and T, and any number of other tin lizzies in the long history of the automobile.

The road continues to wind past the cabins. Follow it and soon you are abreast of another seaside meadow. Privies and water taps herald additional campsites for tent or sleeping-bag backpackers. Each site is so beautifully situated the others are not intrusive.

Finally the road passes some rocky tidepools, all protected. Look but do not disturb. Go with the road back to the parking area. Then wind your way via the simple path there that leads down to the beach.

> *Here is*
> *a different state of being*
> *where a morning cobweb becomes*
> *a fairy handkerchief*
> *where I can lie against sand and*
> *stone*
> *Face the rim of the globe*
> *Feel waves wash over me*
> *and crisp breezes refresh my*
> *skin*
> *Listen to children's laughter*
> *like blowing bells . . .*
> *Smell the spices of the season . . .*

So wrote Margaretta Mitchell. Now everyone can share the experience.

The View from Mount Tamalpais

15

For my money, the twenty-minute scenic Verna Dunshea Trail around the peak of Mount Tamalpais is the most exhilarating walk in the Bay Area. It may well rank with the more beautiful walks of the entire world.

Although good anytime, it is best in the fall when ruffled clouds, as purple-shaded as Edwardian prose, bunch lacily below it in rococo embellishment of the old blue flower of day. From this high trail, one can survey in quick succession all 360° of the compass, yet it is a relatively level walk that even the most motor-tied can enjoy.

Begin this walk in the free public parking lot on Tamalpais's East Peak. (If you come by public transportation, get off the Bolinas-bound Golden Gate Transit bus at Mountain Home Inn and take, perforce, the steep

Throckmorton hogback trail to the same point. Wear cleated boots.) At the outset, notice the picnic tables in the oaks and pines just southeast of the parking area. This grove was just below the terminal siding for the Mt. Tamalpais and Muir Woods Railway.

Walk east, toward the still evident foundations of Tamalpais Tavern, destroyed by fire. Near the adobe style restrooms is a sign indicating the Twenty-Minute Trail goes north. Take it. Within a few hundred yards Lake Lagunitas and the larger Bon Tempe Lake are visible. Meadow Cub, velvety green, lies beyond to remind the walker that grass, as John Ingalls described it, is "the forgiveness of nature— her constant benediction."

If you can take your eyes from the splendor of the hilly terrain below, at the first viewpoint notice the plaque that says "Back to the mountain in the fullness of life" and gives the dates of George Grant and his wife Grace Adelaide, who came instead in the emptiness of death. Star-thorn, manzanita, oak and madrone border the trail, framing tantalizing glimpses of San Rafael, Sir Francis Drake Boulevard, and the bay. The next curve reveals Corte Madera Slough, Point Quentin, the Richmond-San Rafael Bridge and the fields of oil tanks across the bay in Richmond. The East Peak fire trail and the Indian fire trail which peel off below are part of a fire-protection pattern created in 1913 by F. L. Olmsted, of the famous park-planning family. The face of Mount Tamalpais has been blackened by fire many times. Gardner Lookout, the little tower at its apex named for Edwin B. Gardner, long chief warden of the Tamalpais Fire District, is staffed annually until the gauge registers three inches of rainfall.

North Knee is the easily accessible viewpoint a few hundred feet down Blithedale Ridge on the Indian fire trail. The latter is a misleading name since Indians shunned the peak as a place of strong magic until a white man challenged them. According to the historian H. P. Munro-Fraser, the pioneer Jacob Primer Leese first scaled the mountain. Leese found his Indian assistants frightened because "the top of the mountain was inhabited by evil spirits and no one could go up there and come back alive." Chief Marin, considered by his men to be the bravest man in the world, then made the climb and hung his red shirt on the cross. His friends decided he had been 'robbed of his uniform by the Devil himself" until he returned.

When the hot summer wind known locally as the "Devil's Breath" roars off the peak, it is easy to see why a primitive people would fear it. To this day, Indian shamans perform special rituals with a crystal on the mountaintop every twelve years; they consider Tamalpais one of the three enchanted peaks in California.

Look for hazelnuts near the Devil's Slide, which begins in the forefront of the vast panorama of the East Bay. Tamalpa Trail is the next to join the Twenty-Minute Trail. Thereafter the trail footing becomes wooden—old railroad ties set into the cliff. Duck under the rock outcropping and you're on a little bridge overlooking Tiburon and San Francisco

A moment or two more and you have arrived at Sunrise Point, with a bench conveniently placed for viewing and steel cables protecting an even more daring overlook. After a soul-filling gaze, end this walk where you began it, having looped the mountain at an elevation of 2,400 feet above sea level.

Phoenix Lake

16

Marin County's little Phoenix Lake, like the mythical self-regenerating bird for which it is named, has been reborn. A new spillway across its renovated earth-filled dam has just been completed. For walkers, this means that once again there is easy eastern access to that whole network of wonderful wilderness trails on the Marin Municipal Water District lands.

Lagunitas, Bon Tempe, Alpine and Kent lakes all lie linked by excellent trails beyond Phoenix Lake. Quite apart from that, Phoenix Lake has charms of its own, including

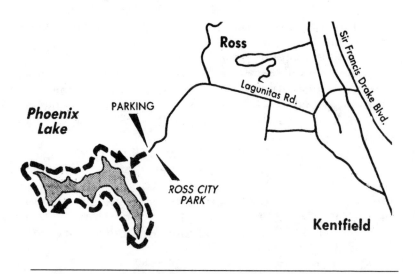

1,500 acres of natural woodland, good fishing, newly-improved trails around the water's edge and a Queen Anne log cabin that may be the only one of its kind.

To sample these attractions, the Phoenix Lake Trail is a logical starting place. Wear flat-heeled walking shoes and bring a picnic in your day pack, if you wish.

Your Alsatian, Weimaraner or cougar is welcome on a leash, but don't plan to come in a truck. Large vehicles, such as trailers; smelly ones, such as trucks and buses; and noisy ones, such as motorcycles, are prohibited at all times.

Take a Golden Gate Transit bus or your own car to the town of Ross via Sir Francis Drake Boulevard. Turn off at Lagunitas Road, passing the attractive Ross Common, and go almost to its end, continuing through the Natalie Coffin Greene Park, at one time Marin Municipal Water District (MMWD) land but now operated by the town of Ross, until you reach a large parking lot in a redwood grove.

From this point, you can take Windy Ridge Trail to Kentfield or the Harry B. Allen Trail to Larkspur. In other directions, the Yolanda Trail, Fish Gulch Trail, Fish Grade and Shaver Grade trails, Madrone Trail and Eldridge Grade Trail all take off nearby, linking with all the Mount Tamalpais trails that adjoin or fall within the MMWD watershed.

To reach Phoenix Lake, walk away from the picnic area toward the outhouses. Turn uphill on the road, which is closed to all but emergency and patrol vehicles. As soon as you are on the bridge, you have left the town of Ross and Natalie Coffin Greene Park.

Soon you will reach a big stand of beavertail cactus and century plants. Uphill from them on a ledge of land is a ranger's residence, overlooking the new spillway. A sign at the overlook announces that Phoenix Lake is open from 8 a.m. until sunset daily.

Go out on the little overlook to examine the picturesque spillway, completed in 1986 to replace an older covered flume, and then head onto the gravel road that tops the dam.

As you cross, look to your left to see the pool where water comes down the spillway from Phoenix Lake to feed Ross Creek. Phoenix, Ben Williams and Fish Gulch creeks all feed into Phoenix Lake, the second lake to be created in the MMWD system.

Former caretaker Clayton (Sox) Stocking, once a general foreman for MMWD and for its predecessor, the Marin County Water Company, once told me he had worked on the original Phoenix dam in 1904. "We hauled in all the dirt by horses, mules, men and hard labor," he said.

Phoenix dam was drained in 1966 after another earthfilled dam, the Baldwin Hills Dam in Los Angeles, broke open. By 1969, the entire earthfill had been reconstructed at Phoenix, the water level had been lowered and—to the delight of walkers and naturalists in conservation-minded Marin County—the watershed was set aside to be used as a park ever after.

As you leave the dam on the broad gravelled trail, look on your right for the single pathway that goes down to the water's edge. Created by the Marin Conservation Corps, the new path was especially designed to give fishermen better shoreline use.

Go down the steps on your right and walk along the shore as far as you can, past benches and trash cans, to see how well this replacement of an old narrow and dangerous trail has been carried out. At the far end, go up the steps on your left and you will be back on the broad main gravel trail.

Continue on the broad trail to your right and look upward for one of the prettiest views of Mount Tamalpais. As you come around the lake, look across the water to locate the smaller Bald Hill, locally known as Mount Baldy. With the ranger's house in the middle ground, it looks like an old-time chocolate box cover.

Soon you will reach Bill Williams Gulch, an area that suffered a major landslide in the big storms of 1982. Look over the left side of the trail to see a new culvert installed after the storm, with the old culvert visible below it.

The big sandbar visible on your right at this end of the lake is also a result of the 1982 storms. Maintenance crews doing the repair work hoped to find a cache of Confederate gold that pioneer Bill Williams is reputed to have hidden in the gulch. So far, it is still Bill William's secret.

When you reach a trail sign that says "Phoenix Dam Trail .6 mi," turn right and go uphill on 55 steps made of old railroad ties. There is a bench where you can pause and rest your legs near the top.

Thereafter, the trail becomes a single path high above the water, passing through native woodlands with maidenhair fern, woodwardia fern, trilliums, huckleberry and the little creeping mint, yerba buena, in the understory.

"Fortunately, eucalyptus never invaded Phoenix watershed." MMWD Lands Division Manager Stephen Petterle told me. "The few eucalyptus that appeared on the periphery of the native forest were killed by frost a few years ago and removed."

Recently, MMWD has destroyed by controlled burning nearly 30 acres of the invasive Scotch broom plant that drives out the native ceonothus and wild azalea shrubs.

Chief Ranger Casey May, who conducted me on this walk, pointed out a great blue heron's nest below us as we climbed with the path.

Pausing a moment, we could hear a fish jump. "As part of a fish habitat improvement project," he told me, "MMWD has installed 1,700 used tires in the lakebed to make a breeding place for largemouth bass. The tires are netted down and fixed to the lakebed. The goal of the project is to create a self-sustaining habitat."

The state Department of Fish and Game, which stocks the lake with fish during the winter, has put 350 bass of breeder stock into the lake, along with the red-eared sunfish that are a favorite food source for the bass.

When you reach a place where steps go down to a sandbar, ignore them and stay on the upper trail, following a sign pointing toward the "New Bridge," which is to the left.

Soon you are in a pretty redwood canyon with the music of water gurgling happily alongside the trail. Redwood logs in the streambed are part of the storm devastation to the watershed.

At the third sandbar, you are at Fish Gulch, the main feeder stream to Phoenix Lake. Continue to the left and observe how steep this canyon is. "A good rain on Fish Gulch watershed can fill Phoenix Lake in a day," Casey told me.

Cross the new bridge over the gully and you come up alongside a meter box that monitors the water flow. Turn right to cross the footbridge alongside it, then turn right again on the road, which is often alive with walkers and joggers.

This land, originally part of Rancho Punta de Quentin, was called Hippolyte Ranch by James S. Porteous, and his wife, Janet, who bought it in 1883 from pioneer Alexander Forbes.

The picturesque Queen Anne log cabin you will soon sight on your left was built later for their coachman, Martin Grant. Believed to be the only one of its kind in Marin, the log cabin has been recommended for restoration and landmark status. If you have any old photos of the cabin, or of the Porteous mansion, which stood uphill (where the ranger's residence is visible) until it burned in 1925, please send them to Petterle, MMWD, 220 Nellen Avenue, Corte Madera 94925.

When you become aware of a log anchored mid-lake for a duck landing, you are in an area that was a tunnel of

Scotch broom two or three years ago. Now completely clear, the trail once again overlooks the lake.

The hollow log you pass is a horse trough. Horses are permitted on the Yolanda Trail, but bicycles must use only the designated "protection roads" used by ranger patrols. Those who venture onto other trails can be cited and their bicycles can be impounded.

The trail soon brings you back below the green house that serves as a ranger station. Having looped the entire lake and finished this walk, you are now in possession of another of Marin County's better-kept secrets.

Larskpur Landing

17

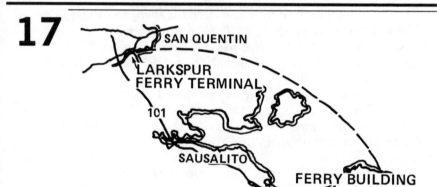

This walk is on water! (Oh, come now, there is a widely accepted report extant that Somebody once walked on water . . .)

Bridges notwithstanding, the swanlike Ferry Building, that mellow colossus of Colusa sandstone, is still San Francisco's most romantic gate. Recently it hatched two ducklings, but both siblings—the Larskpur Terminal and the new San Francisco Ferry Terminal—both built by the Golden Gate Bridge, Highway, and Transportation District, are birds of far different structure from San Francisco's Ferry Building. More than anything else, the new San Francisco

Ferry Terminal is a space-age ramada, an elaborate train on the bustle of a Victorian grande dame.

When the ribbon was cut, loosing the new fledgling from its architects, Enviromental Planning and Design Associates, readers of the "Bay Area at Your Feet" column in the *San Francisco Chronicle* were invited to walk around both terminals and the breadth of the bay between via a half-fare ferry trip. Although it costs more today, the trip is well worth it.

To make this walk, present yourself at the Larkspur Terminal or at San Francisco Terminal half an hour before any sailing time with cash in hand for the roundtrip ticket. (One way is normally $2.20. Children twelve and under and old jokers like me go for less.)

Assuming that you are starting from San Francisco, convey yourself to the watery end of Market Street, preferably by Muni buses 7, 8, 9, 14, 21, 31, or 32, all of which converge at the Ferry Building or near its green apron, Justin Herman Park. When you reach the building, look for the red, blue, and green "wave" signs of the Golden Gate Transit District. These will direct you through the large open arch south of the clocktower and tunnel. In a trice you are on a concrete platform facing the airy steel trellis, trees, and windscreens of the new terminal. Follow the line to your right to the ticket window; then, ticket in hand, meander around at the entry level to see how the waiting rooms are placed. If there is time before your boat puts in, go up to the second level and stroll the long ramp for a fine bay view and an overview of the terminal complex. That big boxy structure at the bay end of the platform is an airvent shaft for the subway tube of the BART system. Golden Gate District boardmember Steve Leonidaikis, who first conducted me on this walk, encouraged the restaurant on its roof. Old ferry hands who yearn for the classic waiting patterns of yore also look in at Sinbad's on the next pad south. It is close enough for commuters to enjoy a meal or drink, and while waiting one can keep an eye out for the ferry approach. It also augurs well for the revitalization of the waterfront between the Ferry Building and the Bay Bridge; where a promenade has been made between these landmarks.

Once aboard the ferry, wander casually around each deck to sample the variations of views, wind, spray, shelter and ambiance. Then pick a spot where you can enjoy the unfurling panorama of the bay. The bridges, the ridges, the islands, the highlands, the cities, the pretties, all come into one's ken in a graceful succession.

After you are well across the bay, as you pass grim old San Quentin, first Muzzy Marsh and then Heerdt Marsh, a preserve of the California State Fish and Game Department, will be on the south. The preserve was rebuilt by the transit district after the Larkspur Terminal construction. Corte Madera Slough is the channel between them that sustains a houseboat colony. Larkspur Landing is the shopping center and apartment development on your right. A pedestrian footbridge over Sir Francis Drake Boulevard leads to it. Wood Island, is the eminence visible behind the lacy geometrics of the Larkspur Terminal.

History buffs, aware that it was 410 years ago that Sir Francis Drake "fell in with a convenient and fit harborough" somewhere on the Bay Area coast, may get an extra thrill when they realize some historians believe this is the area where the old freebooter careened *The Golden Hind.* Drake's plate of brass, which may or may not be the greatest scholarly hoax of our time, was found on the hillslope visible across U.S. Route 101.

When you are ashore at Larkspur, stroll around the traingular terminal here to assess its family ties to the San Francisco structure. It may be an architect's dream, but in rainy weather it is a commuter's nightmare. Then go out towards the parking lot and take the sidewalk which goes left toward the marsh. High tides leave flotsam visible in the pickleweed, but depending on the time of day, you may spot a western grebe, or even a daring clapper rail on the marsh.

Once around the parking lot, follow the line of the little creek below trees to East Sir Francis Drake Boulevard and take a left skirting it. As you walk, notice the little one-block-long frontier town that could be a set for a western movie. This is Buckaloo Flats, which accommodates a handful of shops, among them The Growing Concern, an antique shop and refinishing establishment where oak is prime. The town is totally contrived. Of the antiques, about seventy percent of what you see are old, and thirty percent are reproductions made in the Bay Area.

Persist along the boulevard to find it is possible to cross that complex freeway interchange. The Cross-Marin Bicycle trail makes its way along the waterside on this route poters out at Ross but ultimately will arrive at Samuel P. Taylor State Park and Tomales Bay State Park. (Buses also connect with the ferries and go to Point Reyes and to Muir Woods.)

Walk only as far as the waiting time for the next ferryboat permits, then start back. Miss the ferry and it's a long swim back!

Stinson Beach

18

The splendid three-mile-long crescent of sand at Stinson Beach, variously described as 12½, 15, and 23 miles north of San Francisco, has been called "the best in Northern California." The southern six-tenth mile of it, which had been a state park since 1961, has quietly eased over into the Golden Gate National Recreation Area. To the public "from over the hill," which started swarming into the area to play and picnic 110 years ago when Capt. Alfred Easkoot first put up tents for vacationers, the big discernible change was a pleasant one: the $1.50 daily parking fee was dropped. For the 1,500 or so "natives" who live in the little shoreline village, a recreational community whose only historical *raison de'etre* is the enticing sand strand, the change was also pleasant: traffic no longer tied up Highway 1 while waiting at the park entrance to pay the fee.

There are some other subtle differences. Parked cars that used to clog streets west of the highway while their owners dodged the fee by strolling through the pedestrian gates, now show up in the capacious parking lot instead. Golden Gate Transit buses come into the park to turn around. The antidog law is being enforced. There is a larger staff of life guards and rangers with better equipment, including a paddleboard large enough to bring a disabled swimmer through the surf.

None of this will really matter to the walker who comes north to explore Stinson Beach for the first time. He is in for a thrill. Long before he nears the sand, his anticipation will begin rising. Soon after the Stinson Beach turnoff onto California Highway 1 from U.S. Route 101 north of the Golden Gate Bridge (and once past the schlocky inter-section at Tamalpais Valley), Shoreline Highway reaches an intersection with Panoramic Highway. (Either route will bring you to Stinson Beach). Surprisingly soon Panoramic Highway reaches open countryside, much of it in the Golden Gate National Recreation Area. Follow Panoramic Highway uphill around the shoulders of Mount Tamalpais through the contiguous state park as it weaves through the canyons; the everyday pressures seem to drop away from the most harried city dweller. By the time the road swings downhill at Pantoll ranger station, you will have passed through a refreshing succession of redwood groves alter-nating with vast ridgetop overviews.

The best is still to come. On the curve above White
Gate Ranch, one gets the first enticing glimpse of the long
sandspit below, often framed in a sea that seems to be of a
handhammered silver studded in season with salmon
boats. On a clear day, the Farallones are visible. The road
then descends abruptly. The second curve in the road
makes a drop of perhaps sixty feet below a landmark water
tank, and here the whole view seems enlarged, as though

the air itself were a giant magnifying glass. There, a few miles below, is one's destination, laid out like a map. There are not many roads today whose promise of a worthy end is so soon realized.

Highway 1 is also "Main Street" for the community of Stinson Beach, which takes its name from Nathan Stinson, another early entrepreneur of recreation. Early on, this area was known as Willow Camp, a name commemorated in a local antique store. Later, the Dipsea Inn and the eight-mile trail to it from Mill Valley, gave the area a name. Oddly enough, the name that has stuck commemorates a man who stayed at the beach (albeit surrounded by tents he had raised) for only five years.

Actual beach turnoff into the park is about 100 feet north of the village's major intersection. Follow the beach-trail, once you are parked. Soon a bordering road will take you through trees, away from the parking lot that has covered "Poison Lake." As you pass the grassy picnic and barbecue area, look for a three-story lookout tower, whose beach sign says FOOD. A lifeguard spotter's station is on the top level, rangers' offices are in the middle, and first aid facilities are on the lowest. A snack bar is around on the north side.

Continue strolling south through the dunes to locate a place to plunk your gear. As you walk, observe the jasper seastacks offshore at the point where the strand seems to terminate. These have given the name of Red Rock Beach to the extreme south end, traditionally a little more permissive for sunbathing. Little buildings that look from this vantage like an Irish coastal colony are the controversial Kent Cottages at Rocky Point, which are now pioneer education camp hostels. A southern entrace for the beach could also be in the cards.

When you have reached the cliffs, reverse your direction and start north. Leashed dogs at midbeach signal the end of the GGNRA and the beginning of the county area—the cream colored house is near the boundary. When the crowd thins out, you are alee of Seadrift, the posh second home community which occupies much of the northernmost section of the sandspit. In California, beaches below the mean high tide line are public, but property owners have been known to let their own mean high dudgeon line preempt the legal tide line.

When you reach the end of the spit, you will be at the swift channel separating the venerable village of Bolinas, original headquarters of Rancho Tomales y Baulenas. On the original *diseño* the sandspit was designated simply as *"arenal."* Bolinas residents saw waterfront houses tumble off their pilings during the earthquake of 1906, as did the old hotel and a few boats converted to residences on the sandspit.

Meander back as you will. You may be lucky enough to see a man walking a huge tortoise on the beach, as one did recently. See hang gliders land on the beach or have roses dropped on your head from a low flying plane: one young man took this route to propose marriage to his young lady here not so long ago.

A Walk in the Woods to the Seashore

19

Beautiful Bear Valley, a natural break in Inverness Ridge at Point Reyes National Seashore, is thirty-five miles northwest of San Francisco by way of the weaving, winding, twisting, twining, narrow California Highway 1. From the city, it is faster via U.S. Route 101 and Sir Francis Drake Boulevard. Either way you go, it is an ideal one day excursion.

Seasoned hikers refer to Bear Valley Trail as "an old ladies' stroll" because it is fairly level. It is also so entrancing at least one conservationist, fearful of threatened overuse, has called it "a Yosemite Valley of the future."

This it may well become. Today it is still unspoiled and to the casual walker not in gung-ho climbing condition, Bear

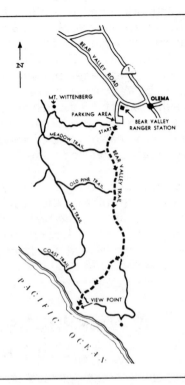

Valley Trail can be pleasurable indeed. It rambles for 4 4/10 miles on an old ranch roadway along two singing creeks which drain in opposite directions, by a magnificent dogwood, through bishop pine, Douglas fir, madrone, laurel, and horsechestnut trees to the ocean. At the shore, cliffs, agate-strewn beaches, blowholes, seastacks, little tumbling waterfalls, tidepools, and wind-worn meadows reward the walker.

Begin this walk on the sunniest day possible, for coastal valleys are gloomy in the fog. Bring a lightweight lunch you can carry easily and a canteen, for there are no concessions. (Nearest source of refreshments is in the little town of Olema.) Leave your dog at home. Horses are allowed on weekdays only, which makes hiking easier and less crowded on the weekend.

Stop first at the handsome new visitor center at park headquarters, designed by Henrik Bull, located beyond what was formerly the barn of Bear Valley Dairy Ranch, Architect Earl R. MacDonald, who did much of the work on the ranch during the 1930s, designed the bunkhouse that is now the ranger station. The milk station has become the park fire station. Trail maps, bird count lists, and such are distributed at the visitors center, which has a fine small museum. Also for sale are postcards, U.S. Geological Survey maps, and paperback books about the area.

After your stop here, look near a white gate for the NPS-brown sign marking the trail. Rules posted nearby indicate the current restrictive stringencies.

Bear Valley has forty miles of hiking trails, many of them a spiderweb of unused ranch roads. More ambitious climbers and physical fitness fans may want to follow Sky Trail west from this point up the 1,407-foot elevation of Mount Wittenburg, then loop south to the coast and return via Bear Valley. Lazier amblers should look for the road south.

At the outset the road follows Bear Valley Creek, which drains in the opposite direction from Coast Creek, thanks to the San Andreas Fault, on whose geologically tender edge this land lies.

Gradually the road rises with the land. After passing a meadow with a few picnic tables, the road parallels Coast Creek. Stop occasionally and listen to the singing water. Each creek and each little streamlet, spring, and falls that joins the mainstream makes its own music, becoming almost symphonic at the ocean.

The meadow has a past history as the location of a hunt club which Presidents William Howard Taft and Teddy Roosevelt visited. At one time an excursion surrey made regular runs from Olema House to the beach via Bear Valley Road at a cost of one dollar per passenger.

Along the path are "the blue forget-me-nots that grow for happy lovers. Within a mile of the Pacific, you reach a designated wilderness. You'll know it by the "No Bicycle" sign. Look also for birds as you walk. The Point Reyes peninsula has had the second highest bird count in the nation.

After passing several subsidiary paths, Bear Valley Trail leaves the roadway in a meadow almost within sound of the sea. Walk out to the cliff viewpoint to reconnoiter, then follow the path south that says "Blowhole—Caution." Here is high adventure. At low tide, the trail gives access to the beach through a windcarved arch. As the tide rises, one can see the ocean at work carving ever more seastacks.

If you come upon a little shard of Ming pottery on the beach, you can chalk it up to the leavings of either Sir Francis Drake's ship *The Golden Hind*, or Sebastian Cermeno's Spanish galleon *San Agustin*. Agates are commoner. Both shards and stones belong to the park.

Plan at least one visit as a spring wildflower trip, when the big dogwood tree near the start of the trail is in bloom. If you want to see the spot where legend has it the earth swallowed a cow in the earthquake of 1906, try the shorter Earthquake Trail. (This is described later in this book, as "An Earthquake Walk at Bear Valley.")

The View from Mount Wittenburg

20

"For pure, unadulterated sea air, full of fog and oxygen, charged with ozone, salubrious and salsuginous, invigorating and life-giving air, that will make the pulses leap and bring the roses to the cheek, one should go to Point Reyes, where it can be had at first hand, bereft of nothing."

So wrote H.P. Munro-Fraser in his authoritative history of Marin County, describing in 1880 the climate of what is now the Point Reyes National Seashore. The walker who makes the climb in spring from Bear Valley to the bald crest of 1,407-foot Mount Wittenburg, a southern highpoint of the Inverness Ridge, will discover at this season the salsuginous sea air is charged with the scent of lupine, California

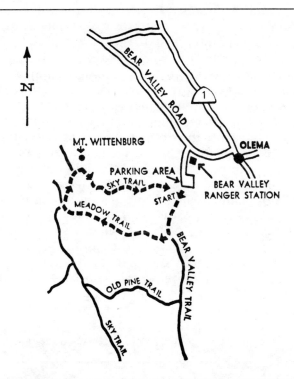

poppies, cowslips, and iris. If the winter's rains have been plentiful, the countryside blossoms with a rare lushness.

Pack a knapsack lunch and canteen, for there are no concessions at Bear Valley. Make an information stop at the Bear Valley Visitor Center beyond the farmhouse that serves as park headquarters. This is about half a mile from Olema, thirty-five miles northwest of San Francisco on "wonderful One," the beautiful narrow coastal highway that is, at this writing, a scenic treasure unspoiled in its interrelationship with the land through which it passes.

Park at the trailhead and walk south on the Bear Valley Trail. Almost immediately, the Sky Trail to Mount Wittenburg takes off uphill. Ignore it for the moment and continue on the Bear Valley Trail to see the "butterfly tree," a great white eastern dogwood across the creek beyond the bridge.

Watch along the trail for five-finger ferns which grow in profusion here. Soon Meadow Trail forks uphill on the right. Take it to make a gentle climb to the peak through a primeval forest of Douglas firs for which Inverness Ridge is noted.

After many long switchbacks through laurel, madrone, bishop pine, and fir, the trail reaches a beautiful grassy meadow where the observant may sometimes spot a mountain badger or a black-tailed deer. The trail, almost lost in deep grass, goes back into the trees at the far end of the meadow to cross Sky Trail soon thereafter on a lower shoulder of Mount Wittenburg. Follow Sky Trail right around a broad curve until a sign indicates the way to the mountaintop and a bare path winds uphill like a great embroidered thread.

Mount Wittenburg was not named for Prince Hamlet's alma mater, according to Erwin G. Gudde's *California Place Names*, but for a man named Wittenburg reputed to have had a ranch here. It may have been at the corral site visible in a little crotch of land below the peak toward the west. A cairn of rock under the seashore blue sign noting the elevation of the crest and another nearby supporting a red,

much-faded rag of flag are all that mark the mountaintop.

On a foggy day, film maker Mark Kitchel says, "On the crest it is like living with gods on Mount Olympus or Parnassus. All you see are other mountaintops." On a fair day, the view is stupendous, with Olema looking like a toy railroad town and Drake's Estero like a map on the land. To Ranger Mark Koening, it makes tangible the concept of plate tectonics as one looks over the wrinkles in the earth's surface.

Look for Mount Tamalpais, Mount St. Helena, and Mount Diablo to get your bearings. When you have gloried in the surroundings sufficiently or have finished your picnic lunch, pick up Sky Trail for a quick return. It winds, a single footpath, through lupine and poppies over the south-easterly side of the mounded crest.

Point Reyes

31

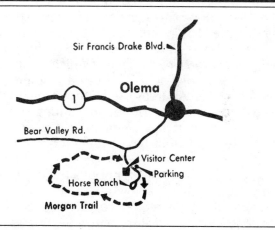

Point Reyes, like any significant land mass, means different things to different people. for the initiate, it represents those great long beaches, gentle peaks, superb Douglas fir forests and the wonderful wilderness feelings of unpressured solitude. But there are also those, especially first-time and one-time visitors, the Elsewhereans, who seek it for its man-made pleasures.

The barn-like new Bear Valley Visitor Center, near park headquarters in Olema, and the new Morgan Trail, which loops around it, passing the Morgan Horse Ranch and its little museum as well as Kule Loklo, the reconstructed Miwok village, were designed with these park users in mind.

West Marin loves its old barns. As well it might, for they call up in all of us a yearning for that uncomplicated time when open fields of browsing cows were not a rarity. If you haven't been up to Point Reyes, or haven't been there recently, consider a walk today on the Morgan Trail. It is easy enough for tots.

Dig out your warm jacket and walking shoes. Pack a picnic if you wish. Then head north from San Francisco via Highway 101 and Sir Francis Drake Boulevard to Olema. Park headquarters is about a mile from the historic Olema Inn, and Jevoys Farm House a restaurant.

Landmark for park headquarters is a big red barn with a "W" on its cupola. This signals the entrance to the park, but it is NOT the visitor center.

Part of the original Shafter Ranch (which was so vast it was divided into 26 parts, each of which was given a letter of the alphabet to distinguish it from the others), "W" Ranch straddles the San Andreas Fault. One corner of the barn was moved 16 feet off its foundation during the 1906 earthquake. Although it has been in use ever since, county earthquake regulations have prevented its development as a visitor center.

Drive on past, and park about a quarter of a mile down the road at the Bear Valley Trailhead parking lot.

On sight, you'll recognize the new brown barn just north of the lot as a visitor center. Inviting as it seems, for this walk save the visitor center for last and look instead for the Morgan Trail sign to the right of the broad Bear Valley Trail, originally a ranch road, on the west side of the asphalt road that leads uphill to the Morgan Horse Ranch.

The trail, a double-width, crushed quarry-rock path, angles off uphill across a meadow, in the opposite direction from the much-used Earthquake Trail.

When you are about 100 yards uphill, abreast of a distinguished clump of fine old Douglas firs, pause a moment to look back down on the valley, with the visitor center in the foreground.

This barn might look familiar to you. Henrik Bull, of the Bull, Volkman and Stockwell architectural firm, which designed the center, may well have taken as his inspiration the Inociente DeGottardi barn built in 1902. It is still standing alongside Highway 1 at the Alan Sieroty State Beach on the east side of Tomales Bay. The major differences between the two buildings are age and the windows in the cupola and in the hayloft door space.

The new grass around the center was a golden wedding anniversary gift to the Harold Bucklins of Inverness from their friends and family as a tribute to Harold's years of work on the trails of the national seashore.

Climb another 50 feet and pause again to look beyond the center at Black's Mountain, known to fans of rock music as Elephant Mountain, almost a twin to White's Mountain a little farther away. This vantage spot should appeal to photographers focusing on the visitor center and the peaceful valley, with its venerable bay trees.

As you continue through a wet area, notice how peeler posts have been used as curbing for the trail to lift it up out of the spongy earth. Come along this slope at dawn and you may spot a mountain badger. When Ranger Harry Carpenter, who supervised the building of the Morgan Trail, and I came this way, a white fallow deer was munching grass in a scene as picturesque as a Christmas card.

You soon cross the Woodpecker Trail. Horse-lovers may want to detour to the right for a quick look at the Morgan horses in the National Park system. The Morgans themselves are the first truly American breed. They are all descended from a strong little horse named Figure, who came into the hands of a Vermont singing master named Justin Morgan in 1795 in payment of a debt. Figure proved to be so useful, and have such stamina, that his progeny have been sought as saddle horses, farm horses, carriage horses, dray horses and war horses.

Soon the trail goes into a forest of bay, tan oak and hazelbrush, which opens into a cathedral-like area of patriarchal firs every bit as majestic as redwoods.

Ignore the service road (it goes to a water tank) and bear right at the crossroads. In another 60 feet, a switchback trail goes uphill to the Miwok village. Bear left instead to the Horse Trail and stay on it. This cut-and-fill section of the trail swoops down to Horse Creek. The new bridge was put in about five years ago. Do not cross it, but bear right on the broad main trail.

Kule Lokio, the Miwok Indian village, will come into view charmingly on your right. Look for a hikers' stile—a gap in the fence—and stroll through the village to see its acorn granary, redwood bark house, tule house, *temescal* and a newly completed Dance House, which is half underground. The big rectangle on the ground is also a dance area, which Inland Miwoks come here annually to use.

At the main sign at the edge of the village, follow the trail into the eucalyptus. Avoid the poison oak on your right. At the next trail sign, bear right. Go left downhill at the service road, and then follow the paddock fence line to the right again. Shortly you will see the visitor center come into view as the trail rounds the gentle curve of the hillside.

"This trail is up for adoption under our Adopt-a-Trail program," Ranger Carpenter told me. "Hopefully, it will be chosen by the Pacific Pioneers of Pacific Telephone Company, who would make it accessible for the handicapped." So far, 10 volunteer groups have adopted trails in the national seashore and have 11 active volunteer trail crews at work, with four more giving occasional work days.

Pause to take a good look when you come to a sign indicating a site restoration project. Much of the road you are on will be grass covered when work is completed. Veer with the path around to the left and come down into the valley.

Complete this walk with a stop at the Bear Valley Visitor Center, with its nutshell view of the wildlife in this vast, wonderful park.

Point Reyes Light, and the Sea Lion Overlook

22

The Point Reyes Lighthouse was established in 1870 on the pitch of the western head of Point Reyes, which has been called the most dangerous shore on the west coast of the continent. Its location is dramatic, overlooking on the one hand a favorite playground of the California gray whale, and on the other, a hangout for sea lions and puffins.

It is a tossup whether it sees more fog annually than Point Barrow, Alaska, or Nantucket Light, Massachusetts. Certainly the cold isolation must have been foggy when that usually factual historian J.P. Munro-Fraser saw it in 1880. The Alley Bowen and Company *History of Marin County* records his impressions in a burst of purple prose:

> In the lonely watches of the dreary, stormy night, with the fury of the wind about him, with the roar and rush of the breakers dashing against the rocks below him, sounding in his ears, with no human soul near him, sits the keeper, true to his trust, faithful to his charge, doing well and honestly his duty, keeping his lamp trimmed and burning, sending forth the ray to guide and make glad the storm-encircled sailor. Then let honor be given to whom honor is due and to these brave, sacrificing men, let us render a just tribute.

Munro-Fraser must have seen Point Reyes at its grim worst. At its splendid best, there are few places in the world more spectacular. The lighthouse closed to the public on May 15, 1967, when the Coast Guard said it hadn't enough

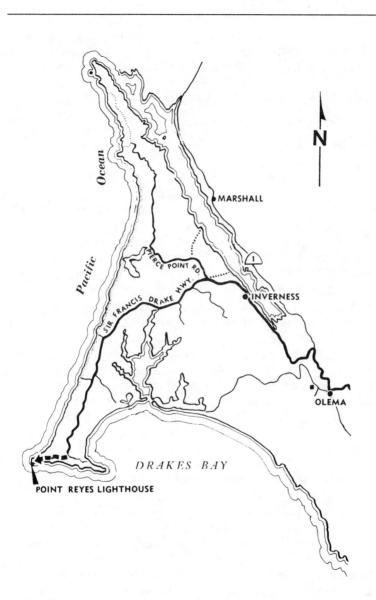

personnel to accommodate visitors. Happily for all of us, it
was reopened by the National Park Service in August 1977.
Walkers can now explore what could easily become the

number one tourist attraction of the National Seashore.

To make this walk from U.S. Route 101, take Sir Francis Drake Boulevard west, beyond Olema, to its end in Point Reyes National Seashore. Here is the parking lot for Sea Lion Overlook and the lighthouse. As the road makes its way westerly you can tell whether the light will be "socked in" or not. (A call to the Visitor Center, 663-1092, or to the lighthouse, 669-1534, will also let you know the forecast ahead of time.) Once parked, put on your hiking boots, gloves, hat and an extra windshirt or sweater. The headland is always breezier than the sheltered parking lot.

At the outset, look for the trail marker that indicates the Sea Lion Overlook, then follow the single path uphill to the fence-enclosed vantage. One time when I made this walk, thirty-seven sea lions and twenty-two pups were visible on the offshore rocks below. Others cavorted in the water like schoolboys on a spree.

When you have witnessed this glimpse of shore life sufficiently, follow the looping trail back through wonderful wildflowers in spring to the parking lot. You can continue your walk on the paved road beyond the car-barrier. As you go, look for the rare "Johnny Tuck," a Point Reyes orthocarpus or "owls clover". En route you will be sheltered by an old cypress windbreak. Through it you can see the great Point Reyes Beach.

As you walk, try to imagine a clipper ship under full sail, coming ashore on the beach in a deep fog. This is what happened to the *Sea Nymph* in 1861, the Russian ship *Novick* in 1853, the *Warrior Queen* in 1875, and to some ten other ships, the last of which was the *Tai Vin* in 1924. Another thirteen ships and an airliner were wrecked on the lighthouse headlands.

Wildflowers along the cliff on your left seem to thrive prodigiously despite the steady onshore breeze. Look for coast buckwheat, mallow, poppies, owl's clover, mimulus, and lupine to bloom here, nurtured by the moisture of fog, long after they have dried up elsewhere.

Be prepared to climb steps. When you reach the lighthouse you are at a prime location to watch the Gray Whale migration, especially between January and March.

You will be at the top of a flight of stairs equal in height to a thirty-story building. George von Physter lists the number of steps as 304 in his book *California Lighthouses*. My own count, and that of Dave Mitchell of the Pulitzer prize-winning *Point Reyes Light*, a West Marin weekly paper which takes its name from the lighthouse, is 429. Preparatory to reopening the station, the Park Service installed new handrails and several rest-stop platforms. After you check in with the ranger, look for the concrete pad on your right for a splendid overview of the whole complex. Murres and puffins have been observed among the cormorants on the rocks below. Bodega Head is the land mass visible to the northwest. The odd dome, which looks like the bald head of a giant Mr. Clean emerging from a cement tray, is an ingenious water recovery system used by lighthouse keepers in the days when transportation of water depended on horse and wagon.

Check with the ranger in the attractive little visitors center-cum-book store before you start down the steps, Park Service orders are to close the light in case of high winds. As you make your way down the staircase, notice the rails underfoot on either side. These were used for a handcart which once brought supplies down to the "wickies" or "coasties" on duty.

The *piece de resistance* of this walk is the light itself, a magnificent, pineapple-shaped first order Fresnel lens composed of hand ground glass bullseyes mounted in brass. More than a thousand pieces of glass make up the lens, to give it the appearance of gigantic glistening diamonds when it is lighted. When refined lard oil lamps lit the lens, a glass chimney carried the smoke up to a ball-shaped opening on the roof. A clockwork drive powered by a weight rotated the lens. Beams could be seen twenty-four miles at sea. The light became electrified around 1916 and has been automated since 1970.

If the splendid isolation makes you yearn to spend a year or so here, reflect, as you make your way back up those ranks of steps, that in 1889 the second assistant keeper went crazy and was handed over to the constable in Olema.

Miwoks

23

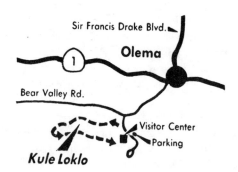

Coast Miwok Indians inhabited Marin County for at least 3000 years before the coming of the white man. "They are a people of a tractable, free and loving nature, without guile or treachery," was the way Francis Fletcher, chaplain of Sir Francis Drake's ship *Golden Hind*, described them in his journal.

When Drake arrived off the Marin coast in 1759, there were at least 113 Miwok villages on the Point Reyes Peninsula. Now the Coast Miwoks are almost extinct, victims of foreign diseases for which they had no immunity.

What few Coast Miwoks remain are shy indeed, but once a year some of them come to Kule Loklo, the Coast Miwok Cultural Exhibit in the Point Reyes National Seashore. The Fifth Annual Native American Celebration is next Saturday, July 13, from 10 a.m. to 5 p.m. Then basket makers, wood and stone carvers, beaders, flint knappers, singers and dancers will enliven the exhibit with the activities their forefathers might have been engaged in when the billowing sails of the *Golden Hind* were sighted off the coast.

The walk around Kule Loklo, which is really a display of indigenous architecture rather than a village, is good any time, but best of all during the celebration. One can then taste foods prepared in the native fashion and, in some few cases, purchase native-made handicrafts.

To enjoy this walk, head north from San Francisco complete with a picnic and walking shoes. The route is via Highway 101 and Sir Francis Drake Boulevard to Olema. Make a right turn alongside the historic Olema Inn, and, immediately beyond it, turn sharp left to reach park headquarters about a mile from the inn.

Follow the road into the National Seashore, driving between the headquarters building and the big red barn with a "W" on it. These were originally buildings on the "W" ranch, part of the Shafter Ranch, which was so vast it was divided into 26 sections, each named for a letter of the alphabet.

About a quarter of a mile down the road is the big new Bear Valley Visitor's Center, designed by Bull, Bolkmann and Stockwell. Park across the road from it in the big trailhead parking lot.

Stop first in the center to see the fine arts display, which complements permanent displays of the wildlife of the Point Reyes peninsula. When you have looked over the spacious center, go out through the main exit, walk east parallel to the approach road and look for the trail sign for Kule Loklo.

Follow the trail uphill to your left, between trees and the paddock fence. Along the quarter-mile path, there are five trailside exhibits describing the Miwoks' culture of the past, their use of their environment, the impact on the tribes of the European arrival, the demise of native tribes and, finally, the current revival of interest in the culture.

The "village" was started in 1976 by the National Park Service, Miwok Archeological Preserve of Marin and the Dixie School District of Marin County. Constructed of native materials, and with methods used by the Coast Miwoks, Kule Loklo was built for the education of park visitors.

Program coordinator Kepa Maly told me, "Kule Loklo isn't really a village, however much it may resemble one. Buildings alone don't make villages. It is people who make villages."

More people, especially Miwok-Pomo families, have begun coming each year for the celebration, and now the project even has a Miwok-Pomo staff member, Milton "Bun" Lucas, recruited by the Bureau of Indian Affairs.

Look near the gateway for a wooden box containing leaflets that describe a self-guided tour of the "village." There is no charge for these or for entering the exhibit, but walkers are expected to return leaflets to the box.

Go into Kule Loklo. If you have ever been there before, you will find the changes are significant. There are many new structures among the older ones. One of these is a "lam-ma," as Miwoks called the sweathouse. Two others are "kotca," which, according to a Miwok dictionary, meant, "a place where real people (as opposed to spirits) lived." Both are larger than earlier dwellings. One is a thatched, the other a redwood bark-slab "kotca."

There is also a new, and bigger, dance structure and an outdoor dance area. Come along at the right time Saturday and you may see fragments of native dances performed or hear a singer intoning a spirit song, a walking song or a gambling song.

"There may no longer be any pure-bred Miwoks," Maly, who is part Hawaiian, told me, "but there are Miwoks carrying English and Spanish surnames that are alive and actively recall what their elders taught them of the Miwok culture. Some of these families have started to come to Kule Loklo for the celebration. We are hoping to develop a docent program in which trainees will be taught by such Coast Miwok-Pomo native Americans." If this is a program that interests you, Maly is the man to see for enrolling.

Stop at the food booth, if you wish. The proceeds help to support the Hitil Child Development Center. When you have enjoyed the "village" to its fullest, look for the trail near the restrooms to return the way you came.

If you would enjoy a longer walk, as you exit, look to the right for a sign that says, "To the Horse Barns." Follow it into the forest. The trail plunges down near a creek (don't cross the bridge), then swings around to the left along the far side of the Morgan horse pasture to come out near the barns where Morgan brood mares are stables. Stop awhile to admire these unique little broad-shouldered mounts.

Morgans are indigenous to the United States. Those bred at Point Reyes are used in the National Seashore for ranger patrols. Like all Morgans, they are descended originally from a strong little horse called "Figure," owned in 1795 by Vermont singing master Justin Morgan. It is the only recognized American breed of horse. Morgan fanciers point out that Stonewall Jackson's horse Fancy, Phil Sheridan's Rienzi and Custer's horse Comanche, who survived the "Last Stand," were all Morgans.

Visit the tack room to see exhibits of horsey paraphernalia. Then head down hill on either the Woodpecker Trail, past that distinguished clump of old Douglas fir trees standing alone in the meadow, or the broader fire road. Either way will return you to the area of the Bear Valley Trailhead parking lot, the tree-shaded picnic area and the Visitor's Center.

The Loch Ness of Marin

24

TOMALES BAY STATE PARK

Whenever another of the outsized footprints of Bigfoot, the elusive monster of the Northwest, is discovered and followed by attendant merriment, I find myself with an almost over-whelming Puckish urge to start a watery rumor. The rumor would be that something resembling the Loch Ness monster had been sighted in Tomales Bay.

Loch Ness, like Tomales Bay, lies in a great long geological fault and is also a firth connected to the sea. There is sufficient physical similarity of conformation that James Black, an early Marin settler, named a western shore community for his birthplace, Inverness, in whose shire Loch Ness lies. So far, my conscience has kept my irresponsible urge in check (if a Scot's conscience does not keep her from sinning, my Grandfather Watson used to warn, it will surely keep her from enjoying it). Nevertheless, I keep hoping that some enterprising junk-sculptor will artfully nail four monstrous old half-track tires to a raft and set it afloat some misty night.

I suspect it is this, as much as the Bishop pines and the cockles, that brings me back every so often for a walk in Tomales Bay State Park, four miles north of Inverness. As local residents know, it is a good walk for the Point Reyes National Seashore visitor who finds himself on Point Reyes on one of those grey days when the fog seems to have a cold edge that cuts to the bone. If there is warmth and sheltered waterside walking to be had on the long peninsula on such a day, it is to be found in the sandy little coves and western shore beaches of Tomales Bay State Park.

Begin this walk with a stop at your local bait shop for a clamdigging license. Bring your clam hoe, picnic and thermos (the nearest shops are at Inverness), pay the day-use fee, park as near to the water as you can, and you are then ready to explore on foot these unspoiled 1,018 acres of scenic excellence.

The big parking area is at Heart's Desire Beach, with two other beaches in easy walking distance. Three-quarters of a mile north is Indian Beach. About one-third of a mile south is Pebble Beach. There are good trails through the woods overlooking the shore, which take off from the parking circle, but if it is low tide, stick to the beach instead and join in or watch the carnival of clammers as they scrabble through the rocks for the succulent prize, *Paphis stamines*, also known as the little-neck clam, hard-shell clam, Tomales Bay cockle, rock clam, and the ribbed carpet shell. Fifty is the limit and they must each be more than 1½ inches in diameter.

Long before either Juan Rodriquez Cabrillo or Sir Francis Drake sailed past the Marin coast, Indians clawed among the rocks of this shore for clams much as people do today. Their name for the water which had filled the San Andreas rift zone was Lake Olemas. Since Tomales means Bay, today we are using the redundant name of "Bay Bay" for this long narrow inlet. As you walk, watch for redwing blackbirds, tule wrens, Wilson snipes, bitterns, and those beachfront clowns—the sandpipers. Herons, ruddy ducks, scoters, grebes, wilets and curlews are not uncommon. Sometimes the great Point Reyes ravens pass overhead. Keep your eye peeled among the rocks and you may stumble on a shell of the rare native oyster. Fences visible in some parts of Tomales Bay protect imported oyster beds under cultivation, both from poachers and from underwater predators.

When you have explored the beach, return to the parking circle to pick up the Jepson Trail, named in honor of the late Willis Linn Jepson, a pioneer conservationist and founder of the School of Forestry at the University of California. From the south side of the circle, it leads uphill through California laurel, madrone, oak and wax myrtle to a splendid stand of Bishop pine, the Jepson Memorial Grove. The Bishop pine, whose cones may hang onto the stem they encircle for fifteen years, has built-in insurance against forest fires. Its cones open and seeds germinate only after exposure to fire.

Take a last look at the bay before you leave. If something that looks like a Loch Ness monster seems to be lurking in the distance, I'd be grateful if you'd let me know.

Marin's Quiet Country Village

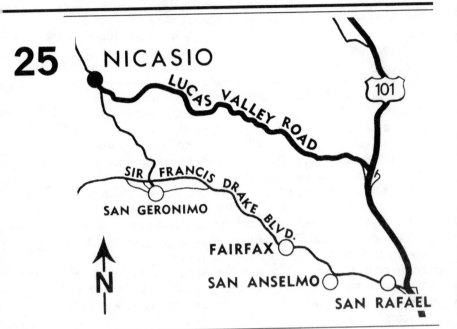

Lovely little Nicasio sits in a basin of hills on a back country road, as fresh and modest as a milkmaid in her Sunday go-to-meeting best. Somewhere, just over the hill, is a villain developer, twirling those figurative long black mustachios. If he doesn't have designs on Nicasio's virgin landscape, it's only because he hasn't seen her yet.

Nicasio Valley has such fragile environmental quality that one misplaced building or signpost could throw the entire ecological entity out of whack. Even a small tract could create a smog basin that would make Los Angeles blush. Fortunately, there is a hero riding to the rescue of this fair village well before she is in distress. It is a research team jointly sponsored by the Marin County Planning Department and America the Beautiful Fund with the cooperation of the Nicasio Property Owners Association. They have come up with a land-use program that could keep Nicasio livable.

To see what an unspoiled countryside looks like, as all

of Marin county looked a scant thirty years ago, take a walk around Nicasio's central plaza. Take the Lucas Valley road just north of San Rafael. After leaving the developing suburbia it meanders west from U.S. Route 101 through bucolic countryside for ten beautiful undeveloped miles. Then, suddenly, one is detouring at sharp right angles beside what seems to be a field in the heart of a miniscule village. Park where you can, preferably in front of Rancho Nicasio.

This was the site of the first house built here in 1852 by Noah Corey, who finished his home with shakes made with a circular saw driven by horsepower. Second building to stand on the site was the three-story Hotel Nicasio, an effort of William G. Miller built in 1867 and the center of Nicasio's social life until it burned in 1940. Glenn Kerch, Nick Kobseff, and Dorothy Mead are the proprietors of the Rancho Nicasio, its general store, post office, restaurant, and swimming pool.

Notice the baseball field and bleachers in the corner of the central square, where a nicely carved sign says George Bill Till Road. Earliest recorded history of the square indicates that it was proposed as the site for a courthouse in the 1860's, when Nicasio had 600 population, two nearby lumber mills, and yearned to be the county seat. It may have

been in use as a plaza as early as 1835, however, when Governor Figueroa granted the surrounding twenty square leagues of land to Teodosio Quilajeaqui and other of his tribe, a grant later rejected by the Yankee Land Commission of 1855. In some respects more enlightened than our own, old California laws required a certain percentage of land for common public use. Like the town, the "Nicasio" Indians, actually Coastal Miwoks, take their name from a convert chief whose name saint was Nicasius.

Walk westerly toward the San Geronimo Road. At the corner, look north to see a village street where Huck Finn or Tom Sawyer would feel at home. Then turn south, following the square past the Druid Hall. A butcher shop, a grocery and a blacksmithy, whose first smith, Thomas Ward, set up his forge and anvil outdoors under a spreading oak tree, have been fixtures along this rural way in the past.

At the next corner, walk east, toward the charming white church, Our Lady of Loretto, which celebrated its centenary in 1965. Abreast of the rose-covered trellis en route, pause to look up in the hills at wind sculptured trees. Planner Al Solnit says Nicasio Valley's flat center bowl was totally filled by stream erosion from the surrounding ring of mountains. Landslides are common in this geologically unstable area.

Turn north at Mary Evelyn Lane and complete the square. If one comes along this way on a weekday, sometimes the only sound is the singing of wind in the trees. Finish this walk inside Rancho Nicasio for a look at a large mural whose central figure is Jose Calistro, last chief of the Nicasio Indians. A mounted buffalo head hangs nearby. Either one would have appreciated Marin County poet Lew Welch's moving words: "This is the last place, there is nowhere else to go . . . at the feet of the final cliffs of all Man's wanderings."

Abbott's Lagoon at Tomales Point

26

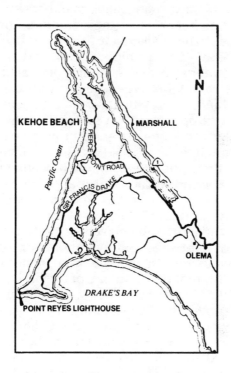

Abbott's Lagoon, a favorite Tomales Point swimming and picnicking spot for West Marin residents for almost a hundred years, has a mystique of its own. Two fine stories of derring do and one of daring don't cling to it. The first happened in 1861 when the clippership *Sea Nymph*, heading by dead reckoning toward the Golden Gate in a thick fog, sailed aground on Ten-Mile Beach near the lagoon. Hero of the day was Carlyle S. Abbott, who lassoed first the ship's captain and dragged him ashore, using a riata and his cowpony, then every other member of the crew but two.

Second was the *Warrior Queen* out of Auckland, whose crew put out in three small boats during heavy seas and rowed all the way to San Francisco rather than try a landing on the great beach after their ship was driven too far inshore. Capt. Henry Claussen, thinking to save them, swam out to the anchored ship only to find men, log, and instruments gone. Instead of bedraggled sailors, he rescued the figurehead of the ship. According to Helen Bingham in *In Tamal Land*, it was standing on the Claussen ranch in 1912. I saw it on a Point Reyes Ranch in the 1950s.

The third and funniest Abbott Lagoon story happened during Prohibition, when the Brock Schreiber family picnicked there and found twenty two-quart square-faced bottles of Holland gin, all neatly packed in individual straw baskets, possibly chucked overboard after a rum-running chase. Beryl Schreiber Jesperson recalls that "Mother hated liquor of any kind, so she played Carrie Nation." While the men almost wept, she broke every bottle on a driftwood log. With delicious irony, several weeks later one member of the family cut his foot badly on one of the broken bottles. The indomitable Mother Schreiber sterilized the wound with gin from another bottle found intact that day.

The walker who goes to explore Abbott's Lagoon, now part of the Point Reyes National Seashore, may not find anything so dramatic on the nearby driftwood beach, but he will surely see wildflowers, wild birds and possibly a herd of goats gone wild.

To make this walk, pack your picnic, leave the dog home, and head north from San Francisco via U.S. Route 101 to Sir Francis Drake Boulevard. Follow the boulevard through Inverness until you are parallel to Tomales Bay State Park. Turn right, or north, on Pierce Point Road and drive about four miles until you pass a sharp right angle that leads into H Ranch. Exactly nine-tenths of a mile past this ranch is a small parking lot, fenced on three sides, on the west side of the road. Park here. Abbott's Lagoon will be the body of water lying off your right.

Go through the narrow hiker's stile. Soon a cowpath takes off to the right through the pastureland and reaches the most passable part of the marsh which surrounds the near end of the lagoon. Cross to find a jeep trail through this part of the meadow. It soon connects with an old ranch road. Bear right on the road, going through the fence where you can, and soon you will reach the narrow neck between the arms of the lagoon, enlivened sometimes by a small waterfall. The removal of an old shelter built long ago accounts for the flattened place at the end of the road. The upper lagoon has long been a favored swimming place.

To reach the Pacific Ocean near the north end of Ten-Mile Beach (sometimes also called Eleven-Mile Beach, Twelve-Mile Beach, and Great Beach), cross the creek near the waterfall, go through the stile uphill, and skirt the shore of the lower lagoon, moving away from the tremendous bare sand dune visable on your right.

When you reach the sand bar that sometimes blocks the lagoon from the sea, look back across the fresh water lagoon to locate a long windbreak of trees. A goat herd, guarded by a ferocious long-horned billy, often frequents the hill immediately north of it. Bear right to find the great driftwood beach and a few fisherman's driftwood wind-shelters. Surfperch and an occasional striped bass are taken on the shore, starry flounders in the lagoon. In years of heavy rain, Abbotts's Lagoon may break through its sandbar, let the tide in, and repopulate itself with saltwater creatures.

To return, climb over the big dune, look for the narrow neck and cross by the waterfall to retrace your steps.

San Rafael, "The Sanitarium"

27

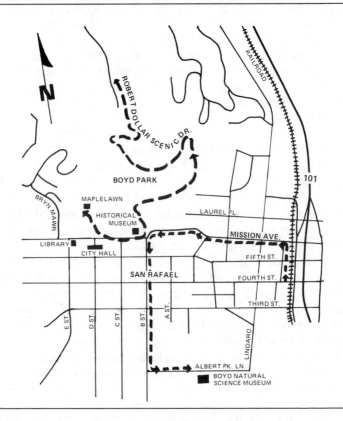

"The coldest winter I ever spent," Mark Twain is said to have written, "was a summer in San Francisco"

For relief, he learned to do what the Indians, Spaniards, Mexicans and Forty-Niners of the Bay Region had done before him—seek the sun—as citywise citizens do today when fog frowns overlong.

Sunny San Rafael, the Marin County seat, which snuggles into a sheltered strath at the north end of San Francisco Bay just before it merges with San Pablo Bay, was just the right distance away from San Francisco for a holiday in the days of horse and oar. The climate was equable, and thereby grew a town.

From the jabbled freeway approach no casual motorist would suspect the pleasures that await those willing to explore San Rafael on foot. Early California called it "The Sanitarium," or "the local Gretna Green," both deservedly and remnants of both facets of growth are still about.

Begin this walk at the corner of Tamalpais and Third Streets, long the front door of San Rafael. Historian J.P. Munro-Frazer identified the tribe of Indians who once inhabited San Rafael as the Jouskionmes, and they built more than one *temescal* or sweathouse. the native version of a clinic, here at the foot of San Rafael Hill near a creek. The conquering Spaniards took their health cue from the Indians. In 1817, when converts at San Francisco's Mission Dolores were dying from measles, VD, TB, and other missionary introduced diseases, Padre Ventura Fortuni came this way to found Mission San Rafael Arcángel as an *asistencia*, a sort of work-while-you-heal resort, hoping it would save his flock. It didn't. The priests' orchard was about 300 yards west.

Walk north alongside the Northwestern Pacific Railroad station, now a senior center, which stands on the site of a triple murder, the most infamous incident of the Bear Flag Revolt of 1846: it was here that the twin brothers, Ramon and Francisco De Haro, and their aged uncle, Don José Berryessa, were shot by Kit Carson at the command of John C. Fremont.

Forbear Fourth Street, the shopping concourse, noting how satisfactorily the hill looms ahead beyond this junction, and continue on to Mission Street to turn west. Under shady trees, past comfortable old brown shingled houses, Mission Street goes not to the reconstructed *asistencia*, well worth visiting, but behind it. Notice 1130 Mission, now the Bagley Apartments. This was the home of San Francisco vigilante leader William Tell Coleman, developer of this valley, not nearly so well remembered as giant Don Timeteo Murphy, a benevolent pioneer. Coleman hired Golden Gate Park engineer William Hammond Hall to plan the streets, which follow topography, "not the cardinal points of the compass."

At B Street, the walker has three interesting choices immediately at hand, three more nearby, and another at the opposite end of B, ten blocks south.

• For mountain goats: turn right and climb Laurel Place to reach the Robert Dollar Scenic Road to the top of San Rafael Hill.

• For children, picnickers, and the indolent: at Laurel go through the elegant wrought-iron gates into the shady dingle of Boyd Memorial Park.

• For history buffs: at the entrance to Boyd Memorial Park, Marin County Historical Museum in the yellow gate house just ahead is open on Wednesday and Saturday afternoons. Near the front porch, notice the great flensing kettle, big enough to stew three missionaries.

A block beyond the museum, on Mission, is Maplelawn, long the home of Artic explorer Louise A. Boyd, now the Elks Club. Next to it is the Robert Dollar house, Falkirk. The Louise A. Boyd Natural Science Museum, about half a mile south of here (Albert Park Lane just off B Street) has a zoo of native animals, including a harbor seal named Easter.

Also nearby are some of the early churches, a handsome library (at Mission and E Streets), fine old homes of sea captains, and the court house. San Rafael may not be a cure for the measles, but there is plenty to see in a day's ramble.

San Rafael's Glass-Walled Movie Studio

28

Delighted by film historian Geoffrey Bell's documentary "Those Daring Young Film Makers by the Golden Gate," several people called to ask me, "Where in San Rafael was the famous glass-walled movie studio located?"

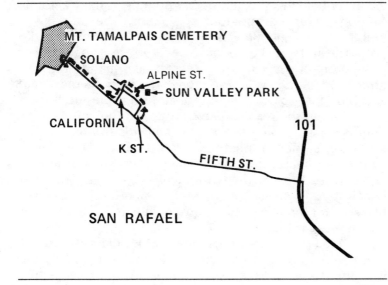

The answer, unlikely though it may seem to some of its young residents today, is Sun Valley. It's a pleasant part of San Rafael, divided from San Anselmo by Red Hill, and one the walker will enjoy exploring not only for its historical overtones, but for its pleasant climate and amenities.

To see for yourself, take U.S. Route 101 north from San Francisco to San Rafael's Fifth Street and K Street. (En route, you will pass at Fifth and H the Victor Building, a little fragment of the 1915 Panama Pacific Exposition floated over from San Francisco and now in use as the clubhouse of the San Rafael Improvement Club.)

Park where you can along Fifth street and try to imagine it as a eucalyptus-lined country lane. When pioneer Alexander Forbes, who owned this part of the rancho named *Santa Maragarita y las Gallinas*, or "St. Margaret and the Hens," developed the Forbes tract, he named this road Culloden Avenue for the famous Scottish battlefield. Immediately to the north, Forbes Hill had a San Rafael Water Company reservoir by 1869. The creek that filled it used to run beside the road.

Walk uphill on K Street to Solano. In 1915, according to

Geoffrey Bell, this was the main entrance to the California Motion Picture Corporation's grounds. The stone wall visible further uphill was a boundary between studio property and the home of a Senator Shortridge. Other perimeters of the studio lot were California Street, Fifth Street and J Street. When you reach the patriotic red, white and blue mailbox that faces Solano, stand beside it for a moment and try to imagine cowboys and Indians, bandits, miners, hanging judges and dancehall girls swarming along this long, golden, sunbathed strath of land. Now it is a community of comfortable family homes whose gardens and children thrive in the same excellent "natural light" that led Herbert Payne, scion of a Menlo Park fortune, to select this spot for the film productions he bankrolled in the days before kleig lights.

Stroll along the winding lane that is Solano and when you parallel the area on your right now occupied by the greenhouse whose cactus garden and fruiting citrus tree make it look like a little piece of Arizona, you are about where the studio offices stood. Continue on until you are abreast of a big Japanese-inspired garden with a romantic crab apple tree. According to cinematographer Bell, it was here, at 139 Solano, that the glass-walled studio stage stood.

You are also across the street from San Rafael's Sun Valley Park. Stroll into it, between the lawns and play equipment. When we made this walk, Bell and I found three-year-old Noah Perrin riding the little hippo as happily as if it had been a mustang. His mother, Mrs. Gail Perrin, said no, she had no idea there had ever been movies made in this valley, and stared in amazement at old movie stills showing star Beatrix Michelena posed against the big rock outcroppings higher up the canyon walls, now surrounded by houses.

Romantic scenery for the Bret Harte story "Salomy Jane" swept from the rocks to Mount Tamalpais in the distance. Continue uphill to see how producer-director George E. Middleton, husband of the star, managed the sweep. Beyond the restrooms, bear right along the bench of land you find there. Once Forbes Road, it now leads to a charming little gazebo with tables and a barbecue pit. As you return from the gazebo, look on your right for a narrow footpath that meanders upward across the hillface. Follow this path to steps and climb them to the junction of Windsor and Chestnut Streets. From the landing, both rock and Mount Tamalpais are visible. Since California Motion Picture Corporation had picked up all the film rights to Bret Harte's stories, they based their westerns on them. In an early Bret Harte adaptation you are likely to see this segue from rock to peak.

When you have enjoyed this distant vista, descend the steps again, swinging toward Alpine Street and the red-roofed water tank. "In the studio's heyday," Geoffrey Bell told me, "stage coaches, broughams, democrat wagons, and buckboards were lined up along here, waiting to be 'cut off at the pass' by Indians or badhats." On Alpine, instead of returning to the park, bear right to California, then left downhill.

If this were 1916, the laboratory for developing film would be on your left when you reach Humboldt Street. Now it is a row of homes. Continue downhill and just before you reach the little clutch of shops, look on the lefthand side of the street. There the one thing unchanged on the valley floor is the creek which was often filmed as it gurgled along, framed against eucalyptus. The studio cookhouse and the dining hall stretched easterly along Fifth.

Bear right on Fifth, which came into being for access to the Mount Tamalpais Cemetery, visible uphill toward the northwest. Stroll toward its white mausoleum, which gives a Forest Lawn feeling, appropriately Hollywooden, to a studio area. Soon you find yourself at Happy Lane. When you reach Sun Valley school, the terrain seems to open into a wide expanse of countryside, with horses, barns and an old farmhouse visible on the hill, a little microcosm leftover from yesterday.

Continue toward the cemetery and it's Look Homeward Angel, as the Marin Monument Company emerges unexpectedly from the trees at 2468 Fifth Avenue. One huge eucalyptus near it may have been planted by San Rafael developer William Tell Coleman, who imported seeds from Australia in 1872.

It is Marin's pioneer doctor, Alfred Taliaferro (pronounced Tolliver in his native Virginia), whom its citizens can thank for the cemetery. Dr. Taliaferro convinced his colleague Dr. Henry DuBois to donate the land. Editor Frank Pixley of the *San Francisco Argonaut* thought it uproarious that a doctor should own a cemetery, and twitted him in print. Dr. Taliaferro, who is buried there, would have made a suitable character for the film company. He often played three card monte at Don Timoteo Murphy's, according to *The Reminiscences of Charles Lauff* and "wore a large rimmed hat, tucked his pants in his boots and used cuss words like a trooper." He also was willing to jump on his horse and ride off in the dead of night to succor the ill or wounded.

When you reach the cemetery, notice that the war veteran's monument stands in a heart-shaped lawn. Stroll in the grounds for a peaceful ending to this walk, surrounded by—well—you could call them shades of the Old West.

Because of popular demand, there occasionally is a showing of "Those Daring Young Film Makers by the Golden Gate" at the California Historical Society, 2090 Jackson Street, San Francisco. Showings are usually free, but since space is limited, tickets must be reserved ahead of time by calling 567-1848.

China Camp State Park

29

"Shlimpy! Shlimpy!" the Chinese door-to-door peddler would call as he walked along, his baskets of fresh-cooked bay shrimp slung from a yoke on his shoulders. It was our most famous street cry. The kids would swarm up to him with a nickel for a paper cone of shrimp to pop in their

mouths like peanuts. Housewives came out in their aprons with saucepans in hand to buy a pound for a quarter by the curbside. The cats came out, too, to get any shrimp that might spill. It was a familiar scene in most Bay Area communities between 1869 and 1954.

The shrimp came from the Bay by way of China camps. At least three shrimpers' villages bearing the name of China Camp were situated on the bay—one in San Mateo County, one in Contra Costa, and the third and oldest in Marin. The Marin village, where a little shrimping has persisted into our own time, is now the 1,500-acre China Camp State Park. It offers some of the more interesting walking to be found along the shores of San Pablo Bay.

To make this walk of exploration, drive north from San Francisco via U.S. Route 101 to San Rafael. Take the North San Pedro offramp east. Instead of turning into Marin County's beautiful Frank Lloyd Wright-designed Civic

Center, continue on North San Pedro Road, meandering through Santa Venetia. When Mabry McMahon planned this development in 1914, he hoped to transform the south fork of Las Gallinas Creek into something resembling the canals of Venice. World War I forestalled his plans, leaving something less grandiose. Swing past MacPhail School and the casual country boatyard called Buck's Launching Ramp at the creek mouth, round the hill and look for a sign in the marsh bordering the bay. It says China Camp State Park. About fifty feet beyond it on your right will be another sign saying Back Ranch Meadows Parking. This is the northern perimeter of the park, purchased from actor Chinn Ho, whose forebears fished here. Park here or along the roadside for the next 500 yards.

Once parked, notice that there is what seems to be a hilly island close at hand on the bay side of the road and another further east. The one farther into the bay is Jake's Island, the goal for this walk. At low tides during the summer, a footpath leads around the near hill exactly at the edge of the marsh, beginning at the six bollard-style posts. Continue walking farther along the road to find a triangular metal gate on the south side of the hill which gives on a broad country lane, bordered part way along by a row of old eucalyptus trees that undulates with the road. This is the route of choice.

As you stroll this dirt road between marsh and hillside, look uphill to see where park aides and rangers have been working to heal up the ugly erosion scars left by trailbikes, motorcycles, and other offroad vehicles, the curse of the wilderness. Oak and bay trees stud the hillside. Wild roses sport a shy pink blossom here and again. Pickleweed stands beyond the eucalyptus, habitat of food for bay shrimp.

Suddenly one rounds the hill and discovers that the road winds through the marsh. It is passable except for about an hour at the highest winter tides. Look north, or left, to discover part of an old duck blind and catwalk, possibly left by Jake, the hermit for whom the island was named. No one seems to recall the rest of his name today.

Don't be alarmed as you walk up the far hill if there is a heavy smell of skunk. This is skunkweed, *Navarettia squarrosa*, a little blue spiky plant underfoot which seems to prefer paths. When you reach the end of the trail, bear left for a great view toward Hamilton Air Force Base. The shards of Jake's long abandoned cabin still stand at trail's end. Rangers removed this and other habitations on the bayside points of the park to allow view parking in some cases, picnic access in others. Look east to discern the remains of a shrimper's pier. Then take the other fork of the short island trail to overlook Rat Rock and several little bays between this point and China Camp. Restaurant, pier and shacks at China Camp fishing village are still used by Frank Quan, as they were by his father, Quan Hock Quan, who introduced the conical shrimp net which does not take bass. Earlier shrimp fishermen used bottom nets, which harvested indiscriminately, and were a *bete noir* to sportsmen, who prompted legislation to prevent such fishing. According to *California Fishing Ports*, Bulletin 96 of the state Fish and Game Department, there were 245,000 pounds of shrimp landed between 1949-1951. The catch in 1951 was 97,000 pounds. Now, some thirty years later, efforts have been made to renew California's fishing industry.

When you have enjoyed this sample of the new park, return to your wheels and continue along San Pedro Road to the south end of the preserve to see what is left of China Camp itself. Restored as an historical site, largely through the efforts of the Marin Chinese Cultural Group it is a place of pilgrimage for many Chinese. There is bay shrimp for sale at the restaurant counter on weekends.

As you walk downhill from the upper parking lot below the China Camp sign, try to envision the hillsides around dotted with tents for refugees after the 1906 earthquake. Unwelcome elswhere because of the six cases of bubonic plague known to exist in Chinatown at that time, 10,000 Chinese were brought here from San Francisco in sampans and shrimpfisher's *lorchas*, as the specialized junks used for shrimping were known.

Not all the past history was so valiant, of course. There were times when boatloads of Chinese immigrants would hover beyond the Golden Gate until nightfall, then make their way to China Camp to let passengers disembark illegally.

Chinese left the camp to build the railroads, dig the wine tunnels, produce bricks at nearby McNear's Brickyard, start restaurants, laundries, and mine the played-out gold fields for jade. Go around the little restaurant building, still unchanged, to see a display of the shrimping operation in its heyday. Nobody really knows how many men fished here, although the estimates go from 250 to 10,000. Residents were each required to pay one dollar a month rent. When the rent was due, boats simply sailed for Richmond's China Camp loaded with overnight visitors until word arrived that the rent collector was gone.

Frank Lloyd Wright's Marin Masterpiece

30

If architecture is truly "frozen music," as Friedrich von Schelling suggested in the ninetheenth century, the finest

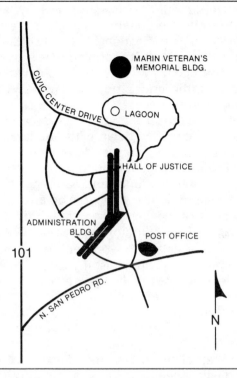

concerto in the Bay Area is the Frank Lloyd Wright creation just north of San Rafael.

The first movement, the County Administration Building, was completed in 1962. At its dedication, one rainy October day, Dr. Theodore A. Gill, president of the San Francisco Theological Seminary, said in language almost as unique for a cleric as the building itself is for a county seat, "This is the kind of event that could tear you up if you let it."

It can still tear you up. Quite possibly it will always tear up the person of receptive mind who walks around it with eyes open to the artist's vision. If ticky-tacky boxes, monotonous cubist nightmare towers and slurby roadside wastelands have left you disenchanted with the way mankind defiles the lovely land we live in, come some leisurely day to the Marin Civic Center and take this walk to renew your hopes.

Beauty was Frank Lloyd Wright's primary inspiration. A

building, he felt, should belong to its terrain, to its time and to its use. Whether you begin this walk at the bus stop off U.S. Route 101, or in the parking lot or any other point, stop first and take a good look. It sits on not one but two hills, and a road goes through the middle of it. From whatever aspect it is viewed, it fits the landscape, a triumph few buildings are allowed to achieve.

Notice at the outset that it is composed of arches that out-Chirico Chirico. They begin with one large arch at the lowest level and reach a crescendo of arches that become circles and a dome at the roof. Go to the center of the lowest arch to find the main entrance and pause again, this time to look up at the bubble of sky above. You are indoors before entering a door or leaving the outside. This is one of the special charms of the building.

A sweep of escalator beyond golden doors urges one upwards immediately, but resist if you will, to walk first on the lowest level where a mall of gardens makes a handsome indoor avenue. The machinery of the building, the heating plant, plumbing guts and such, normally buried deep underground, lie behind those imposing doors marked "Private."

Take the escalator to the second level. Notice how the bubble of daylight seems to beckon one upward invitingly. Then walk to the railing of the central court, to look down first, then upward. The open court makes this building seem bigger and more spacious than it is. The floors, incidentally, are what Mr. Bennett Raffin, of Rothschild, Raffin and Weirick, the contracting firm that built the building, calls Taliesin red, a hue the famous architect derived from the *kaibab*, or old red limestone, of his beloved Arizona home.

If it is a weekday, walk north to the cafeteria at the end of the second level to see the outdoor garden and pool contained in that great retaining wall which looks from outside like a ship with one scupper.

Stairs lead up to the third level, where the well is wider and the building longer. The chambers of the Board of Supervisors and the Planning Commission, two bodies frequently embroiled in stormy sessions before this visionary center became its present happy reality, fill much of the north end.

It is on the fourth level that the building becomes most lyrical. It is again longer, its wells wider, and its dome is filled with the public library. Walk from one end to the other to see how variably the school department, the California room, and the veteran's offices fill their quarters. The windows in the roof are one of the best surprises, but small details of many kinds delight the eye at unexpected places. Try to remember, as you walk, the county buildings of an earlier time, smelling of ammonia and entrenched bureaucracy. This, the mind says, regarding the heart-lifting vistas through each window and down each corridor, is how things should be. The master, as his students and admirers will always think of him, put it into three words: form follows function.

Open Space

31

"Nature has been generous to Marin," says the Marin County Open Space District informational leaflet. "Everywhere are grassy meadows to picnic in, wooded trails to explore and beautiful wooded groves to enjoy. There are rolling hills, green valleys and bayland marshes . . ."

There are also such spectacular scene-stealers as Muir Woods, Mount Tamalpais, the Golden Gate National Recreation Area coastline and the even wilder Point Reyes National Seashore. It's a cornucopia of natural treasures that could have led residents to ignore more modest terrains. But not in Marin!

Thirteen years ago, in a general election, the county approves—with 69 percent of the voters in favor—what may well be the most distinguished program in the nation for preserving and protecting strategic open space. The goal was to create a buffer of green between each of Marin's 11 cities and towns.

Now there are 20 open space preserves, with 6000 acres of land under the management of the Marin County Open Space District. Trails within the preserves are open to the public. Open space preserves are often so accessible that Marin County residents can step outside the back door and be on a trail.

Open space trails are also unusual because they are built in part by volunteers and in part by the remarkable Marin Conservation Corps. This is an organization that couples environmental awareness with the development of skills in the county's young people through work experience and education. As part of their training, young trail builders go on backpack and camping trips, learning how to enjoy the land they work on.

A pleasant sample of an open space preserve can be enjoyed by a walk along the two-mile trail that encircles Novato's Deer Island—a 200-foot-high hill surrounded by fields and fens. For bird watchers, the island is one of the handiest observation places one can find overlooking the West Bay marshes.

To make this walk, pack your day-bag with lunch, liquids and a field guide to western birds, as well as your binoculars. Then head north from San Francisco on the Golden Gate Bridge and Highway 101, past Novato to the San Marin-Atherton exit. Turn right on Atherton Avenue, right again on Olive Avenue and left onto Deer Island Lane.

There is parking near the end of the lane at the entrance to a farmhouse now occupied by Open Space District rangers.

Look for the number 305 on a gate. Alongside it is the Deer Island Open Space sign. It announces that this trail is open for public use and the enjoyment of walkers, horse riders and dogs on a leash; prohibited are smokers, guns, fires and wheeled vehicles of any kind. The preserve is also open for camping by special advance permit which can be obtained from the Marin County Recreation and Park Department, whose offices are in Civic Center, San Rafael.

Step over the high coaming, go through the hiker's stile and turn right.

As you come up over the rise near the farmhouse, corrals are visible in the foreground below, a reminder that despite the marsh that surrounds it, this land has long been grazed. According to historian J.P. Munro-Fraser's 1880 "History of Marin County," Deer Island had been settled as early as 1840.

Later, farmers built a small landing so dairy products could be shipped to San Francisco by barge on Novato Creek, which is visible winding through the marsh in the middle ground. Off in the distance, Highway 101 is the ribbon that sparkles with motion in and out of trees, hills and buildings below Big Rock Ridge.

"This is oak savannah," Karin told me as we approached a grove of gnarly old coast live oak trees. "Open Space District purchased the upper 130 acres in 1978 and another 10 acres in 1982. Most of the preserves we buy are upland ridges, so we can help cities retain their individual identies."

The trail seems to change subtly when you reach a mossy, square old cistern. "This is where we started new trail work this summer," Jock told us. "The kids really take pride in their work. They like to come back later with friends and be able to say, 'Look, I helped build this.'"

The smaller hill off to the right is nicknamed Fawn Island because of its size and proximity to Deer Island. Both hills were once regularly surrounded by water at high tide.

As late as 1928, shrimpers, set liners and sardine fisherman found this marsh and its sloughs good pickings.

After you pass the big rocky gully, continue to the left on the old roadbed, following the foot of Deer Island. When you reach a pair of crossing paths, stay on the main trail. Just beyond a little gully, you are back on another portion of the trail build by the Conservation Corps this summer.

Soon the trail swings around to pass another lovely

grove of oaks and a big windersheared bay tree. Logs that have been left along the trailside are intended to serve first as convient benches for walkers; later they will become homes for small woodland creatures, and finally they will disintegrate naturally into the soil.

As you leave this grove of sensuous trees, which is sure to be a favorite picnic spot during Novato's hot summers, look off to your right to see the black Point cutoff, Highway 37, and the tracks of the Northwestern Pacific Railroad, visible across the flood plain. The big squares filled with water closer at hand are tertiary sewage treatment ponds, so carefully handled there is no odor.

A gray squirrel ran across the trail as we paused. Big raccoon prints, deer scat on the trail and scuttering quail were more evidence of wildlife activity on Deer Island.

When you round the curve into another shady nook, you will see fencing to protect walkers from the foundations of another cistern.

Rancho maps dating to 1854 at the Novato Historical Society show another residence on this side of Deer Island. An 1891 article in Sausalito News announced a new milking barn hero. Members of the pioneer DeBorba and Nunes families of Novato subsequently farmed here.

The hills of the Black Point peninsula, visible as you swing around the next curve, were the scene of "considerable gold excitement" in the 1850s, according to Munro-Fraser, until it was discovered there wasn't enough gold in the quartz vein to make it pay.

Veer upward on the next path to the left after you pass the two old concrete water troughs visible downhill. All too soon you will be back at the little parking lot and your wheels.

Stafford Lake

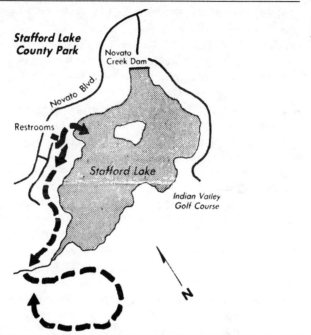

Stafford Lake County Park

Novato Creek Dam

Novato Blvd.

Restrooms

Stafford Lake

Indian Valley Golf Course

N

32

Inevitably there comes a time in winter when the "early morning fog along the coast" is still thick at noon and looks as though it will hang around all day.

Then it is time to head for Marin County's Stafford Lake, once again sparkling in the Hicks Valley. Closed in 1984 for draining so that an over-population of carp which was muddying northern Marin County drinking water could be reduced, Stafford Lake now has a resident colony of largemouth bass and red-ear sunfish, usually found only in Florida fresh waters.

This is not so surprising as it may seem at first. Stafford Lake is located about eight miles west of Novato. The weather in Novato is so clement that flyers often can find blue skies there when every other airfield in the Bay Area is socked in. This climate pattern has made Stafford Lake a good location for a warm water fishery, and for walkers, a rare place in the sun.

To make this walk, leave your dog at home and head north from San Francisco to Novato on Highway 101. Take the DeLong Avenue exit, go over the freeway, and turn right on Novato Boulevard, which leads directly to the lake.

Within a few blocks you have left urbanity behind and are driving through rolling meadowland along a valley carved by Novato Creek.

Just beyond the dam, one comes upon Stafford Lake. It is named in honor of the Dr. Charles D. Stafford, a Novato veterinarian, who served as first chairman of the North Marin Community Water District and was instrumental in tapping Novato Creek as a source of water for his home community.

Drive in, turn left and head for the closest parking lot. Except for senior citizens, there is a parking fee. From October 1 until March 31, the fee is $1.00 a day. During the rest of the year, the fee increases on weekends to $3.00 per car. Opening and closing hours vary with daylight during the year.

Once parked, go around the restrooms to find on the outside wall a large carved map of the lake.

Leaving the map wall, as you face the water, look downhill on your right to locate a gorup picnic area that can accommodate 40 people. An even larger picnic area is visible near the trees across the lake, near the west end. If you come along here on the right day, you may discover members of the Los Altos Hunt Club, formally dressed in hunting "pinks" and top hats. At those times, shouts of "Tally ho" and "Gone away," followed by thundering hoof-beats and the yelp of hounds, make Stafford Lake seem like a bit of Old England.

Turn left. The wooden structures nearby are wind shelters, each containing a couple of picnic tables. The larger concentration of tables is a group picnic area, available by reservation number for all three group areas is 499-6387.

Walk toward the little bridge. Notice the miniature inlet immediately below where dead branches and tree trunks are visible in the water. This is a fish habitat constructed so bass, sunfish and a few schools of mosquito-fish can hide.

Once you reach the little peninsula, look across the water toward Stafford Lake's island. Its trees contain Marin County's largest heronry. According to ornithologist Helen M. Pratt of the Point Reyes Bird Observatory staff, great blue herons first began nesting on the island in 1962, ten years after the lake was completed. At last count there were 29 nests.

Often the lake surface is alive with gulls, who come inland to cleanse the salt from their beaks. Migrating waterfowl also stop here, including about 50 Canada geese, usually residents of Goose Lake in Northern California, who have been wintering at Stafford Lake between November and March.

Park supervisor Jack Golan, who conducted me on this walk says several of the Canada geese, perhaps permanently injured, and one Ross goose, have become permanent residents. Birders also may sight a pair of golden eagles and a Swainson's hawk, which are frequently seen above the park.

Indian Valley Golf Course occupies the land visible across the lake beyond the dam. If you think you see an outdoor elevator among the trees, your eyes are not deceiving you. It takes golfers up to the ninth hole in the 18-hole public course.

Retrace your steps to the upper parking lot and continue walking west through the park to the lower parking lot. Restrooms, picnic area, and volleyball court and a baseball field lie between the lot and the shoreline.

Because of the demand for such recreational amenities in Marin, these facilities will be duplicated immediately to the south of the present site. State funds of $385,000 have been appropriated for the expanded facilities.

The walker has a choice of two trails at this point, depending on the status of construction and land-contouring work.

One goes along the water's edge. The other goes uphill through live oak, deciduous oak and bay forest. If there has been about 10 days of rain, the approach to either trail turns into a soggy marsh and hikers may require waterproof boots.

If you are game to try either trail, both of which begin in the same way, look for the sign for the Nature or Loop trail at the south end of the parking lot. A chain shuts off the trail approach to cars to prevent teenage drivers from tearing up this old ranch road when it is muddy. Go through the hiker's stile alongside and turn left, going around a large berm of earth cleaned from the lake bottom in the recent fishery rehabilitation.

Thousands of carp were removed by a Southeast Asian fisherman at that time and sold commercially. An 8-foot long sturgeon, often compared by local fisherman to the Loch Ness monster, also was discovered at the bottom of the lake. California Academy of Sciences expert John McCosker estimated that the huge fish was at least 60 years old.

Continue around the berm and, in a moment, you reach Terwilliger Pond, which was used as a holding tank for 70 native turtles when the lake was drained.

At the trail junction, go to the right and follow the fence line left. At the large oak, turn left just past the little shelter, built to contain equipment for a Campfire Girls' camp here. Cross the bridge over the creek, looking out for nettles on the right as you leave it.

Ignore the road and go to the right. Jimson weed was growing in the pathway when I made this walk, half obscuring the footpath. Look for this footpath, which follows the highest ground between two small ponds.

Thereafter, it winds through a marshy area, crossing the creek on three little bridges built by the Marin Conservation Corps. At the park limit sign, go left. When you have crossed the third bridge, go through the hiker's stile.

You are now at the base of a small hill. Look to the right to locate an old Miwok Indian campground further upstream. Then look for the trail sign at the foot of the hill and follow it to the left. The loop trail is 1.9 kilometers, or 1.2 miles, long and encircles the hill beside you.

As you climb, looking down on the serene water surrounded by the rounded hills of Hicks Valley, you may find,"the peace that passes all understanding" that walkers often experience in unspoiled country.

All too soon, you will be back at the marsh and stile. The way back is the way you came.

Sonoma County

Petaluma Adobe

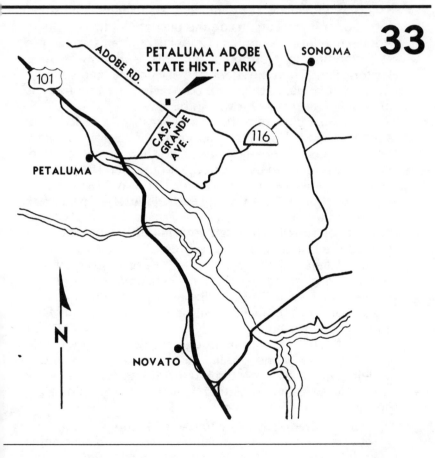

PETALUMA ADOBE
STATE HIST. PARK

SONOMA

ADOBE RD.

101

CASA GRANDE AVE.

116

PETALUMA

N

NOVATO

33

Envision California of 1834 as a gigantic chessboard on which the Czar of Russia was challenging Mexico. "Check," said Russia from her toeholds at Fort Ross and Bodega, convinced they balanced Monterey and the Presidio of San Francisco. "Checkmate," replied Mexico, plunking the fortress known as the Petaluma Adobe down on the lovely land of Sonoma county. And that was that. Russia picked up her pieces and retreated back to Square One.

Like the half-remembered scenario of a Jennette MacDonald-Nelson Eddy musical, it all seems a little far-fetched until you step inside the big patio of the Petaluma Adobe, the finest example of Colonial Mexican architecture still standing in Northern California, and now a State Historic Park. Then the sheer size of Gen. Mariano Vallejo's Casa Grande makes the script convincing, even though it is now only half the size it was in his day.

The lazy days of autumn are ideal for a visit to the sunbaked limbo of Alta California's once great military headquarters. Thirty-eight miles north of San Francisco, Petaluma is reached by way of U.S. Route 101. The adobe is almost four miles east via California Highway 116 on a knoll at the junction of Casa Grande and Old Adobe Roads. Park in the lot, pay your fee and, letting imaginary guitar strains of "Cielito Lindo" play through your mind, start up the path toward the bridge over Adobe Creek.

In Vallejo's time 66,622.17 acres, or more than 100 square miles, comprised Rancho Petaluma. Although the name always sounds to me like a new motel or a flower-shaped pink light bulb, Petaluma is an approximation of the Suisun Indian Language for "O Fair Vale." In Spanish, it means "flat hills." From the bridge, picnic tables are visible on either side of the stream bed. The statue of General Vallejo you reach as you climb upward was donated by the Old Adobe Fiesta Association, which annually holds a big outdoor barbecue in the courtyard.

Pause when you have climbed high enough to see the whole patio, to take in its outdoor kitchen, blacksmithy, ramada, carreta, and candlemaking trypots. When I visited here once, Santa Rosa Girl Scout and Brownie Troops 36 and 136 were baking bread in the ovens. It tasted great.

During the school year, fourth grade school classes studying colonial history often stay overnight in the upper level of the adobe, living for twenty-four hours as the Mexicans did here.

When you are abreast of a roped-off area, the flooring of a building section now gone, take a good look at the vast F-shaped structure that still stands. The vanished east wing was equally large. Bear left at the ovens to reach the front veranda, which has mission grapes twining on its massive columns. As many as 160 Indians often worked that many ox teams simultaneously, cultivating Vallejo's 2,000-acre vineyard.

Go into the visitors center, which has cases depicting the life that once flourished here, and pick up the leaflet describing the monument. Mexican music forms a pleasant background as you stroll at will from room to room. Each is now furnished with the appropriate looms, gristmill, and artifacts in use in the adobe's heyday. Go up either staircase to find the general's apartment, the only one in the building which had a fireplace. In other rooms, only the three-foot-thick walls warmed the occupants in winter, as they cooled them in summer. Verandas on both sides protected the adobe clay from dissolving in the winter rains. After its original thatched roof blew off in a storm, Vallejo hired George Yount, for whom Yountville is named, to reroof the building with handsplit redwood shakes.

When you have inspected both floors of the interior, go around to the far side to find whitefaced Hereford cattle, live chickens, and the burro, who answers to both the names of Chiquita and Flower. Hides drying on racks behind the adobe were known as "California bank notes" when Vallejo's men shipped them out from Petaluma Creek to San Francisco Bay.

For the one fee, resident ranger A.J. Ebbatson says, you can also visit on the same day other nearby historical parks—Sonoma's Mission, Vallejo's home Lachryma Montis, Fort Ross, Jack London's home, or Benicia Capitol. Traffic being what it is, don't expect to do all six in one day, but it would be possible to take in one, or even two more after visiting Rancho Petaluma.

Petaluma's "Iron Front" Victorians

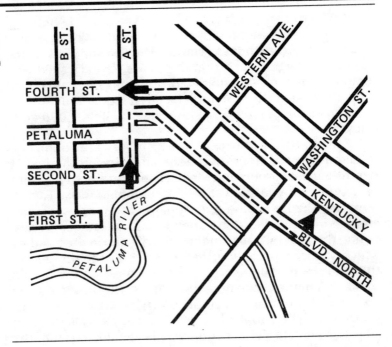

Tap with a coin what appear to be elaborately carved wooden cornices or moldings on many a Victorian storefront in graceful old Petaluma and you may be rewarded with a metallic ring. You've discovered one of the many "iron front" buildings for which the city is becoming increasingly renowned. Petaluma, once the wealthiest city in Sonoma County, probably has more distinguished "iron fronts" than anywhere else on earth.

Most "iron fronts" were made in San Francisco (where, as in Santa Rosa, which also once had many, few survived the great quake of 1906). An early attempt at prefabricated construction, they were also a forecast of things to come in the building trade. Usually foundry-made of cast or sheet iron in sections small enough to cart and ship, the iron sidings were customarily ordered only for the street side of a building. Once at the site, they were hoisted into position and bolted to an underlying brick or wooden wall.

A bicentennial walking tour of Petaluma's "iron fronted" structures introduced in 1975 by Mayor Helen Putnam, was so successful that it has subsequently been expanded and elaborated on by the City of Petaluma's Cultural and Historic Preservation Committee jointly with Heritage Homes of Petaluma. Free copies of a leaflet and map are available by writing the Petaluma Chamber of Commerce, 314 Western Avenue, Petaluma 94952, or telephoning them at (707) 762-2785. It is the better part of wisdom to write ahead for a copy if you are an architectural buff. Don't expect to be able to pick one up on a Sunday.

With your folder tucked into a pocket, transport yourself north from San Francisco to make this walk. It would be the most fun to go by boat via the Petaluma Creek, as the "iron fronts" themselves went to Petaluma. Alas, this is now a freight-only line. This leaves the seeker of public transportation dependent on Golden Gate Transit. Using your own wheels, take U.S. Route 101; turn off on Petaluma Boulevard and head westward to reach the junction of Second and B Streets near the Petaluma Creek turning basin.

Site Number One on the walking guide is the depot of the old Petaluma-Haystack Railroad, the first such line to be built north of San Francisco. In 1864, a twenty-six horse-power locomotive carried both passengers and freight between the depot and the steamer dock three miles away at Haystack Landing.

Look north to discern a stone warehouse, once occupied by John McNear's grain mill, which is still supported on one side by a stone wall built in 1850. It now has a rabbit-warren of shops and restaurants. Walking away from the river on B Street, as you approach Center Park, imagine hitching posts where the trees now stand. In 1823, when El Camino Real passed through Petaluma, this was the hub of the town as Mariano and Salvador Vallejo knew it. In the north end of the park, look for the mission-trail bell that marks the route of El Camino Real, then follow Petaluma Boulevard to discover the McNear Commercial Building, built in Period style in 1911. Next door, is site 5 on the tour, built by John McNear in 1886, and described as "the lightest and most graceful of the iron fronts in Petaluma." Leaves and delicate human heads are indicators of the then-new Beaux Arts style of design. The McNear building is architecturally the same on both ends, one fronting Petaluma Boulevard, the other Fourth Street.

Across the street, the recently painted brick commercial building is a Neoclassic creation of Petaluma's own most noted architect, Brainerd Jones. Designed in 1920, it has served as a post office and was at one time part of Petaluma's Chinatown.

The next block of Petaluma Boulevard brings you up to Western Avenue, where the Masonic Building, an outstanding iron fronted High Victorian Italianate, has been a landmark since 1882. The Seth Thomas Clock in the tower is an original that was shipped via the steamer *Pilot*. The tower was rebuilt in 1934. Hyman and Appleton were the architects of the Mercantile Trust. The Odd Fellows Building, immediately north of the bank, has been classified as a "Second Empire style with mansard roof." It too boasts an iron front.

The most distinguished row of iron fronts of all, however, is the south side of Western Avenue, between Petaluma Boulevard and Kentucky Street. Built between 1881 and 1885, they have been described by David Gebhard, Roger Montgomery, and their coauthors in *A Guide of Architecture in San Francisco and Northern California*, as "unmatched," and have been honored by both the California Heritage Council and the New York organization, Friends of Cast-Iron Architecture. Finest of the lot is the Mutual Relief Association Building, "partly because the crisp cast-iron decoration has been further delineated by being painted green and set against a tan background." Look for the plaque at the base, which announces that the decoration was cast by the Pendergast Foundry in San Francisco.

When you have admired the *tour de force*, return to

Petaluma Boulevard and continue to Washington Street to see a dozen more distinguished buildings en route. Then cut alongside the park on Mary Street to Kentucky to check out some interesting Italianate and Stick style buildings before bearing left to find another of Petaluma's iron fronts with pressed sheet-metal roof cornices and friezes.

Site 17 is the Gwinn Building, a stucco false front with Chicago style windows, but purists will say it is easily surpassed by the McClay Building, the most elaborate iron

front on the block. In 1866, it was the Opera House, where Mark Twain made his lecture "On the Sandwich Islands." Still in print, it was panned at the time by a local reviewer, now forgotten, who wrote, "As a newspaper correspondent, Mark Twain is a racy and humorous writer, but as a lecturer, he falls below mediocrity." Artemus Ward, Josh Billings, Robert Ingersoll, and Bayard Taylor came off better in the eyes of critics when Petaluma was a major stop in the Chautauqua circuit.

All together, there are twenty-six sites on the Old Petaluma Walking Tour. Most of them are distinguished architecturally but pop cultists will also dig two local landmarks. One is a Coca Cola sign from the days when Petaluma was the "Egg Basket of the West." The other is an increasingly rare prefabricated metal gas station built in 1925.

Burbank Garden and Juillard Park

35

Luther Burbank, the plant wizard of Santa Rosa, gave "scentless flowers perfume, tasteless fruits flavor, dry colored blossoms, or those with a single hue, brilliant and variegated garments." He also created a spineless cactus, the Burbank potato, the 'Gold,' 'Wickson,' 'American' and 'Climax' plums, the 'Splendor' and 'Sugar' prunes, and any number of daisies, poppies, roses, callas, gladioli, and dahlias. Today it is impossible to go into a plant nursery without seeing seeds, seedlings, or plants in gallon cans descended from the great horticulturist's experimental hybrids.

Fortunately for all plant lovers, the nucleus of his

gardens in downtown Santa Rosa had been preserved as a park and declared a National Historic Monument. It is open free to the public daily. It is also so handy to the freeway that the adjoining Juillard Park makes an ideal rest stop or picnicking place for the northbound traveller.

To make this green-thumber's walk, take an hour's drive north on the big spine of U.S. Route 101. The downtown offramp leads into Santa Rosa's main drag, Fourth Street. Turn right on Santa Rosa Avenue and park as near as you can to Sonoma Avenue. Then walk toward the leafiest oasis in sight. This will be the former home of Luther Burbank, occupied long afterward by his generous widow, and surrounded by the fruits of his labors. The great naturalist is buried under the deodar nearest the greenhouse. Walk along the picket fence until you reach a brick pavilion, constructed in 1959 by Leland Noel and the Santa Rosa Recreation and Park Department at the urging of local garden clubs. Bronze commemorative plaques usually share the interior with cyclists resting from the relentless Sonoma sunshine during summer.

Walk through the pavilion. Immediately beyond, stop for the stunning vista of a waterfall and pool seen across a sundial which sits in a tremendous copper lotus within cool lawns. Admire, then bear right around the circular brick walk, through labelled plants arranged in handsome flower beds. Under the big linden tree near the fence, pause again to look across Charles Street to the Park Apartments, which follow the classic design of an early California hotel. Then continue on to the big red eucalyptus. Instead of heading for the waterfall here, tempting as it is, go right, to find behind the hedge three large raised beds near the gardener's work area. This is an idea many gardeners may want to incorporate in their own backyards. Then look for the glass and redwood garden house. If it is open, go in and sign the guestbook. If not, peer through the windows to locate several large photographs of Burbank. One taken at the Panama Pacific International Exposition with Thomas A. Edison, Henry Ford, Harvey Firestone, and their spouses certainly gathers, as if in one handful, the men who shaped contemporary America. Pause a while by the reflecting pool on which it fronts, then start toward the big cactus garden visible behind the greenhouse and carriage house. Recent literature says Burbank did not like to tweeze the gloccids from the big prickly pears he was hybridizing, so he simply asked the cacti to stop producing them and they obliged. Whether the story is apocryphal or not, it is known that Burbank talked to his plants.

When you have enjoyed the many treasures of the garden, return to Santa Rosa Avenue by way of the pavilion. Look across it to locate Juillard Park, but for the moment walk north. Abreast of the blue mailbox, you have reached the lovely new Sonoma Avenue linear park, part of Santa Rosa's civic center redevelopment. Go through the path around the fountain and follow the line of it east paralleling Sonoma Avenue for a block. The nearest building across the street by the three flags is the police headquarters. The terraced red one is the new federal building. Retrace your steps after you reach the little footbridge to return to Juillard Park, known for its beautiful chain of graduated ponds and for the church built from one redwood tree, now a museum. Beyond A Street is yet another contiguous park, now called Burbank Playground, suitably named for a man who loved children as he loved plants. It is as though Santa Rosa has taken to heart his words that "the planted and tended tree is as sure a sign of civilization as a revered flag, a church spire, or a schoolhouse belfry."

Sonoma Plaza

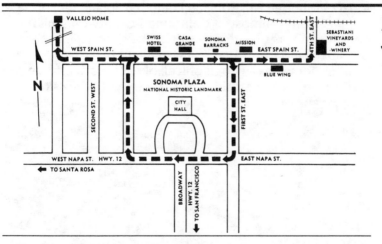

36

Indian Summer comes like a song to Sonoma.

A dust-devil pirouettes along Spain Street, flirting with a few dry leaves that join the dance, giving it a crisper whisper for a moment. In the air, the promise of the grape harvest hovers like a kiss.

Unhurried, the season settles on Sonoma as the much-educated Henry Adams would have the Indian Summer of life: "a little sunny and a little sad, and infinite in wealth and depth of tone."

Sonoma Plaza is a National Historic Landmark, an eight-acre patch of public land surrounded by ten historical buildings that have witnessed the unbelievable transition of California from wilderness to bewilderedness. Stroll it once, some uneventful day when time has her way with you, and you will find yourself beguiled, like a youth newly in love, and possibly determined, as many thoughtful visitors have been, that not another stick or stone of this sleepy pueblo should change.

Old Chief Sem Yet Ho, Mighty Arm of the Suisun tribe, strode bare-armed around this square. Fremont, the undisciplined; genial General Vallejo, winegrower Agoston Haraszthy, the raw Bear Flaggers, Mammy Pleasant, Jack London and Fighting Joe Hooker all passed this way.

They came in the wake of Fr. Jose Altamira, who on July 4, 1823 founded Mission San Francisco Solano de Sonoma, last and northernmost of California's twenty-one missions. The mission, restored and open as a State Park Historic Landmark and a museum, is an excellent place to begin this walk. Sonoma has a geographical joke: its plaza is bounded on both east and west sides by First Street. The mission is on

the northeast corner of First Street East and East Spain Street.

Ranged around the plaza are the Blue Wing Inn, once a hotel; Sonoma Barracks, headquarters of the Bear Flag party; servants quarters of Casa Grande, Gen. Mariano G. Vallejo's first adobe home; the Swiss Hotel, built by brother Salvador Vallejo and still operating as a restaurant; Salvador's home; Ray House, officer's mess for Stevenson's Regiment in 1847; Fitch House, built by Jacob Leese, second settler of San Francisco; a Bear Flag monument; a children's playground; and a city hall, which unexpectedly houses a delight of more recent history, the airplane model collection of the late Gen. Hap Arnold.

Sonoma is also known in our time for its cheeses. A favorite outing for many San Francisco families includes a purchase stop for cheese on the plaza, another for fresh bread, and one for wine at August Sebastiani's, culminating with a picnic either at another state park, Vallejo's home, Lachryma Montis, a short half mile northwest of the plaza, (via a walking trail that begins near Depot Park off First Street west at the train tracks and also goes to Sebastiani's tasting room) or at Buena Vista Winery, two miles east on Old Winery Road. Buena Vista was originally Haraszthy Champagne Cellars, built in 1856 by the California "father of viniculture."

The leisurely stroll around Sonoma's plaza, browsing for old bottles, treasures, or paintings, reading the historical markers on the old adobes, puzzling over the funeral notices occasionally tacked up on telephone posts, and luxuriating in an absence of pressure is there to be had anytime except the weekend of the Valley of the Moon Vintage Festival.

The Vintage Festival is usually in September. Then sleepy Sonoma wakes up to play, parade and pray. The grapes are blessed, queens are crowned and kissed, folks dance, wine is tasted and the harvest is celebrated with tribal rites. Oh, Summer, you old Indian Summer . . .

A Bigger Jack London Park

37

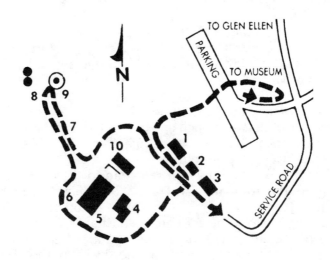

"Who will reap what I have sown here in this almighty sweet land," Jack London wrote of Beauty Ranch, the 1400-acre Sonoma County spread where he raised purebred livestock. "You and I will be forgotten. Others will come and go; these, too shall pass, as you and I shall pass and others take their places, each telling his love, as I tell you, that life is sweet."

And sweet indeed it is in the wine country, where the Jack London Historical Park at Glen Ellen has been expanded from its original 39 acres to 800. The walker who goes to enjoy it will find in addition to the long established trail to the Wolf House ruins and London's lava-rock covered gravesite, there are new trails accessible along Asbury and Graham creeks, up the friendly little 2200-foot peak that is Sonoma Mountain, around fine old vineyards, down to a charming little lake and to what was once Jack London's working ranch.

Of these, my favorite is the ranch trail, partly for the architectural surprises it offers, among them the actual cottage where London lived and died on the ranch, the remains of the Kohler and Frohling winery, and oddly enough, a round sty of rock known as the Pig Palace, designed by London himself.

To make this walk, transport yourself north from San Francisco, via Highway 101. Take 37, the Sears Point cutoff, then 101 north to Big Bend to pick up Arnold Drive (which parallels route 12) into the town of Glen Ellen. At the north end of the main shopping street, bear left on the London Ranch Road following the State Park sign. Be prepared to pay your $3 per vehicle fee, or $2 if you are a silver-haired senior. If you bring Rover and Towser, there is an additional tail-fee of 50 cents per dog; they must be kept on leashes and you need proof they've had rabies shots. The grounds are open from 8 A.M. to Sunset daily, the Museum is open from 10 A.M. to 5 P.M. daily, except on Thanksgiving, Christmas and New Years.

At the outset, stop in Charmain London's House of Happy Walls, handy to the parking lot, to see how the writer actually lived, and to pick up a trail guide to the ranch. Mementos of his many travels and triumphs abound. Looking into the office, it is easy to envision him writing the daily thousand-word stint, preparing lectures, reading proofs, answering the ten thousand fan letters per year, negotiating with his agents and publishers, drawing up plans to construct the Piggery, generating new ideas. But it is when you peer into the viewer to see a motion picture film strip flickering as London rides one of his big horses or hugs a prize pig that the immense vitality of the man comes across. Then one sees him truly as he viewed himself, a sailor on horseback.

After you have looked upstairs to see the clever Inglenook window seats that could double as beds, go across the parking lot to find on the opposite side the trailhead for the ranch trail, a one kilometer stroll under gracious old trees. Building Number 1, built of stone by Chinese laborers in 1884, was the Kohler and Frohling sherry building. The famous piano manufacturer, Charles Kohler, and his partner John Frohling acquired their Tokay Vineyard in 1875. The following year, 1876, they pressed

45,000 gallons of wine in Glen Ellen. By 1888, they were growing 250 acres of grapes on the nearby hills.

Site 2 was built in 1914 by Italian stonemasons and the stones protruding from the walls were deliberate, a style in contrast to the Chinese preference of stones flush with the walls. Although it looks charmingly rustic enough to have served as a guest cottage, London designed it for composting manure, much of it gathered from Site 3, the stone barn where six of the prize Shire workhorses dwelt.

From the barn swing south-westerly toward the cottage, built in 1862 by State Supreme Court Justice Jackson Temple. Nearest wing was a winery building that served as dining room while Wolf House was abuilding. Go around to the far side to find the room, added on in 1914 after Wolf House had burned, where Jack wrote *Valley of the Moon*, and *Little Lady of the Big House*. "I liked those hills up there," he wrote. "they were beautiful, as you see, and I wanted beauty . . . and I was content with beauty for awhile. It pleases me more than anything else now, but I am putting this ranch into first class shape and am laying a foundation for a good paying industry here." Look in each of the three directions the windows face to see the beauty he meant.

Then swing around to the front of the building to see the minuscule room where he died of uremia on Nov. 22, 1916, two months short of his 41st birthday. For a man who planned on mammoth lines, it is ironic that he died in a sleeping porch so small one wonders a bed would fit in it.

Wine buffs will find the huge foundation at Site 5 equally astonishing, for exactly the opposite reason— immensity. The huge building built by Kohler and Frohling to house their winery came down in the 1906 earthquake. London rebuilt it to house his guests, ranch hands and carriages. A fire destroyed the wooden upper stories in 1965 during the time when London's nephew, Milo Shepard was operating the big ranch and vineyard.

"Watch my dust!" London wrote. "Oh, I shall make mistakes amany; but watch my dream come true . . ." Walk through the eucalyptus forest to see two of his mistakes, the forest itself, mistakenly planted to the tune of $50,000 in the expectation that it would be a hardwood crop, and the two abandoned silos—never necessary to California farming, as they are to northern snowbound farms.

It is the Pig Palace that will dumbfound most visitors. The circular shape was to save labor, a central feedhouse surrounded by 17 pens. Each family of pigs had their own quarters, including a front patio, private feed and water troughs, roofed pen and backyard, all more spacious than many hotel rooms. The old Kohler and Frohling distillery, Site 10, and the blacksmith shop, which looks rather like the home of the witch that baked Hansel and Gretel, were used by London to store farm machines.

When you have finished the loop, swing back along the service road to return by way of Wolf House. The dining room designed to seat 50 guests stands stark and open to the sky. A redwood tree grows through the front stoop. It may not be the Acropolis, but it is the Bay Area's most romantic, bittersweet, melancholy ruins.

Sugarloaf Ridge State Park

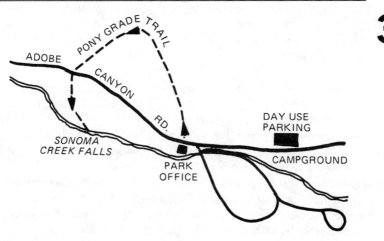

38

If you ask a native of Sonoma or Napa Counties "How do you get to Sugarloaf?" he may, with a twinkle in his eye, send you north, south, east or west, with absolute honesty. for between them, the two adjacent counties have a surfeit of sugarloaves. There is Sugarloaf Mountain, Sugarloaf Hill, Sugarloaf Peak, and Sugarloaf Ridge.

This ambiguity of nomenclature has kept Sugarloaf Ridge State Park, a choice scenic oasis for hikers and horsemen, somewhat secret. Nestling between Sugarloaf Ridge, Bald and Red Mountains (both also have similarly named hills and peaks nearby), the park has twenty-five miles of trails through 1,500 acres of the volcanic Mayacamas Mountains. Confusingly named or not, it is too inviting to stay under wraps forever. Since the motorcar is restricted to a main road and two parking lots, the walking in Sugarloaf Ridge State Park is pleasant indeed.

The ridge lies about an hour north of San Francisco, midway between Sonoma and Santa Rosa off California Highway 12. To explore the state park, take U.S. Route 101 north to the Black Point cutoff (Highway 37), then take Highways 121 and 12 to Sonoma. North of Sonoma, Highway 12 pokes through that succession of mineral springs resorts—El Verano, Boyes Springs, Fetters Hot Springs, and Agua Caliente—that grew up when it was fashionable "to take the waters." As you go through them, try to envision the nobs and nabobs of San Francisco arriving by train to be met in fashionable landaus, stages, and surreys. It was here one came during the "Gay Nineties" to bake out aches and overindulgences.

Just beyond the little town of Kenwood, take Adobe Canyon Road right, or east, for 2½ miles (after spotting Pagani Brothers Winery for the return trip). This narrow road, too small for buses, campers, and trailers, winds alongside Sonoma Creek to the park, merging with Bear Creek near the entrance.

Just past the check station, park at the day-use parking lot (there is a campground lot farther into the park) and head back on foot down the road about 100 yards. On one side of the road will be a sign indicating "Falls Trail—Falls ½ mile." On the other side will be a sign saying "Pony Gate

Trail—Park Entrance 1¼ mile." To enjoy the best approach on both trails, make a loop that begins with the Pony Gate Trail on the uphill side of the road and returns via Falls Trail.

Go off uphill through oak, bay, madrone and chaparral. Beyond a beautiful bay tree, the trail reaches an open meadow. Thereafter, Pony Gate Trail climbs gradually and easily. Near its apex, make a little digression uphill from the trail to see Red Mountain, elevation 2,530 feet, to the near north. It is the one with radar on it. Mount St. Helena, 4,344 feet in elevation, is farther north.

When you have enjoyed the exhilarating volcanic vistas, rugged with canyons and convolutions, return to the trail and continue downward to Sonoma Creek, crossing at the road to reach Falls Trail.

Falls Trail is shorter and steeper in one place. It is also contrastingly wooded and dark, going through silvery and jade green pines and some snags of burned redwoods. Gradually it zigs and zags to the falls. If one comes early enough in the day, there may be black-tailed deer, foxes, bobcats, coyotes or raccoons along the trail. Still existing within the park, rangers say, are even the rare mountain lions whose howling gave the Mayacamas Mountains their Indian name.

Annadel State Park

39

October's bright blue weather lingers longer in Sonoma. And crisper. The hillsides wear great splashes of red and gold. Swallowtails and red-admirals drift by lazy as falling leaves. Adding zest to this seasonal parade are all the pungent smells of Indian Summer on the air. Highwines. Woodsmoke. Ripening fieldflowers.

One of the most enticing places for walkers to enjoy this mellow season is on the trails of the 4,900-acre Annadel

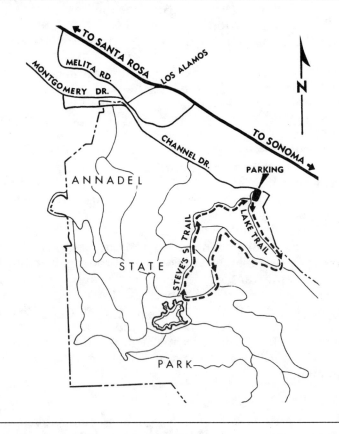

State Park. Undeveloped, its thirty-five miles of old ranch roads have been reserved for hikers and horsemen. Although it is just six miles from Santa Rosa, Annadel is so well hidden by peripheral development that unless you know it is there, you could pass it unknowingly.

To explore this gentle land, leave your dog at home, pack a picnic knapsack, a canteen and your hiking boots and a handful of quarters. Then head north from San Francisco via U.S. Route 101. Turn east on State Highway 12 and drive toward Sonoma for 5½ miles. Turn right on Los Alamos Road, make a second right on Melita Road, then left on Montgomery Drive, following the spillway of Santa Rosa

Creek. After half a mile, turn left on Channel Drive, which follows the opposite shore of the creek, backtracking past a dam and two small reservoirs. When you reach the motley collection of trailers established as residences for state park rangers, stop to pick a trail map out of the dispenser, price 75¢. Then continue on to the parking lot beside the automotive barrier.

Once parked, seek out the enlarged map under glass to scope out the two routes to Lake Ilsanjo, whose odd title is not an Indian word but a contraction from the names of Ilsa and Joe Coney, earlier owners who built the lake hoping to create a golf course there. Of the two routes, Steve's S (for Secret) Trail, named for the Coney's grandson, is the steeper. Elinor Guilford, who lives at nearby Oakmont and hikes these trails regularly, recommends it for the return trip, a descent rather than a climb.

Go uphill past the privy and bear left on Lake Trail, the old gravel road. About fifty yards along, you will pass the end of Steve's S Trail, to note for your completion of this loop expedition. Continue through the manzanita and valley oaks that dot this pastureland until you are parallel to a stump on your left. The valley on your right at this point, concealed behind trees, was once an obsidian quarry used by Indians: here Pomos created arrow and spear points. Chips underfoot on the road often show flaking along the edge, but perfect specimens of arrowheads are rare.

At the second set of big boulders, bear right uphill on Lake Trail, ignoring the Two-Quarry Trail, the route to Ledson Marsh. Trail signs are square, much like mileposts of an earlier day. Bear left when you reach the fork at the hitching rail. Soon the Douglas fir forest, which provides comfortable shade through the hot Sonoma summer, gives way to oak and beautiful mossy rocks. Ms. Guilford, who conducted me on this walk, says the name Annadel, like the Lake's name, was coined. Annie Hutchinson, daughter of Samuel Hutchinson, who bought much of the land from Juan and Ramona Carrillo de Pacheco Wilson, grantees of old Rancho Guilicos, of which this was part, was the "Anna" joined to "dell" (or valley) perpetuated here. local conservationists would like to honor Santa Rosa businessman

Henry Trione, who worked to bring about the park, in a similar manner somewhere within Annadel.

Soon one reaches a rise from which Lake Ilsanjo is visible below and Bennett Mountain beyond. Look across the meadow downhill to locate Santa Rosa on your right. A bicycle trail, a little too far for all but the most gung-ho hikers, connects one corner of Annadel with Santa Rosa by way of Spring Lake and Howarth Parks.

Ignore No Burma Trail [sic] at the fork and stay with Lake Trail. Feral black pigs, which usually inhabit Pig Flat at the far end of the park, have been seen seeking water in this area. Ranger Bill Krumbein says, "We are trying to eradicate them because of habitat damage." Like the commoner black-tailed deer, they run from people, frightened. At the next fork, a junction with Steve's S Trail, go downhill to the lake. In the manzanita grove, again take the right fork and suddenly you emerge at a lakeside meadow fitted with hitching racks and privies. Fishermen often catch bluegills and black bass on the shores of this lake, once the headwaters of Spring Creek.

When you have rested, dined, fished or played long enough, take Steve's S Trail back. It will lead you through dense Douglas fir forest, past old cobblestone quarry sites and down to the parking lot.

Hood Mountain Regional Park

40

When Sonoma county awakened to population pressures it planted the seed that has grown into the Bay Area's newest park system. Now ten diverse parks, every one pleasurable, receive visitors, and four more are in the offing. Of those already open to the public, perhaps the most inviting to city dwellers is Hood Mountain Regional Park, a hike-in or horseback park exclusively, where the wild white

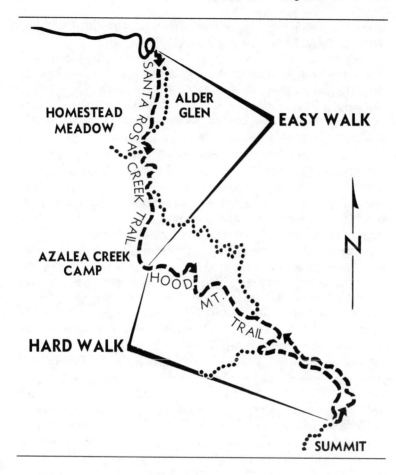

azaleas bloom in the spring. At 2,730 feet, Hood Mountain is the highest peak overlooking the Valley of the Moon. The 4½-mile trail to Gunsight Rock, beyond its crest, is rugged enough to break in climbers who want to be in shape for backpacking in the Sierra Nevada.

For those whose aims are for a more modest Sunday walk, an ideal outing is the trail to Azalea Creek Camp, a matter of two miles.

To make this walk, transport yourself complete with picnic lunch in a knapsack and stout lug-soled hiking boots, north from San Francisco via U.S. Route 101. At Santa Rosa, take the Sebastopol/Sonoma offramp to California Highway 12. Past the Sonoma County Fairgrounds, Highway 12 makes a left on Farmer's Lane and a right on Fourth Street, just past St. Eugene's Cathedral. Follow 12 to Los Alamos Road (a brown sign below the green roadsign indicates both Annadel and Hood Mountain Parks) and turn left. Climbing all the way, you will reach Hood Mountain Regional Park at the end of Los Alamos road five miles later.

Park, check into the ranger station to pay your day-use fee, and pick up a trail map. One look at it will show you that the 1,968 acres in the park are threaded on a main trail to Mount Hood, crossing valleys and ridges in a lofty length of the Mayacamas range. At the outset, follow the Santa Rosa Creek trail downhill from the south end of the parking lot to Homestead Meadow. It is a footpath that parallels and later joins a fire road. If roadwalking is your preference, the fire road passes the corral of Wilikos and Molly, park horses used by Ranger Gary Greenough to patrol the area.

Homestead Meadow is the grassy open space visible below as you descend, outlined on one upper slope by an old grapestake fence. Under the large oak, there was once a smithy for shoeing horses. Although the Mills family that pioneered here has long been gone from this site, the one member still left in nearby Windsor recalls there was once a milkshed under another oak. Its last use was as a wood-cutter's shed. As you walk through the valley, the bucolic feeling of nineteenth-century ranch life that swells in the mind almost calls for the background music to "Cimarron." At almost any moment, a Conestoga wagon could come around the bend of imagination, or a cowpoke amble up on his pinto.

Bear left at the fork. At the gate near Santa Rosa Creek, bear right. This is the narrowest part of the park, with private land on the left. Pause a moment to look at the point where the east and north forks of the creek join. Early settlers knew that such junctions usually created a shallow gravelly shelf in the water that could be forded. Eleanor Guilford, who often conducts Sierra Club hikes on the Mount Hood trails, says she forded it barefoot when the park was first opened. About thirty feet below the fork, look for the footplank to cross the east fork, which flows all year long. If the weather is warm, children often seek out shallow ponds downstream for wading. Ignacio Vella of Sonoma says there are also some deep holes where any member of the Izaak Walton League could spend a productive hour or two a-angling along Santa Rosa Creek.

Continue on the main road; you are now on the Hood Mountain Trail. Stay with it as you make the gentle climb. Occasionally old logging roads veer away from the main trail into the fir forest, last logged in the 1950s. Ignore them, for they soon peter out. The Skyline Trail, which goes off to the left, then swings across the opposite ridge to terminate finally at Mount Hood, was constructed by Santa Rosa college student Wade Eakle.

Rockhounds will be fascinated with the variation in outcroppings visible along the main trail. Mount Hood, which the Wilikos Indians called Mount Wilikos, was not an actual volcano, but rather a volcanic tube or neck. Lava flow can still be detected under manzanita brush and buckbrush in some areas. Capt. William Hood, like almost all of the earliest Sonoma County pioneers, was related to the Carrillo-Vallejo family, if only by marriage. He owned this land, originally part of the Rancho Guilicos granted to Don Juan Wilson in 1850.

Soon the trail swings down into Azalea Camp, where there is a broad flat meadow near the creek. Named for the native *Rhododendron occidentale*, or western azalea, which dots the streambanks here, lighting up the woodlands with great splashes of creamy white blossoms, it has four campsites. Three are for families and one for groups. Overnight fees are modest, but reservations must be made by calling (707) 539-9903 a week to ten days ahead of use.

Those who are game to go the next two miles, making the steep climb from the lowest park elevation of 700 feet at Frogpond Flat to the peak of Mount Hood, will be rewarded with vast views of the Pacific on the west, the Sierra foothills on the east, San Francisco fifty miles to the south, and much that lies closer at hand. Gunsight Rock, which ultimately will also have hikers' or horsemen's camps, is a quarter mile farther than the peak.

The returning walker can take Summit Trail, a footpath which loops back to the main trail for the upper lap, then Manzanita Trail, which does the same thing in the midlevel manzanita forest, then complete the return trip from Azalea Creek Camp, as less ambitious walkers will, via the main fire road, Mount Hood Trail. Plan to be back in the parking lot before 8 P.M., when the park closes.

A Russian River Trail

41

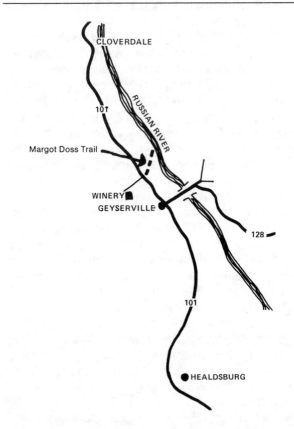

In 1880, Geyserville, already twenty-five years old, had one store, one post office, one saloon, one hotel and one blacksmith shop. *The History of Sonoma County*, published that year by Alley Bowen and Company, summed up the little town in a sentence: "Geyserville is not so much a place as it is these establishments."

Historians might have mentioned the vineyards that had recently been planted nearby by August Quitzow in the shadow of Geyser Peak. After nearly a hundred years of grapegrowing for other vintners, Geyser Peak Winery began retailing its own wine under the Voltaire label and opened its grounds to visitors. For walkers, the change heralded several unexpected pleasures, among them a trail through vineyards to the banks of the Russian River. To my delight, it was named the Margot Doss Trail. Present owner Henry Trione says he plans to keep the trail open.

To enjoy this unusual walk by the river once called the Slavianka, transport yourself approximately fifty miles north of San Francisco via U.S. Route 101. The handsome Geyser Peak Winery buildings, designed by Keith Associates, are west of the new length of freeway, but the river and the trail are on the east side. It is one of the few places a walker can get down to the shores of the river. Take Canyon Road offramp into Geyserville, population now 1,610, and drive one mile north of the beautiful old red barn at the junction. There, under a tree by a big old white house, is an inconspicuous half barrel with a sign that says Geyser Peak Winery offices. Drive in short of it and continue past the buildings to find a circular parking lot about 100 yards farther on the right. Park here, put on your sneakers or hiking shoes, take your picnic daypack, and head east on the dirt road toward Geyser Peak. At 3,470 feet, it is the most conspicuous landmark in the area. As you walk toward the mountain, the Russian River reveals its course by the screen of willows and buckeye trees which outline the meanders of the water. Once they also concealed the Indian village called Pipoholma. Later, Russians trapped furs along the river.

In about the length of a city block, the tracks of the San Francisco and North Pacific Railroad, now called the

Northwestern Pacific Railroad, and nicknamed The Nowhere in Particular, cross the field. Railroad buffs may have the unexpected fun of counting and naming ownership of passing box cars. Two or three trains pass daily at all seasons and many more during the apple, pear, plum and grape seasons when Geyserville turns into a major shipping point. If there is a train in sight, be sure to wait for it to pass before crossing the tracks.

When you reach the fenced water treatment plant, follow the trail left around it. Recently planted vines that line the trail include the white varietals for which California is famous, Chenin Blanc, Pinot Chardonnay, Johannisberg Reisling. At the trees, follow the trail to the golden sands on the river bank where there is a little crescent of shore on which to sun and picnic. If you find a bright red rock among the river pebbles, it may be cinnabar, which once created a little miners' rush in this area during the Gold Rush days when quicksilver was used to refine gold ore. Be cautious about going into the water, for there is no lifeguard and you enter at your own risk. As any passing canoeist could tell you, the Russian River is tricky. Each winter season its swift current creates new deep holes, leaves uprooted trees as treacherous underwater snags, and changes its course. A sand bar that is on the east side of the river one year, for example, may be one curve farther along and west of the river the following year.

If you are game for a longer walk, retrace your steps to the border of the vineyards and bear left along the jeep road through the trees until you reach a bordering fence line where the river curves. If the day is cool enough, one can follow the roads bordering vineplanted fields (recross the railroad tracks at the main dirt road near the settling ponds). If it is sunny and hot, as the Alexander Valley so often is, return as you came, shaded by the riverbank trees. Final reward, of course, can be a stop at the Geyser Peak Winery for a tour. Connoisseurs of the grape will also find tasting rooms open at Nervo, Pedroncelli and Souverain, off the highway en route back to the city. Horticulturists may seek out the Rhodazalea Gardens in the village of Geyserville. And anyone may puzzle over the unusual wooden fence nearby, made to look like great metal links.

Armstrong Redwoods, near Guerneville

42

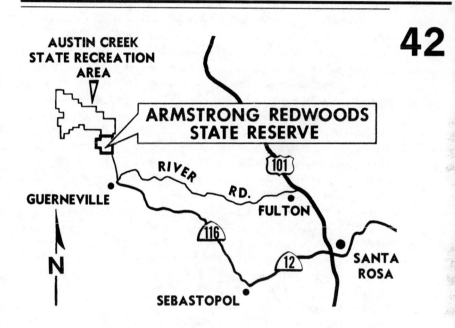

Armstrong Redwoods State Reserve is more than sixty years old. My curiosity piqued by news that people on foot can enter the park free as an encouragement to excluding motor-cars from the redwood grove, I went north to Guerneville to walk around Colonel Armstrong's living testimonial that a lumberman can love trees for their beauty as well as their board feet.

It was heartening to learn that no matter how low the nearby Russian River may get, the 680 acres of Armstrong redwoods, fed by underground wells and the water of Fife Creek will not have to shut out visitors even in drought years. Whether the adjoining 4,200-acre foothill preserve, Austin Creek State Recreation Area, long a favorite of horsemen, hikers, and fishermen for its primitive camps, will be open or closed always depends on fire danger. Some years it closes for several days. Even when it is open campers must pack in their own water. Since campsites are limited and on a first come first serve basis be sure you have a reservation if you plan to camp overnight.

Actually, Sonoma County is so close to San Francisco that one can enjoy "the redwood experience" in a day's trip. The quick route is north via U.S. Route 101. Past Santa Rosa, cut west toward the coast on River Road. At Guerneville, once known as Stumptown, you are two miles from the park via Armstrong Woods Road. This is the only way in and out of the Armstrong Redwoods.

At the ranger station, park and put on a sweater, no matter how warm it seems. Indians, who wore less clothes than we do, named this grove of redwoods, "The Dark Place" and avoided it for its silence and chill. Trails used by Indians are high on the steep canyon walls where sunshine could filter through the pointed treetops. Since it was logged selectively long ago, trees are not nearly so dense as in the forest primeval, but it is shady.

Pick up a trail guide at the entrance kiosk. A nature trail has been prepared to route the walker past the most interesting flora in the park, which includes the rare redwood orchid, *Calypso Balbosa*. Botanists may want to ask the ranger on duty to mark recent blooming locations on maps. None were in bloom when I was there, but we saw yellow violets and white trilliums.

Start out on the Pioneer Trail. Watch for cars in the narrow canyon mouth for the first 100 yards of the trail. The paved road separates and rejoins again twice. At the point it rejoins first, look ahead to see the top of the Parson Jones Tree, 310 feet tall, 1,300 years old, and named for Colonel Armstrong's son-in-law, W. L. Jones, a Congregational minister. The road rejoins and separates again around the fenced tree. Geographically, this land is essentially a ravine with two valleys carved by arms of Fife Creek which come together to form a Y. The right arm and trail go to a picnic area and beyond that to Austin Creek. Take the left arm, which reaches the Parson Jones Tree. After reading the legend, follow the split rail fence around Parson Jones to the right. The concrete pads you see underfoot cover water valves for the simple gravity supply system.

The trail passes through second growth redwoods. Some of them form what Ranger John Melvin, whose father was a "chopper," or logger, describes as a "goose pen picket" circle around a long departed tree. "Early pioneers in the area used to tack fencing to them to pen up their geese," he explained. To him, a fallen limb by the trail is a "widow maker," because loggers have been killed by them. In 1975, snow closed Armstrong grove and brought down many limbs.

At the fire hydrant, cross the road and continue to Luther Burbank Circle, a rest stop whose benches are 25-foot long logs. James B. Armstrong, Colonel of the 134th Ohio Infantry, longed to see his grove made into an arboretum and botanical park and named his friend, the great plantsman, as chairman of a committee to bring it about.

At the sign saying "Icicle Tree," bear left. Icicles are long burls, some of whose tips were once vandalized by burl hunters who sought them for souvenir sales. Behind the tree, leave the foot bridge and climb momentarily with the trail. Look for wildflowers along the rise. It soon drops again to the valley floor.

Shortly you reach the fenced tree called Colonel Armstrong, at 14½ feet in diameter the fattest in the grove. It is 308 feet high and its age is estimated at 1,400 years. The trail dead-ends, both literally and figuratively, at Colonel Armstrong: he didn't live to see his dream of a park come true. It was his loyal daughter Lizzie Armstrong Jones who, in 1917, arranged for the grove to become a county park for the modest sum of $80,000. It has been a state park since 1934.

The parking circle nearby serves the Forest Theater, a 2,000-seat amphitheater prepared by the federal WPA during the Great Depression of the 1930's. The foot-stomping country music of the "Parson Jones Group," famous here for outdoor performances, can be heard

Saturday nights during summers.

If you are game for a climb, from Forest Theater, take the nature trail beyond the Coon Tree; it goes up the steep side slope, and circles back to Parson Jones Tree. If you prefer to stay in the level cathedral atmosphere of the great grove, follow the creekside trail back through the valley floor to complete this loop.

An Educational Excursion at Salt Point State Park

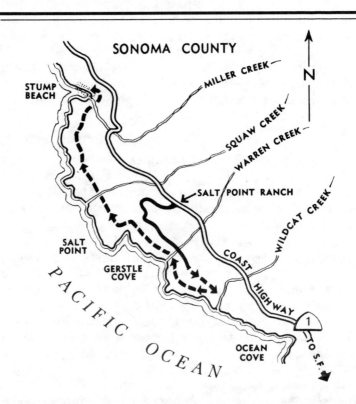

For stimulating walking on a winter morning, few places can match the 6,000-acre Salt Point State Park, the southern section of old El Rancho German on the beautiful Sonoma coast.

Here a dozen little coves and inlets, each more unusual than the last, are set about by sea stacks, natural bridges, caves, tide pools, underwater paths, rocky bluffs, long meadows, small forests, a beach and the estuaries of four creeks. It is a shoreline so ecologically rich it has become a living laboratory for school camping, conceived as an educational as well as recreational facility by both the state park system and Sonoma County educators.

To explore it yourself, head north on California Highway 1. Turn west off the highway about seven miles past Fort Ross. Main access is at Gerstle Cove, a coastal Fish and Game Preserve. Park, pay your $2 day-use fee and walk south, crossing Warren Creek to see wave-cut bluffs that look like great eroded bones, brains or tiki gods. Others, as Dr. Frank Kortum, a Petaluma veterinarian, said as he conducted us on this walk, "look like great dinosaurs waiting to come alive at some future date."

When you have clambered about the enticing water-worn crevices as far as Wildcat Creek, turn back. This approximates at the shore the southern boundary of Rancho German, granted by Pio Pico to Captain Ernest Rufus in 1846. It was also the waterfront perimeter of the 3,000 acres in old Salt Point Ranch. This is land so lean agriculturally, says Dr. Kortum, it would support only 200 ewes. In Indian days, it may well have supported twice that many Pomos, the talented basketweavers who lived here on acorns, elk, fish, seaweed and, in a pinch, roasted grasshoppers.

There are 4,300 acres of shoreline, forests and meadows included in Salt Point. Over 100 camping areas have been sited, many of them east of Highway 1. More important, certain coves are sealed off for five-year periods to reestablish the normal balance of natural life. Until they were denuded by the Eskimo-like Aleuts brought to nearby Fort Ross by the Russian-American Fur Company, these rocks were frequented by great herds of pelagic seals and sea otters. As you walk north, try to envision the Aleuts' bidarkas, or sea-going kayaks, bouncing on these dangerous waters. Whalers, too, have plied this coast, setting up their flensers and trypots on the shore. Little lumber schooners of the "Scandinavian Navy" dodged in and out of the little dogholes here to load not only redwood logged nearby, but great square building blocks quarried for San Francisco. Notice the area Salt Point itself still has many discarded building blocks, lying lichen-softened on the ground. William Benitz, one of John Sutter's friends, was the quarry-master here.

Highwaymen, stagecoach robbers, bull-teamsters, woodsmen, railroadmen, fishermen and rum-runners have all pitted themselves against the deep gorges of Salt Point at one time or another. Like the walker, they must have been relieved to reach the smooth sandy Stump Beach at the mouth of Miller Creek, named not for the big redwood stump there, but for D. Stump, an early Salt Point township sheriff. If your legs are still stout enough, go down the old farm road to the beach and look along the lower cliffs on the north side for fossil shellfish. Bullpine Camp, named for the Scotch pines planted along this coast sixty years ago by W.P. Frick, is at the north edge of Salt Point Ranch. Stop here for directions to the redwood grove and the rhododendrons if you come back again in the blooming season. According to Bruce Walker, whose family owned Salt Point Ranch for three generations, the native rhododendrons are comparable to those at nearby Kruse State Preserve.

Fort Ross

44

One of the unique walks of the nine Bay Area counties is around Fort Ross, a remnant of Imperial Russia's former foothold on the North American continent.

For years it has come as a delightful shock to first-time venturers making their way along wonderful Highway 1 to

FORT ROSS

JENNER

RUSSIAN RIVER

SANTA ROSA

SEBASTOPOL

COTATI

PETALUMA

PACIFIC OCEAN

N

1

101

SAN FRANCISCO

sight the odd blockhouses and two-towered Russian Orthodox chapel silhouetted against the sky. Soon the reason for the Monroe Doctrine becomes clear. History slaps abruptly when one suddenly arrives within the wooden palisade of the fort.

The Christmas holiday season, when the whales are migrating, is the best of times to make this sea-coastal walk. Pack a picnic. Gather up your children, spouse or friend, a duffel-coat, and comfortable flat-heeled shoes. Transport yourself via U.S. Route 101 to Cotati or Santa Rosa, then cut west to Jenner on California Highway 12, the road that rambles beside the Russian River, long a favorite with steelhead fishermen. To the Russians, this river was the Slavianka. Early Spaniards called it the San Sebastian.

The three acres on which Fort Ross stands has been a

State Historical Monument since 1906. There is a $3.00 dollar admission fee, $2.00 for seniors, dogs are not allowed in the Fort. Since 1962, when the state purchased another 356 acres of land from the pioneer G.W. Call family, a natural seaside park has surrounded the stockade. There is a parking fee for use of the area.

At the outset, park your motorcar and walk over to the nearest eight-sided blockhouse. Its original counterpart was built in 1812 at the direction of Ivan A. Kuskoff, commander of the Russian-American Fur Company which leased this land from the resident Pomo Indians for three blankets, three pair of breeches, three horses, two axes, and some beads. Pomos from the nearby village of Mad Shui Nui were soon employed as otter hunters to supplement the Aleuts who had come with Kuskoff from Alaska. Within two years, they exported 200,000 otter pelts.

The only known Battle of Fort Ross took place in 1844 after the Russians had left. It was a siege in which armed white men approached to "run the Indians out of the Fort." After evacuating their families, Indian braves held off the attackers with cannon and muskets, then at midnight slipped into the hills. The self-righteous attackers captured an empty fort, to which the Pomos returned after they left.

Locate the seaward sally port abreast of the stone monument that summarizes Fort Ross's subsequent history. Go through it, beyond the privies to the fence line for a look at the sea meadow and the sloping cliff. Four ships were built at the boat landing that once stood below. San Francisco's Sacramento Street took its name from one of them, renamed, which anchored at its foot. Look across the creek for ruins of a tannery.

Return to the stockade for an inspection of Fort Ross Chapel, the charmer of this expedition. Unlike most Orthodox churches, this one never had a saint's name. It has been restored thrice, once after earthquake damage in 1906 tumbled the 1828 original and twice, after fire demolished the restoration. The front six-sided tower housed three bells, one of which is now in the museum collection. The rear dome is over a round hollow cupola in the ceiling of the chapel. Originally the rafters were sixteen matched, naturally bent limbs from madrone trees. Services are conducted here on Russian Easter, Memorial Day and the Fourth of July.

Cross the highway to visit the commander's house, now a museum. It was here that the journalist Alexander Rotcheff, last commandant of Ross, brought his young wife, the Princess Helena Gagarin, with whom he had eloped from St. Petersburg. Mount St. Helena may be named for her. The French traveller Duflot du Mofras in 1841 described their choice library, French wines, piano forte, gardens and glass house. Back of Fort Ross on the mountain side were 700 horses, 800 cattle, 400 fruit trees and "a vineyard of 700 stock, all of which were in good bearing condition." Some of the fur hunters did not return to Sitka after John Sutter bought the property. One of them was a Finnish captain, Gustave Nybom, who established Inglenook Winery.

If the excellent museum exhibit about the sea otter makes you yearn to get down to the water, continue this walk south of the Russian River along any of the ten miles of beaches which make up the Sonoma Coast Park. Try to imagine little bidarkas, or kayaks, afloat in the surf, in which one hunter would hold a screaming baby otter captive while his companion harpooned the parents that came to the rescue. This is how they decimated the herds which only now are becoming reestablished. At 700 dollars a pelt, even a Czar felt otters were fair game; and the Czar was, after all, the president of the Russian-American Fur Company.

Napa County

Napa Old Town

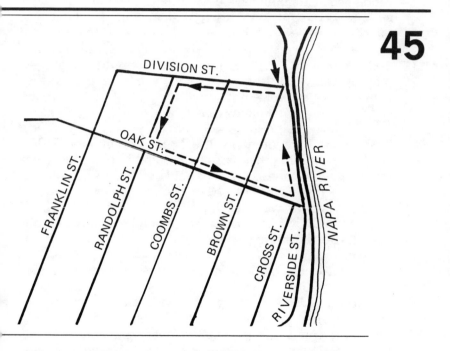

45

By a bend in the river, where rushes are growing . . . Napa new and old stand side by side. On today's side of Division Street is the busy new library, late Bauhaus monolithic without, spacious and well-lighted within. Across from it, under shade trees surrounded by generous lawns, stands yesterday's beautifully proportioned old homes in which Sinclair Lewis, Teddy Roosevelt, or your great grandad would have felt comfortable.

Just a few years ago, little cities such as Napa were ripping Victorian veterans down with a vengeance, replacing them in the false name of progress with block, schlock and ticky tack. Now the word "heritage" vibrates in the valley, and Napa, newly aware of the legacy left her by captains of riverboats and captains of industry alike, has become a leader by looking backward creatively. Preservation and restoration have been progressing simultaneously with new construction. This could have pitfalls, of course, for the scale of old houses and new is often disproportionate. Understanding this, Napa relocates its fine old building or finds new uses for them. Firm in the belief that one of the vital forces keeping a city viable is the convenience of choice homes within walking distance of its heart, the city encourages renovation.

This makes for some very fine city walking, indeed. Responding to a demand, the Napa Community Redevelopment Agency has issued five architectural walking tour leaflets. As long as supplies hold out these are available free through the agency at 1559 First Street, Napa 94558.

My favorite walk is Number One. For students of architecture, Victoriana buffs, city planners, librarians, and even those who thought you can't go home again, it is an unexpected pleasure.

To make this walk, transport yourself north from San Francisco to downtown Napa. Park as near as you can to Division and Brown Streets. At the outset, examine the library finished in 1974. Gianelli and Associates were the architects. If it is open, go inside, bear right, and look out through the tremendous windows for views toward the river that are as striking as murals. If it is not open, stand facing the street on the outdoor conversation pit by the flagpole and look toward your left. The river, rushes and all, is behind the traffic barricade and may one day be revealed here in Napa's proposed linear park. The Migliavacca winery stood where the library is now located and the Migliavacca home, since relocated, was in the concrete pad at the water's edge beside the old brick warehouse. Look across Division Street to get the spacious flavor of trees, lawns and modest building that give a foretaste of grander edifices nearby. Look to the right to locate the slender spire of First Presbyterian, an all-wood Gothic church built in 1874. Walk down the ramp and go one block toward Coombes Street, named for Nathan Coombes, who in 1848 laid out the town on eighty acres given him in payment for building an adobe home for Nicolas Higuera, grantee of Rancho Entre Napa. He created the grid of streets facing the river. Later grids also faced the river at other bends, creating Napa's interesting street complexities.

Cross Coombes and Division Streets and continue west to see 1211 Division, house number one on the tour, an elegant Eastlake style Victorian, now the law offices of Coombes and Dunlap, Attorneys. Architect Bill Jeffries made the addition at the rear to accommodate his offices.

Look on your right to see an early Gothic cottage. At Randolph Street, bear left, passing the stunning Second Empire home of Dr. Ethel Priest. Not every home is listed, but the guide indicates it has been prepared "to encourage awareness of other buildings within and surrounding the tours that possess these basic styles."

At the corner of Oak and Randolph, the houses grow grander. One prize is 486 Coombes, the next corner east, designed as a private home by William Coxhead. Go up close to the entrance to see through the trees the sign "Cedar Gables Inn," evidence of a later use. Then continue on Oak Street to reach Churchill Manor at 485 Brown, and its neighboring mansions, numbers 445 and 443, with their stunning roof lines and columns. Winchester Arms, a Queen Anne style at 492 Randolph, and the mansard-roofed Second Empire style at 1120 Oak, are also elegantly unusual. When you have examined them in detail, go north on Brown to pass other fine Victorians before you reach the river again at what was once called Levee Street and is now Riverside Drive. Before returning to your starting point, pause by the barricade at Brown and Division to notice that the tule rush grows here: the river is still as viable as the town.

Yountville

46

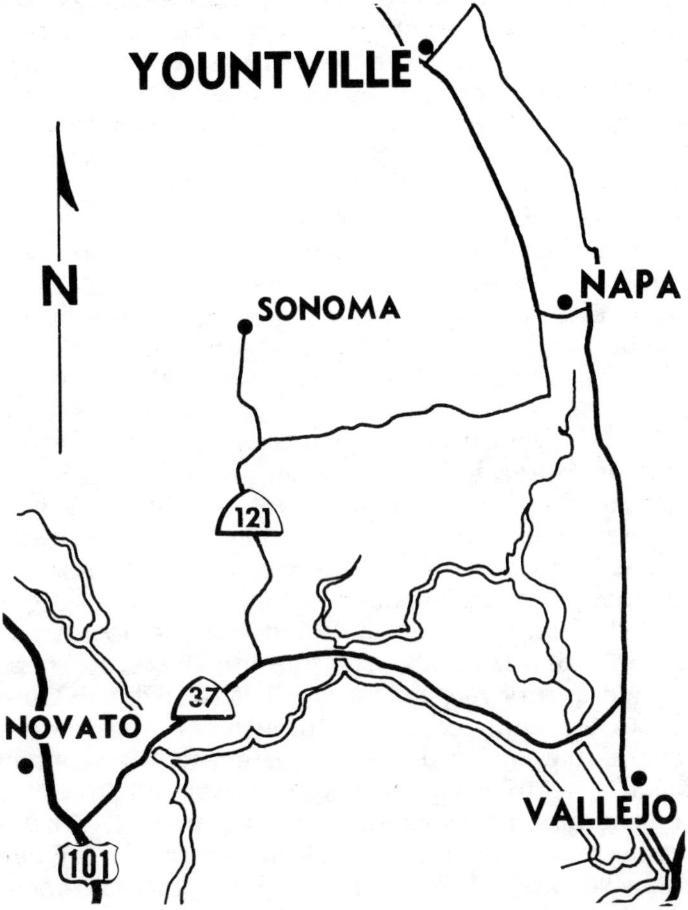

YOUNTVILLE

NAPA

N

SONOMA

121

37

NOVATO

VALLEJO

101

   A free wine-country walking guide, one of the late-appearing legacies of our recent national bicentennial, was published on old Yountville, the pioneer village of Napa County. If you have been building up to a spring pilgrimage to the vineyards, it is a little lagniappe that could make your outing very special indeed. Second in a series of such walking guides by Napa Landmarks, the folder is available, as long as supplies last, by calling (707) 255-1836 or by dropping a self-addressed legal-sized envelope to the landmarks office at 1834 First Street, Napa 94558. It is the better part of wisdom to get a copy before you head north.

Leaflet in hand, head north from San Francisco via U.S. Route 101. To reach "The Wine Way," California Highway 29, take the Napa turnoffs on Highways 37 and 121. Yountville is nine miles north of Napa. When the 6-foot 7-inch tall pioneer George Calvert Yount, known later in life as Jorge Concepcion Yount, set foot in the Napa Valley around 1833, this route was an Indian trail linking villages of the Caymus, Mayacamas, Ulacas, Soscol, Napa, and Callajomana Indians. According to C. A. Menefee's *Sketchbook*, published in 1873, Yount estimated there were from 10,000 to 12,000 Indians then living between Napa and Clear Lake. A thousand of them settled in a rancheria, or village, on the 11,840-acre Caymus Rancho granted Yount in 1836.

The great Gottlieb Groezinger wine buildings, now renovated as a rural Ghirardelli-*cum*-Cannery called Vintage 1870, make a landmark signaling Yountville on your right. Turn off and look for parking. If you haven't obtained the Old Yountville Walking Guide by mail, copies may be available here, or at Yountville City Hall, or at Thomas Bartlett Interiors.

Leaving your wheels at Vintage 1870, Stop 3 in the leaflet's list, head south toward the train station, now called "Whistle Stop." Architecture buffs will recognize this as typical 1888 period Southern Pacific. It houses a cluster of shops. Stop 2 on the tour is an even earlier depot, built in 1868 by the Napa Valley Railroad Company. It was wine that prompted the grander of the two. Within five years of Groezinger's purchase of the Boggs vineyards in 1870, he had more than 150,000 vines bearing, five-sixths of them imported European stock. The odd little traingle of land at Washington and Yount Streets, Stop 4 on the tour, was a leftover piece of land from the Groezinger addition of 1874. The genial wine-maker intended it as a flower garden and, 100 years later, so it is.

Bear left, or north, on Yount Street to reach the

Magnolia Hotel, built in 1873 and restored as one of Yountville's two charming country inns. Magnolia, incidentally, was the name of an even earlier Gold Rush stage-stop inn en route to Sacramento, as well as the name of pioneer orchardist William Nash's Magnolia Rancho nearby. (The other inn is Burgundy House, which started as a winery. In its time, the latter's colorful history has included uses as a speakeasy, a school, a bordello, an LSD factory, and an antique shop.

Cross Finnell Road and there you are at Yountville School, Stop 6. Or perhaps one should say schools, plural, for the school with the bell, constructed in the 1920's sits in front of Old Yountville School, built in 1881, which in turn was added onto a pre-1860's building. For that matter, the bell itself came from yet an earlier Yount School that once stood on the Silverado Trail.

Cross Yount Street again at Webber to locate Stop 7, the Yountville Community Church, established as Baptist in 1876, when the area was famous for its outdoor camp meetings. This southern end of Yountville was known as Sebastopol until 1867 and was one of the four California Sebastopols named at the time when the British and French had the Russian seaport of that name under seige. Others were in Tulare, Sacramento and Nevada Counties and no longer exist. In contrast, Sonoma County's Sebastopol began life as Pine Grove. Citizens of Yountville changed the name of their town after the death of George Yount, to honor him.

When you reach Madison Street you will be at the boundary of the four-block-square Yount townsite and . . . Ah, but there is so much more to see in Yountville especially by hot air balloon that we must not betray all the secrets here. After all, half the fun of exploration is making discoveries yourself—and here is a charming place to do it.

A Vineyard Walk in St. Helena

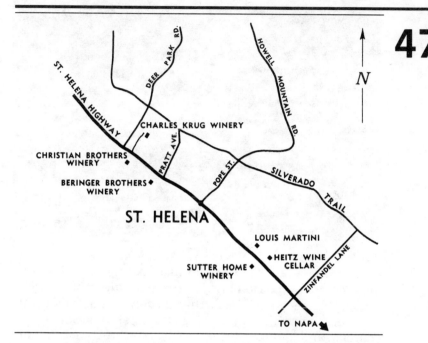

47

"Is there a good vineyard walk?" more than one reader has asked. The answer, of course, is that there are many, all beautiful at the harvest season, when fruit hangs heavy on the vines and its bouquet puts an edge on the air.

During Wine Week, which usually falls between October and November, as the grape crushing comes to an end, the wineries are especially festive. My choice is St. Helena, where it is possible to visit eight wineries in one day, all within walking distance of one another, passing through the remarkable avenue of elms en route.

Begin this walk at the venerable Charles Krug winery at the northern edge of St. Helena, whose main street is also Caliornia Highways 29 and 128. Charles Krug planted his first vines here in 1861, on what was part of the Carne Humana land-grant to his father-in-law, Dr. Edward Turner Bale (builder of the grist mill which still stands a few miles

down the road north of Fremont Abbey winery). Krug was a pioneer newspaper editor and first commercial vintner in the area. He purchased his vines from his friend and former employer, Agostoin Haraszthy, father of California viticulture. Notice the fine valley oak trees that shade the chateau and grounds. Near what was Krug's horse and carriage barn, and is now a rackhouse, is one reputed to be 240 years old. Now owned by the Mondavi family, the winery employs twelve people to conduct tours, with a tour starting about every twenty minutes. Pullman Car No. 2979 standing in the vineyard is an auxiliary wine tasting room.

From tne Krug winery, walk back to the highway through the vineyards and cross to the walk that borders Christian Brothers Wine and Champagne Cellars. Follow the handsome stone wall south until it is interrupted by the grottolike arch that marks the winery entrance. Observe the handsome stonework on the old winery as you approach it. This is reputed to be the largest stone winery building in the world. It was built in 1888 as a cooperative venture, philosophically about fifty years ahead of its time. With this and other wineries, the Christian Brothers, a teaching order, support several schools, St. Mary's College among them.

Return to the stone arch and walk south through the impressive canopy of irreplaceable old elms, once jeopardized like so many of our treasures by a plan for a freeway and saved by wine lovers, growers and conservationists. Savor this shady avenue as a triumph over the highwaymen. Near the end of the lane of trees is the entrance to Beringer Brothers, Inc., renowned for the underground tunnels cut long ago by Chinese laborers and still in use for aging wine. William Mooser, architect of the tower building at Ghirardhelli Square in San Francisco, designed the interesting old house, now used for offices and wine tasting. Beringer is still in the hands of the family who first planted here in 1876. Bordering the road beside the winery buildings behind the house is a line of oleanders trained as trees, most of them greater than the average San Francisco street tree, and almost unbelievable for their variation of reds and pinks while in bloom.

When this fine old estate has revealed its charms, continue south again. In a short time, you will be in the center of town where there is a quaint little park behind the municipal buildings in which to rest or picnic. If you are still game for more wineries, follow Highway 29 to the south edge of town to see the establishments of Louis Martini, Sutter Home, V. Sattui and Heitz Cellars. And the walks that are described next in this book will take you to several other wineries and vineyards.

Silverado Museum, Dedicated to Robert Louis Stevenson

48

"Sighteeing," wrote Robert Louis Stevenson in *The Silverado Squatters*, coining an aphorism that has since become immortal, "is the art of disappointment."

In 1880, when he went by railroad to honeymoon in the

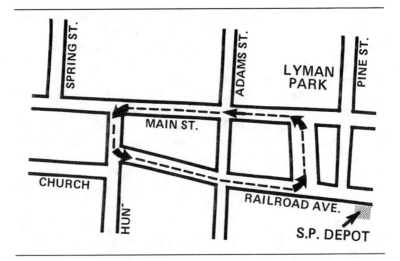

abandoned bunkhouse of a silvermine on the slopes of Mount St. Helena, the towns in Napa valley below

> were compact, in about equal proportions, of bright new wooden houses and great and growing forest trees; and the chapel bell on the engine sounded most festally that sunny Sunday, as we drew up at one green town after another, with the townfolk trooping in their Sunday's best to see the strangers, with the sun sparkling on the clean houses and great domes of foliage humming overhead in the breeze.

An erudite walker in search of Stevenson's traces in the Napa Valley would do well to start in the little town of St. Helena, for an old photograph shows Stevenson reading a galley proof, his hand on the head of a 'tame cat of a dog" that could easily be his pet Chuchu, while sitting on the doorstep of the St. Helena Star. Today, a block away, facing the railroad track his iron horse had rattled along, is the small, privately endowed Silverado Museum, dedicated to the author. In production six miles north on "The Wine Way," Highway 29, is the Schramsberg, one of the two wineries Stevenson visited and described in his essay "Napa Wine." The lane leading to it is little changed since Stevenson walked up to the veranda.

To make a Stevenson pilgrimage, transport yourself via U.S. Route 101 and California Highways 121 and 29 to St. Helena. Park on Main Street near the corner of Adams and Main. Begin walking southeast from this corner. Within 100 feet, you will be at the site of the *St. Helena Star* where Stevenson was photographed. A foodland parking lot now occupies the space. But take heart. Continue a few hundred feet to the present location of the *Star*. "F. B Mackinder—Built 1900" it says on the door. Come on a weekday and, if he is not too busy, publisher Starr Baldwin, direct descendent of Mackinder, may show printing buffs and Stevenson fans the old hand press, chase, wooden type, and other paraphernalia shown in the famous photograph. When we went, a young poet, Bill Berkson, an artist, Joe Brainerd, and I found the cordial welcome here Stevenson must have received almost a hundred years earlier.

When you have marvelled at this quaint old building, look across the street to see the odd Masonic Building with its iron pillars. Other stone buildings are discernible on the street. Continue southeast to Hunt Street, then bear left for one block to Railroad Avenue, then left again to the middle of the block to reach the Hatchery, a building lovingly restored like San Francisco's Cannery, that contains shops. Immediately beyond it is the Silverado Museum, the hobby of Bibliophile Norman Strouse. It contains a collection of Stevensoniana, including a lock of his hair, a desk he wrote on, photographs, plaques, artifacts and manuscripts second only to the Edwin Beinecke collection at Yale.

Browse, admire and wander here to your heart's content. Then bear northwest along Railroad Avenue to find an old-fashioned public park, complete with band shell, where one can picnic under the trees. Walk through the park to reach Main Street again. Eight wineries—Charles Krug, Christian Brothers, Beringer Brothers, Louis Martini, Heitz Cellars, Freemark Abbey, Sutter Home, V. Sattui and Carbone Napa Valley Winery—are all within walking distance along St. Helena's Main Street. To see the famous lane of trees that conservation-minded St. Helena citizens saved from a freeway, walk north. It begins after you pass Pratt Avenue, Walkers of the calibre of Stevenson, whose

Travels with a Donkey were made on foot, or of his fellow Scot, John Muir, can continue north six miles to the entrance of Schramsberg, which now produces only champagne, to walk its memorable lane. The less energetic may want to dally at the nearer wineries to taste St. Helena's famous wines before strolling back.

A Vineyard Walk in the Napa Valley

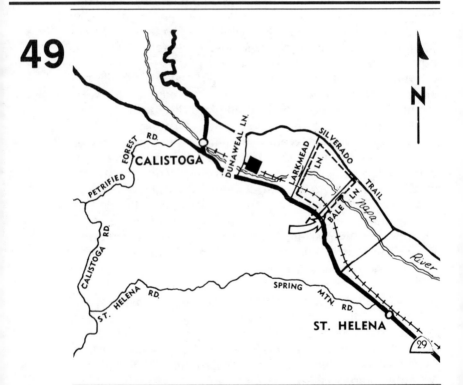

Napa Valley, a long narrow trough bounded by the Mayacamas Mountains on the west and a series of lava ridges that issued long ago from Mount St. Helena on the north and east, means "wine country" to Northern California natives. Thirty wineries are ranged on or near "The Wine Way," California Highway 29. Most of them offer winery tours through cool cellars and tasting rooms rich with Mittel Europa atmosphere. But where, a reader who is deep in a wine-grape identification course has written to inquire, can a walker stroll past vinyards to test his knowledge?

Almost all of the wineries have grapes growing nearby and will let walkers examine them on request. For a real vineyard walk, however, my choice would be a 3½-mile loop walk that begins at Bothe-Napa Valley State Park, goes east along Bale Lane, and turns north on the Silverado Trail to return on Larkmead Lane, with a stop for fun en route at Hanns Kornell's Champagne Cellars.

To make this walk, pack a bottle of suntan lotion and toss a broad-brimmed hat into your car, for the climate that makes the grapes grow can also scorch skin. Transport yourself north from San Francisco via U.S. Route 101 and, at the Black Point cutoff, take California Highway 37 to Sears Point; then take California 121 and 12 toward Napa and Highway 29. Bothe-Napa Valley State Park is about eight miles north of St Helena on Highway 29. Park, pay the modest fee, notice the location of the swimming pool for future reference, then start south along the fence bordering Highway 29.

Bale Lane, named for Dr. Edward Bale, nephew-in-law to Gen. Mariano Vallejo, meets Highway 29 at the park boundary. In 1846, this land was part of his Carne Humana Rancho and was often travelled by pioneers who brought their grain to be ground at Bale's 40-foot-tall water-wheel-powered gristmill, a landmark farther south that is well worth a visit by history buffs. Grape and wine buffs should cross the highway instead and walk seven-tenths of a mile northeast along Bale Lane to Silverado Trail. As you do so, a broad pasture will be on your right, wine grapes of several varieties on trellises on the left. Soon you pass the Sterling Bear Flats Ranch. Notice as you walk the fine old stone house, the barns and the country ambiance. The stream you cross is Napa River, navigable by canoe all the way to San

Francisco Bay.

At the Silverado Trail, named in commemoration of the old stagecoach route and mine celebrated by Robert Louis Stevenson in *The Silverado Squatters*, bear left or northwest. Once past a cluster of buildings, the route again passes vineyards including grapes that are French Colombard, Petite Sirah, Gamay, and Cabernet Sauvignon. Look underfoot occasionally. The bright-eyed may spot a chunk of obsidian or even an arrowhead. The black volcanic glass in the road-shoulder gravel comes from nearby Glass Mountain, visible on the right. The Napa Indians who once lived along this riverbottom used it for spears and gamepoints.

Notice the beautiful oleander driveway entering Rancho de las Flores, home of gentleman grape-grower Gary Gielow, one of an increasing number of people attracted to the valley since agricultural zoning has protected it from random subdivision.

Resist the temptation to bear left through the long *allée* or avenue of grapes a few hundred feet farther and continue instead to Larkmead Lane, beyond some road-straightening endeavors. As you turn, look right, uphill, at the odd vertical power-line right-of-way on the hillside, which makes an ugly swath through the underbrush.

Smudgepots along the road, like sentinels, indicate that frost can be a problem to grape-growers. Look right to see Diamond or Spring Mountain with Mount St. Helena beyond it. The first creek you pass is Dutch Henry Creek. The second is Napa River again. The Hanns Kornell winery, whose old stone building was once operated by Felix Salmina, and which is reputedly the winery owned in her flamboyant days by Lillie Hitchcock Coit, is just beyond the river. Purist Hanns Kornell turns every bottle of champagne on the riddling racks by hand. Its coolness is a great respite for the walker on a hot day.

When you are rested, continue on Larkmead Lane, past the Chenin Blanc and Cabernet grapes of Christian Brothers. The white Moorish citadel visible up on the mountain northward includes a tram and Sterling Vineyards. Turn south on Highway 29 again. Once past the general store and

Ritchie Creek, walkers can cross a wooden footbridge and enter Bothe-Napa Valley State Park to complete this loop.

Bothe-Napa Valley State Park

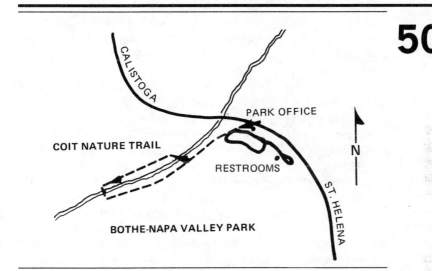

50

If, like the poet Countee Cullen, you "have a rendezvous with Life when Spring's first heralds hum," consider a springtime walk in Bothe-Napa Valley State Park to see the buds of April bursting anew. Life's classic symbols of rebirth burgeon here on the Coit Nature Trail, a gentle two-mile walk along Ritchie Creek where San Francisco's most famous fire buff, Lillie Hitchcock Coit, spent her carefree childhood summers.

To make this walk in the heart of the Napa wine country, transport yourself north from San Francisco via U.S. Route 101 and "The Wine Way," California Highways 29 and 128, through St. Helena and about one mile past the historic Bale gristmill, a part of the park which was recently restored, thanks to the generosity of the California State Parks Foundation.

Once at the main gate, oldtimers may remember Bothe-Napa Valley State Park as Paradise Park, privately operated for many years as a commerical campground. During the hot summers its swimming pool has long been Mecca for valley children and travellers alike. Park near the park office to pick up a self-guiding trail map, then look for the trailhead north of the entrance road. It veers off the service road into a hardwood forest.

Point 1 on the trail indicates bay, buckeye, and the deciduous black oak and broadleaf maple trees here. Periwinkle is the item of interest on Point 2. The guide mentions that periwinkle is a cultivar, or introduced plant, "common in the park along streams and shady areas," and that it was introduced from Europe by pioneer settlers. First settler on this land was a Britisher, Dr. Edward Turner Bale, to whom Rancho Carne Humana was granted in 1843 after his marriage to Maria Ignacia Soberanes, a niece of Gen. Mariano Vallejo. The two-league grant included the entire northern end of the Napa Valley, encompassing all of what is now St. Helena and Calistoga as well as a dozen or more wineries and several hundred vineyards.

At Point 3 notice the madrone whose thin red outer bark sheds annually. The trailguide points out that high quality charcoal made from madrone was used for gunpowder. Native Wappo Indians ate the scarlet berries. It also makes a walker's friend, a stout alpenstock. If you've never hugged a tree, here's your chance. The guide also says, "If you hug this green giant, you will find it quite cool."

Point 4 announces the coast redwood, which tends "to follow the fog belt along the Pacific Coast." It suggests that the walker "Take a break here—sit down on the log bench and try to become a part of the forest life around you. Though busy, its pace is quite different from that of our civilized world." You might see gray squirrels, which are common in the park here. From my own observations, though the pace may be different, the busiest times for raccoon, fox, and deer on park trails are often comparable to the busiest times on commuter freeways—morning and evening.

By the time you reach Point 5, you have left the riparian, or stream-associated environment and are in another woodland of oak, manzanita, blueblossom or ceanothus, and poison oak. Stay on the trail to avoid those shiny pink and fresh green poison oak leaves, no matter how inviting the milkmaids, wild iris, or fritillaria may be. Between trailmarkers 6 and 8, the trail is steep. The less spry can return to the main service road and follow it directly to Point 8, rendezvousing with more agile members of a family group there.

Point 8 was once the site of "Lonely," the home of Dr. Charles Hitchcock, who bought 1,000 acres of Rancho Carne Humana in 1872. His daughter Lillie shocked rural neighbors by riding astride in the days when it was lady like to ride side-saddle, almost as much as she shocked here Telegraph Hill neighbors by running to fires as mascot of Knickerbocker Fire Company 5. Eucalyptus and black acacias visible near the trail were planted by Lillie, as well as fruit trees in the family orchard across the creek. Always interested in horticulture, Lillie was quite possibly the first woman winemaker of California and the label for her Larkmead winery was celebrated in its time. The fountain and pool were built in Lillie's day here, but the park maintenance building was originally built by Reinhold Bothe as a recreation hall for his summer resort clientele in 1929 after "Lonely" had burned. the commercial campground became a state park in 1960.

Ritchie Creek tumbles, rushing, babbling, murmuring down into the park from Diamond Mountain. After you cross it to reach Point 9, look for small trails that lead from the creekside to the water's edge. Pawprints on the shore can tell you where animals come down to drink. If you feel an invisible fence as you walk between Points 10 and 14, you are right. On the left side of the trail, the riparian habitat is wet, cool, and lush with growth. On the right side, the deciduous hardwood forest is warmer. There is almost no overlap of plant communities between the two—a classic lesson for gardeners.

Native Indians used acorns from the grove of oaks in Point 11 for their staple food, but not before grinding and leaching out the bitterness in several washings in the running water of the stream. The resulting mush turned out to be porridgelike soup that would never sell at MacDonald's.

Point 12 may seem to need cleaning to the uninformed visitor. "You may wonder why wood gathering is not permitted in the park." The trail map explains, "The minerals and nutrients in the fallen wood are eventually broken down and returned to the soil. Insects, slime molds, and fungi speed up this process of decay, helping to recycle the elements important to new plant growth. To maintain this beneficial relationship between the living and the dead, leaves and downed wood must lie where they fall." If you are brighteyed, you may find arrowpoints or chips along this length of the trail.

By the time you reach Point 15, you are in a climax forest dominated by Douglas fir, which grew up after giant redwoods were logged here in the last century. At that time the faster growing Douglas fir was considered less important. Today it is one of our most widely used construction timbers because of its strength and straight grain. It is also the most popular West Coast Christmas tree.

Point 16 brings you back to the beginning of this easy hour's walk. If the awakening green of spring whets your appetite for more hiking, the park has half a dozen more trails to explore. Historians will also want to visit the site of Napa County's first church and the adjoining cemetery where early pioneers are buried. It is beyond the campground and picnic areas. If you forgot to bring a picnic, St. Helena, four miles south, offers the choice of wines from eight wineries within its city limits and good locally made cheeses go with them.

Calistoga

51

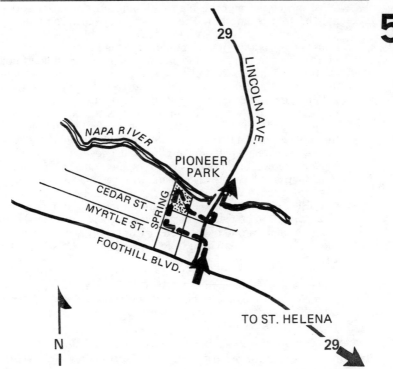

"It is difficult for a European to imagine Calistoga, the whole place is so new, and of such an occidental pattern," Robert Lewis Stevenson wrote in 1880. "The very name, I hear, was invented at a supper party by a man who found the springs."

That man, as residents of Napa County are quick to tell you, was the Mormon millionaire who refused to tithe, Sam "Gold" (Gold from the American River!) Brannan a great admirer of the New York resort, Saratoga, unconsciously coined the spoonerism: "I want it to be the Calistoga of Sarafornia." Everyone loved his slip of the tongue so much, he decided to use it for the name of the resort.

Calistoga had one street in Stevenson's time. As he described it in *The Silverado Squatters:*

> The railroad and the highway come up the valley about parallel to one another. The street of Calistoga joins them, perpendicular to both—a wide street with bright, clean low houses, here and there a verandah over the sidewalk, here and there a horse post, here and there lounging townsfolk. Other streets are marked out, and most likely named, for these towns in the New World begin with a firm resolve to grow larger; Washington and Broadway, and then First and Second, and so forth, being boldly plotted out as soon as the community indulges in a plan. But, in the meanwhile, all the life and most of the houses of Calistoga are concentrated upon the street between the railway station and the road. I never heard it called by any name, but I will hazard a guess that it is either Washington or Broadway. Here are the blacksmith's, the chemist's, the general merchant's, and Keng Sam Kee, the Chinese laundryman's; and here, probably, is the office of the local paper (for the place has a paper—they all have papers) and here, certainly is one of the hotels, Cheeseborough's, whence the daring Foss, a man dear to legend, starts his horses for the Geysers.
>
> It must be remembered that we are here in a land of stage-drivers and highwaymen; a land, in that sense, like England a hundred years ago. The highway robber—road agent, he is quaintly called—is still busy in these parts.

Stevenson, who has been described as "the man who brought the sunshine to San Francisco," was an astute observer. Today there is a freeway where the railroad used to run. We have gas stations instead of smithies and call the chemist's a drugstore. Both stage-driver Sam Foss and the road agents are long gone, but for all that, the reader of *The Silverado Squatters* could still find his way around Calistoga from Stevenson's description.

Indeed, it would make an ideal introduction for the walker who may like to avail himself of a stroll through Calistoga. To make this walk, from San Francisco head north on U.S. Route 101, cut east on California 37 to California Highway 12 and 121, following it to "The Wine Way," California Highway 29, to Calistoga.

Instead of calling the main street Broadway, as Stevenson humorously anticipated, Calistoga called it

Lincoln. Park where you can along Lincoln. Then return on foot to the intersection of Highway 29 and Foothill Boulevard. There behind the service station sign, one can find a plaque commemorating John York, who had the fun of raising the Stars and Stripes the first time it flew over what is now Sacramento, then Sutter's Fort. York was a member of the Grigsby party, the first emigrants to cross the Sierra Nevada by covered wagon; when he arrived here, local Wappo Indians called the site Colaynomo or "oven place" for the hotsprings underground, a name not so different from the present one. To Stevenson, Calistoga seemed "to repose on a mere film above a boiling, subterranean lake." Most of Calistoga's homes today have steaming hot water piped in from the springs.

Look uphill to the right of the York marker to see the Winans vault. Made of rock brought from China, it is a mausoleum containing the remains of Sam Brannan. Recross the highway carefully, then walk northeast on Lincoln Avenue to see at the northwest corner of Myrtle Street a house built in 1876 by Charles W. Ayer, remarkable for its puzzle-work. Never heard of puzzle-work? It is simply "wooden decoration cut with a jigsaw."

Two blocks northwest on Myrtle brings one to the mansion built in 1878 by H.H. Francis. It has walls 2½ feet thick, a bellcast mansard roof, and pedimented gable dormers. One of its tenants, Judge M.E. Billings, may not have hanged Jeff Davis from a sour-apple tree, as the Civil War song threatened, but he certainly watched him surrender to Ulysses S. Grant. Billing's regiment was Grant's escort for the occasion.

Bear right on Spring Street to the Napa River where pioneers entered the town. The crudely hewn steps on the north bank are remains of Calistoga's first crossing. Swing through Pioneer Park and return to Cedar Street to find one of the charming five-room cottages from Sam Brannan's original spa, recently moved here, and Judge Palmer's elegant "House of the Elms."

Take Cedar southeast half a block to Lincoln, and cross the bridge over the Napa River, lingering on it a little if you will, for free-running rivers are a rarity in towns today. Then continue northeast on Lincoln.

Like Stevenson, the walker should wind up at Brannan's Hot Spring Resort, as Pacheteau's was called when Brannan owned it. Gliders in the sky may lure you even further. As Stevenson described in at 5 A.M. on a foggy morning, it was "beautifully green" and he "found the thermometer had been up before me and had already climbed among the nineties," and he remarked that there was "something satisfactory in the sight of that great mountain that enclosed us to the north." The mountain is St. Helena. Stevenson fans who are eager for more walking may want to seek out the monument to him in the Robert Louis Stevenson Memorial State Park on its slopes.

East Bay

Contra Costa County

A Berkeley Loop to Indian Rock, Mortar Rock, and John Hinkel Parks

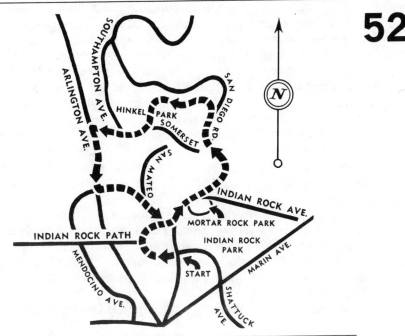

52

Not long ago, a poet at play took me for a walk through North Berkeley, a loop about two miles long, encompassing Indian Rock, Mortar Rock and John Hinkel Parks. En route, we played a walking game in which landmarks and streets became anything their appearance suggested. This had the effect of taking us through the higher altitudes of a country of our own construction.

Unless one has seen it in the rainy season, with torrents of water rushing down, it would not occur to most people to think of Marin Avenue as a rapids. But so it became in Professor David Bromige's walking game. He also saw Oxford Street as a trail and San Diego Road as Happy Valley, which lies above an allied realm called, of course, Unhappy Valley. Author George in "Earth Abides" saw it as the last place man inhabited.

The key to this enchantment lies in leaving your preconceived notions behind and really looking at what is about you. Begin this walk, as we did, where the headwaters of Shattuck Avenue meet Indian Rock Avenue, about a block uphill from The Circle, a convenient stop on the AC Transit bus number 7.

Walk uphill to Indian Rock, the huge irregular rock mass looming overhead, scale it via the rear steps, then sit a while on its eminence. Inspired by the knapsack and by the ropes clinging to an outcrop that are often used here by Sierra Club rock-climbing classes, imagination can make this a very tall mountain, elevation 17,000 feet. "It's an allegory," David said. "See the climbers below struggling up one face when they could easily be walking up the steps on the other two sides." From the peak, the Albany pimple seems to be a closer echo of Mount Tamalpais in the distance. "The cloud of fog under the Golden Gate Bridge looks like cars could be sucked into it," suggested Sherril Jaffe, another poet in our caravan.

Go down the southern steps, then bear left or east to find a siren and two tall metal posts posing as harmless eucalyptus trees. "Every five minutes the siren says 'All right, everybody off the rock,'" David proposed. "No, no," Sherril counterposed. "I think it says 'Enjoy yourselves, dammit, enjoy yourselves.'"

About 300 feet downhill on the right is the entrance to

Indian Rock Path. Enter it and loop the rock base, ignoring the straight segment that goes west (it drops four blocks to Solano Avenue). Soon you will come out in a grove of leptospermum that look like dinosaur trees guarding a rocky hobbit grotto. Go up the stone steps past two stumps, and emerge on San Mateo Avenue. Cross it, go uphill on Indian Rock Avenue and there, midblock at the bend, is Mortar Rock Public Park, announced by a plaque in the stone on your right.

For another spectacular view, climb the steps, bear right, then left around to the top. Here, viewed from a ring of trees enhanced by natural bonsai growing from crevices in the rock, the great bay vista becomes a dramatic backdrop for the interplay of fog "whenever Mr. Gilliam or somebody else lets it through the Gate." Hurry down, for the steps, David says, are there only one minute a year. If you are fast enough, you may surprise a hive of Indian ladies grinding pinole in the mortars that give this ornamental vest pocket park its name.

Then cross Indian Rock Avenue to come out opposite San Diego Road. Take it to a lower altitude, say "16,000 feet." After passing the Roman wall of an abandoned yard and an Aztec cactus prickly pear, look across from 801 San Diego for steps that lead down into Hinkel Park. Turn right at the first landing to find a great view bench. Then look down the cliff to see Hinkel amphitheater where, at certain times, another poet's imagination lets loose a Tibetan traveling troupe in performances of Dan Moore's Magic Floating Opera.

Clinging to the cliffs, pass the hollow tree (what, no mail for me?) to reach a musical creek (tuned by Pan). Look both uphill and down, then continue through the primeval forest to reach Berchtesgarten, a chalet. Here, if you feel inclined, you can come out of the balcony to play Hitler (*Achtung, Sieg Heil!*) or like a peacemaker plead with the multitudes of trees below (I beg of you, lay down your arms). But they only shed their leaves. Continue downward through the oaks (does that distant train whistle mean the Midnight Special will shed its everloving light on me?) to find swings and teeter-totters. Walk to the left to descend through the amphitheater to its stage.

Veer toward the picnic tables for a fast loop back to Indian Rock via Somerset to Southhampton, then left at Arlington to Mendocino Path. Take Mendocino Path uphill. No, you are not imagining the toucan and the racing pigeons in the Japanese garden aviary on the left, nor the bigfoot print in the path. At San Mateo Avenue, bear right to return to Indian Rock. First one to the cave can be the hermit.

The Wildcat Peak Trail

53

Chiseled in low relief into a sandstone scarp some-where on the southwest face of Contra Costa County's Wildcat Peak is the imprint of a hand, possibly an Indian hand, and the date 1810. Unless wind and rain have had their way with it, there is no reason to believe the hand isn't to be rediscovered above Wildcat Fault by any brighteyed, adventuresome climber.

According to the naturalists at the Environmental Educational Center of the Charles Lee Tilden Regional Park in which Wildcat Peak is situated, however, no one has reported seeing it for the last twenty years. Can it still be seen?

To seek it, of couse, one must explore the terrain of Wildcat Peak. This in itself is a pleasant adventure, rewarded by a stupendous view from the crest or possibly a glimpse of a gray fox or a coyote.

The walk proper begins in Indian Camp for those who arrive by car. For those who come by public transportation, it begins at the junction of Grizzly Peak Boulevard, Wildcat Canyon Road, Spruce Street, and Canon Drive. The handsome Shepherd of the Hills Lutheran Church is a good landmark. Indian Camp (now a parking area but once used by the Costanoan Indians in their shell trade) is about two-tenths of a mile downhill on Canon Drive.

The Environmental Center, opened in 1974, is ahead. Swing left at the tennis courts to find the great weeping red gum trees and the parking areas. Wildcat Creek will be on your right, Jewel Lake on your left. Surrounded by 700 acres in which no vehicles or picnickers are permitted, the lake is hidden in blackberry shrubs and willows. Follow the Jewel Lake service road, and the wooden catwalk over the marsh passing Jewel Lake Meadow and its watering trough, until you reach a rustic wooden bridge at the dam and spillway of Wildcat Creek. This is a good place to pause for a look at the lake, to listen for the phalarope, or spy the baby coots and baby ducks to be found here in June.

Wildcat Peak Trail, marked by a green mountain on a brown stake, takes up across the road from the bridge. It is a steep trail which reaches the Rotary Club International Peace Monument at its crest. The nearby Peace Grove of young *Sequoia gigantea* is about forty-five minutes of open country climbing. A loop following the Peak Trail up and a fire road and service road down circles the area in which the Indian hand is known to be located. Old Indian Trail itself lies within this circle, but thanks partly to the Wildcat Fault, it is a more rugged climb.

Peak Trail mounts through coast live oaks (and some poison oak) and under a chain of those anomalous scenery-defacing power line towers which I think of as Geckos. Gecko is a word once shared with me by writer Graydon Walker, who says it derives from the initials for "gas and

electric company oaf." An oaf is a changeling. In the other-wise uncluttered country, my mind is stuck with Graydon's word, as the country itself is stuck with Geckos marching like militant Martian invaders.

There are several bare sandstone slabs from the old underlying Pliocene seaway for the climber to scramble before he reaches the semicircular stone monument. Any of them is a good place to rest and observe the emerging panorama. Finally the bay is revealed, from the San Francisco airport to Novato. Near at hand are Kensington School, a surplus Nike missile site, an old quarry. To the east, the unspoiled watershed of San Pablo dam and reservoir lies beyond the young sequoia grove at one's feet, where there are markers to Adlai Stevenson and John Foster Dulles, among others. Mount Diablo stands majestic in the distance and sometimes there is a hawk's-eye view of the redtailed hawks circling below.

Jewel Lake

54

The idea of walking in the rain conjures up some dismal visions for many people—serfs slogging through the steppes, refugees fleeing a bombed city, the homeless milling about Civic Centers, or an odd man out, collar up, pipe down, on a wet slummy street.

If you are dressed for it however, and have someplace warm and cheerful to go afterwards, rain walking can be very satisfying. The Japanese, who have made an art of sensual appreciation, take rain walks to enjoy the sound on an umbrella, the bejewelling of moss, the splatter of droplets on a still pond.

Rain gives many places in the Bay Area a special quality.

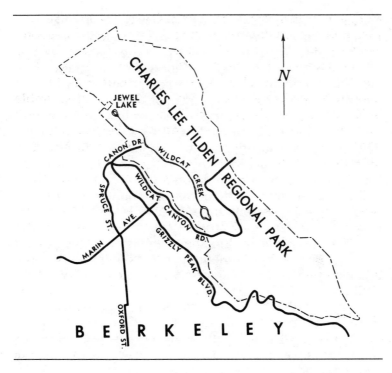

One of these is Jewel Lake in the East Bay, in the nature area that unites Wildcat Canyon and Tilden Regional Parks. Rain or shine, there is always something of interest to see and enjoy on the Jewel Lake Trail, a mile-long walk that can be done by spry grandparents, toddlers, and people in wheelchairs.

To make this walk, if it's raining, provide yourself with boots, rubbers, a poncho or other rain gear. Otherwise your Sunday duds, including ordinary flat heeled shoes, are fine. Then transport yourself to Albany, abreast of Golden Gate Fields. From Highway 80, go inland on Buchanan Street. It swings to join Marin Avenue before you reach San Pablo Avenue. Cross San Pablo and continue uphill on Marin Avenue, past the Circle, to Spruce Street. Near the Kensington City Limits where Spruce meets Wildcat Canyon Road and Canon Drive you reach the Tilden Regional Park spruce gate. (This is also a stop on the AC

Transit #7 and #67 buslines, whose Sunday service has been curtailed, alas.) Drive down Canon, turn left at the foot of the hill, and park as far north as possible.

When Spring is springing all about, first you may want to visit the attractive LIttle Farm, complete with windmill, white fences, red barn, museum of old farm equipment and any number of new chicks, kids, lambs and other live animals. Then look for the trail that goes across to the Environmental Education Center. Go inside to see its small museum. At most seasons, there is usually a fire burning in the little amphitheatre and sometimes a ranger giving a lecture. Pause at the little bookstore counter to pick up a map of the trail or purchase a Jewel Lake Trail booklet, devoted to balance of nature.

Then walk out toward the lawn visible through glass doors opposite the main entrance. Go out, cross the lawn and look for the duck marker that indicates the Jewel Lake Trail.

Post number 1 on the self-guiding trail indicates the gardener's friend, the native Botta Pocket Gopher. If you think he is a pest, consider the great service the gopher does by pushing up weed-free loam ready to scoop into a clay pot without sifting.

Stellar jays and their adaptation to eucalyptus and pine forests, rather than native oak and bay woods are the items of interest for post number 2 (try to ignore the corporation yard, all too visible on your left. Instead look on the right side of the trail for post #3, a bay tree planted to honor longtime park naturalist Joshua Barkin. The trendy new trail guide by his successor, Tim Gordon, gives Josh's recipe for pasta sauce using a bay leaf for flavoring.

Fescue (lawn grass to most of us) thick with ladybugs— which naturalists call ladybeetles, is the subject of Post 4. The big swarms come to this meadow in June. It's a home ladybugs fly away to.

Turn left downhill, leaving the eucalyptus trees and you soon reach a two-plank bridge that crosses a rivulet in Wildcat Fault. About 500 feet further, you reach a second bridge with a handrail which crosses musical Laurel Creek and is a great place, according to the booklet concerning

Post 5 to look for "The Green-eyed Dogs of Winter" mating. These waterdogs are California newts. Since the adults return to breed in the pools where they were born, sometimes there is an informal parade of newts heading across the path toward the water.

Bear left up the steps to reach a grove of coast live oak trees. The path goes below an old road, with the creek visible on your left far below. En route, at one point it is "low bridge" under an oak bough. When you reach an area with new planting on your left, Jewel Lake Trail has been rerouted. Don't inspect Post 6 too closely: It signals poison oak. Cross the old road, and follow a nice little split rail fence through the eucalyptus forest.

Surprisingly it brings you out at a little clearing where the native bunchgrasses, favorite food of the blacktail deer have survived despite the inroads of the man-introduced eucalyptus. Hopefully more of these young "weed trees" will be cut back to let the bunchgrasses proliferate, for seed from it is short supply elsewhere. But weeds or not, the eucalyptus grove with its unique pungency and rustling silver blue scimitar-shaped leaves almost seems like a conversational party in the rain. Stop to look at a nearby tree if it is raining to see how each leaf drops a continual mini-stream of water down to the tree roots below.

When you become aware of ducks quacking in the distance, Jewel Lake is near at hand. In a moment you are crossing a service road and paralleling a feeder stream. Man-made Jewel Lake was first dammed in the "water wars" of the 1880's, when part of the huge *Rancho del Sobrante*, originally granted to Juan Jose and Victor Castro in 1841, was divided by court settlement. The largest part went to land speculators, a water company and the township of Orinda.

Post 9 signals a wall. According to the guide, "During the Great Depression of the early 1930's, stonemasons built the basalt wall on your right to stop erosion of the ravine. The wall held but the fill failed: an aqueduct collapsed." Post 10 calls attention to the aqueduct. Jumping spiders and fox squirrels like to hang out nearby. After an epidemic of mites between 1917 and 1923 killed many of the native western gray squirrels; there were none of the happy scamperers here for almost 40 years. Finally in the late 60's, the fox squirrel, which had been successfully introduced a few years earlier at Oakland's Lakeside Park, were brought to this area.

Notice the restrooms across the park road, which also serves as a horsemen's trail, then plunge into that tunnel of trees below the road from it. It takes you along the water's edge onto the Jewel Lake Trail's most enchanting feature, a long catwalk that zigzags over the marsh like a Japanese bridge. After 100 years of sedimentation, what was once a three acre lake has now shrunken to a one acre pond surrounded by dogwoods, alders and willows, all blooming in springtime. Marsh plants pop up through the mud below. Shelf mushrooms adorn fallen logs. Mayflies and dragonflies skim in the filtered sunlight. Look closely and you may spot raccoon tracks or spy a turtle, a bullfrog or a stickleback. Linger awhile looking at raindrops on the water. You may discover a diving beetle deserving his name or a giant waterbug whirling in this enchanting wildwood.

All too soon you are out of the marshy area. Follow the signposts back to the Environment Education Center again, to warm up by the cheery fire. As you leave, breathe deeply a time or two for a last whiff of the new-washed air, then shake the rain from your shoulders and go home refreshed.

Stephen T. Mather
Redwood Grove

55

"When California was wild, it was the floweriest part of the continent," John Muir wrote in 1901. This may still be true. If Muir were to come striding back through the East

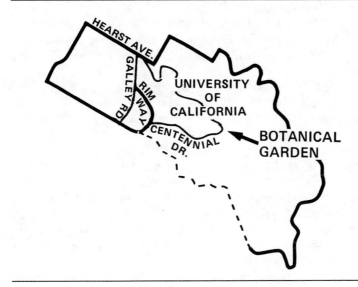

Bay hills almost any year in which spring follows abundant winter rains, he could easily write the same thing, for such springs bring fantastic flowers.

One of the pleasantest places to see flowers both wild and tame in bloom is the University of California Botanical Gardens, thirty-two acres growing 8,000 different species, most of them collected from seeds grown in the wild. It is open to the public at no cost from 9 A.M. to 4:45 P.M. every day of the year but Christmas. Spring is a riot of color in the Rhododendron Dell, the California Annual section and in the New World Desert, to which an information center has recently been added. There is another newly created five-acre garden where the colors are softer and subtler. This is the Stephen T. Mather Redwood Grove, shut off to the public for forty years and now underplanted to create a natural coastal redwood plant community.

To enjoy this treasurehouse, pack your picnic and transport yourself to Strawberry Canyon on the U.C. Berkeley campus. From San Francisco, the route lies across the Bay Bridge, then north via the Eastshore Freeway (Interstate 80) to University Avenue. At the far end of

University, turn left at Oxford one block to Hearst, then right to Gayley Road. It leads to Rim Way, skirts Memorial Stadium and joins Centennial Drive, climbing all the way. When you reach the Botanical Gardens, park where you can.

At the outset, sign the guest register and pick up a free trail map. Since redwood trees have a quieting effect on all of us, plan to shed your freeway stress by strolling first in the Stephen Mather Grove. To reach it, cross Centennial Drive in the crosswalk, go through the big gate, pass the greenhouse and head for the pond, focal point of "the Miocene Forest." Sugar maple, black walnut and tree of heaven may seem oddly unrelated to redwoods, but their fossil ancestors grew in association with them ten million years ago. The modern descendants of eastern trees learned how to adapt to colder weather when climatic changes drove the redwoods out.

Before you cross the bridge, pause to read the tribute that Stephen Tyng Mather, an early graduate of Cal, received when he was awarded an honorary degree of LL.D. from his alma mater in 1924:

> Mountaineer and statesman, lover of nature and of his fellow men. With a generous and farseeing wisdom he has made accessible for a multitude of Americans their heritage of snowcapped mountains, glaciers and streams and falls, of stately forests and quiet meadows.

Mather, John Muir and Newton Drury, for whom another glade nearby is named, all started as journalists. Mather's appointment as first director of the National Park Service also came from an ex-reporter, Assistant Secretary of the Interior Franklin K. Lane. Ironically, the 300-acre arboretum Mather's friends began here after his death in 1930 was truncated by the Depression and by World War II. Fences between the arboretum and its uphill neighbor, the Lawrence Berkeley Laboratory, finally came down in 1970.

Follow the trail and soon you are above the Calvin Townsend Amhitheater, named for a philanthropic alumnus. Although redwoods here are all about forty years old, size is not a reliable indicator of their age. The 2,200-year-old tree found by Emanuel Fritz in Humboldt Redwoods State Park had a diameter of twelve feet. Other trees with the same or greater diameters have been demonstrated to be only a fourth as old. Round the back of the amphitheater and come downhill with the path. Forest duff under the trees is shredded bark, which provides the right medium for compatible underplanting.

After you pass the Drury glade, you reach in quick succession the Emanuel Fritz glade, named for the former forester; the Agnes Roddy Robb glade, named for a longtime secretary to university president R.G. Sproul; and the Knowles Augustus Ryerson glade, which commemorates a horticulturist.

When you reach the pond at the bottom of the slope, veer away from those shiny downhill roofs (they're atop the Atmospheric Aerosol Research Laboratory) and start back uphill on the opposite side of the pond, From Bed 919 there is a pleasant view uphill toward the outdoor classroom.

Soon you are back in the sunlight. Recross Centennial Drive for a quick look at the collection of two dozen or so aloes that surround the waiting bench for bus riders. Then wander past the parking lot and greenhouses toward the educational center. In addition to a generous bench and directions, it offers a fine selection of modestly priced booklets, many prepared by the botanical garden staff.

If you have never seen cactus in bloom, this is the place to do it. From the educational center's entrance level, the overview of the bold and bristly desert plants is fine, but go below and look upward for a really sensational panorama. Then meander as you will, seeking out the rhododendrons and native wildflowers, for no matter how often you return to this lovesome spot, there is always something new and unusual to see.

Lake Anza

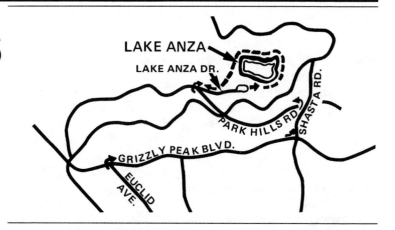

56

"I know a lake where the cool waves break . . ." and its name is Anza. A nine-acre mountain pond in the heart of Tilden Park's 2,065 acres, it is the East Bay's favorite swimming hole. In these days of governmental economies, if there is one lifeguard left on the staff of the East Bay Regional Park District, he's sure to be assigned to scenic Lake Anza.

On a drowsy summer day when the whisper of cattails and the lapping of lake water can take one back to childhood, a loop around Lake Anza is also a joy for the walker.

To make this walk, transport yourself, complete with picnic and swimtogs, to Berkeley. (BART and a shuttle, and AC Transit buses 7 and 67 serve Tilden Park.) On your own wheels, from University Avenue take Oxford left to Hearst, then right on Hearst uphill to Euclid, then left on Euclid for about two miles, then right on Grizzly Peak Boulevard (about a mile and a half) to Shasta Gate. Within Tilden Park, bear left on Park Hills Road to Lake Anza Drive. At the end of Lake Anza Drive, park, pay your fee and locate a convenient spot to stake out your blanket and picnic. Loaf a while to get the lay of the land.

When Capt. Pedro Fages and Father Juan Crespi came

this way in 1772 with "six Catalonian volunteers, six leather-jackets, a muleteer and an Indian servant," they found Wildcat Creek already tame countryside, supporting a Costanoan Indian village nearby. Four years later, Jose Joaquin Moraga and Capt. Juan Bautista de Anza, for whom the lake is named, came along Wildcat Creek and recorded meeting the same Indians.

"Did you ever stand on the top of a high hill in the early morning, when the eastern sky is beginning to put on its morning robe of variegated colors, with all the blended shades of an artist's palette, and watch the town, nestling in the valley at your feet, wake up after its night of slumber? Here a chimney sends its spiral of blue smoke straight in air; then another, and another, like the smoke of Indian scouts signaling to their tribes." So wrote W.E. Hutchinson in 1915 while exploring Wildcat Canyon for his book *Byways Around San Francisco Bay*. There were still trout in the streams for him to catch, but by then the Indians were gone.

The dam you see at the lower end of the lake was built in 1939, bottling up part of Wildcat Creek to supply water for the links of the eighteen-hole golf course uphill to the south. As you look up at 1,913-foot Vollmer Peak to the south and 1,250-foot Grizzly Peak to the north, try to envision 2,000 soldiers swarming over the fulvous hills between. They were stationed here during World War II. Known as Wildcat Canyon until it was renamed in 1934 for Maj. Charles Lee Tilden, first president of the park district's board of directors, Tilden Park in its time has been a watershed, a quarry, an abattoir, and a pasture for cattle from Mission Dolores. Many of its buildings were constructed by the Civilian Conservation Corps crews of the Depression years.

When you have lazed long enough in the summer sun, stroll past the changing rooms and concession stand to pick up the path that loops the lake. Walking around the south end first, you come in rapid succession through willow woodland, rocky outcroppings, streambed meadowland, swampy rushes and cattails—a microcosm of the entire park.

Bear left at the dam and cross the weir. The music you hear drifting toward you comes from the nearby merry-go-round, an antique built in 1911, the most charming one in operation in the Bay Area. Originally operated in the Los Angeles area, it has been a favorite mid-park ride for East Bay children since 1948. Other great rides for children were the little railroad at the north end of the park and the pony rings at the south end, now gone. If the familiar organ music brings out the child in you, bear left on Lake Anza Drive and follow the oom-pah-pahs until the big colorful carousel with its stunning hand-painted horses looms ahead. Pink fluffs of cotton candy for sale at the merry-go-round may bring frowns from dentists and natural food fanatics, but it's all part of the nostalgic mystique of summer fun at Tilden.

After you've ridden a lunging zebra or stately deer, stroll back the way you came, to pass through the orchard and return to the little sandy beach. Redwing blackbirds may call as you suntan there. A sparrowhawk may quiver overhead. Turkey vultures circle, like the scavengers they are, patrolling the hills on their thrice daily pickup beat. Butterflies, dragonflies, damselflies and occasionally a flying frisbee enliven the sand. Trees creak and sigh as though one were a thousand miles from civilization, instead of just over the hill from Berkeley and Oakland.

And then there is the girlwatching and boywatching, all part of the good life in a California summer scene. If that doesn't refresh you after a twenty minute walk around the lake, you can always swim.

Grangers' Wharf, in Martinez

57

If the Martinez waterfront has a genie of place, it must surely be Jennie Cardanalli, daughter of a fisherman, wife of

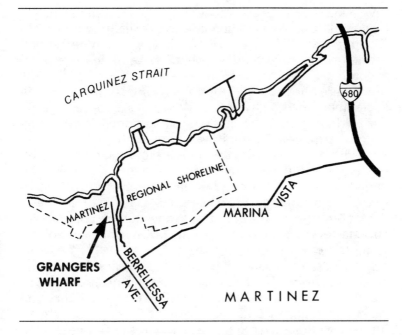

a fisherman, and mother of Contra Costa County Supervisor Nancy Cardanalli Fahden. There are not many people who can get a supervisor out on foot into a debris-strewn marsh to pick up used beer cans and old plastic bottles, but Jennie Cardanalli is one of them.

The result is the Martinez Regional Shoreline Park, 308 acres along the Carquinez Strait, one of the few places in the Bay Area where a walker can get down to the banks of the Sacramento River to stroll or fish. It is no coincidence that the park has grown where the Sicilian fishing community of Martinez once docked their feluccas, and dried and tended their nets.

Grangers' Wharf received the salmon, bass and shad brought into Martinez for canning. It was a cooperative venture originated by Dr. William Strentzel, president of Alhambra Valley Grange. A country practitioner and orchardist, he is better known in our time as John Muir's father-in-law.

In its heyday, the spring salmon run in the Sacramento

River would average about twenty fish per day per man. The bigger fall run, which began in August, might go up to 100 fish per man daily. Two of the Bay Area's nine salmon canneries were located in Martinez, and inasmuch as, according to Slocum's *History of Contra Costa County*, there were about 2,500 fishermen taking salmon along the Sacramento in 1882, Grangers' Wharf was a lively scene. By 1957, when commercial fishing was forbidden from Pittsburg to the Carquinez Bridge, it was all over.

Within a few years, the area around Grangers' Wharf looked like the Dogpatch dump. Jennie Cardanalli, who hadn't seen it in years, cried when someone took her down to the old wharf area a few years ago. Cleaning it up was a job for bulldozers. She didn't have one. But she got a bucket and started to pick up the trash. Inspired, other women came to help.

To see the park that womanpower subsequently delivered from the trash, transport yourself from San Francisco to Martinez via the Bay Bridge, thence on California Highway 24 toward Walnut Creek and north on Interstate 680 to Martinez. Just short of the George Miller, Jr. Bridge between Martinez and Benicia, take the Marina Vista offramp west to Berrellessa Street, bear right and follow it to its end near the water. It will cross the Southern Pacific tracks, a spur originally brought into Grangers' Warehouse at the encouragement of Dr. Strentzel. If you come along at the right time, an Amtrak train may be stopping at the station here. This would be an ideal way to come to the shoreline via public transportation if trains ran often enough. AC Transit's Marina Vista bus from the Concord BART station is the alternative.

At the outset, go through the hiker's stile beside the road barrier, noting the Grangers' Wharf sign that acknowledges the park as part of the Martinez Regional Shoreline, presently being constructed as a cooperative project of the city of Martinez, the State Lands Commission, Shell Oil and the East Bay Regional Park District. When completed, it will have two miles of trails along the water, stretching as far as the bridge visible on the east and linking in the west with the shoreline trail to Point Pinole.

Look underfoot in the walkway, made of red bricks, many broken, to see a thrifty re-use. They were salvaged from the site and relaid by citizens of Martinez. Resist the temptation to go off to the right to see the bocce ball courts. Instead, like Dorothy in the *Wizard of Oz*, follow the brick road. In a short while, the trail divides. Bear left on the gray gravel for a while. Hulet Hornbeck of the East Bay Regional Park District, who conducted me on this walk, pointed out that the pickleweed marsh here is "six times more valuable to the basic food chain of life than the most valuable agricultural land there is. Because men make only an indirect profit from them," he continued, "many of the shortsighted do not realize its great value and would like to exploit what few marshes remain in California. What they don't understand is that when the marshes are done for, so is man."

The little ark on the trail is still occupied by an oldtimer whose tenancy there is limited. Continue past it to the end of the trail to find a little sandy beach. Trains in the distance shunt by busily on weekdays beyond the park boundary. Look uphill to locate, in the live oaks and eucalyptus on the hillside, an old Italian cemetery that would make a natural addition since it is in the "viewshed" of the park.

As you look at the wide panorama on the far shore, try to envision ferry boats on the water. The first, the biggest and one of the last ferries across the Sacramento ran between Martinez and Benicia at various times. In honor of the martini, believed to have been named for the town of Martinez, the last of the car ferries used to fly flags bearing a red cocktail glass on a white background.

When you have looked your fill, retrace your steps to the red brick path and continue on it as far as Arroyo del Hambre locally known as Alhambra Creek. Its headwaters are in Briones Regional Park, about four miles south, and at one time supplied the Alhambra Water Company. Both parks are used for educational purposes so that kids can understand how little streams feed into rivers from the hills.

Bear left at the creek to find at the river's edge, beyond the cattails, another sandy beach where egrets, sandpipers, and marshhawks are sighted. Benches are so subtly designed, they almost look like driftwood that may have come in on a high tide. If you come along this way on the Fourth of July, you will find a bass-fishing tournament underway. You may also find a plaque honoring the farsighted men who first planted stripers in the strait. "The fish came in milk cans from New Jersey," Supervisor Fahden recalls.

When you return to the main trail, continue along the creek to look for a place where another gray gravel trail ends on the opposite shore. Since the bridge is in place, walkers can continue on to the Martinez picnic areas near the marina from this point. To make a loop back to your wheels instead, stay on the creekside path to emerge beside the bocce ball courts, or if you persist on the trail almost to the parking lot, to the barbecue placed by the Jaycees, for fish-fries, of course.

Point Richmond

58

The community of Point Richmond sits on the Contra Costa like a little piece of San Francisco that floated across the bay and stranded itself when the tide went out.

An urbane, attractive oasis in the vast and otherwise depressing industrial steppe, it perches on hills that climb up from the water, like Sausalito, gently tree-shaded and eminently livable. At its heart is a focal triangle of unusual shops and restaurants. On its shore is a new public park, one of the rare waterside parks on the bay. The walk of exploration along the East Bay Regional Park District's Miller-Knox Regional Shoreline makes a pleasant Sunday.

Begin the walk by transporting yourself with fortitude via California Highway 17 as if you were going to cross the

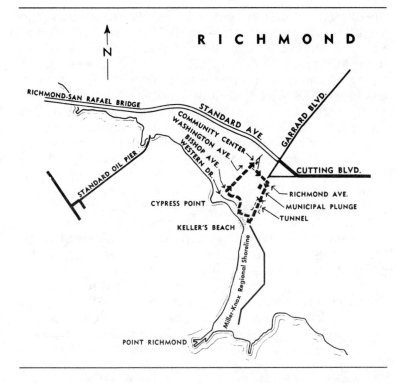

RICHMOND

N

RICHMOND-SAN RAFAEL BRIDGE

STANDARD AVE.

COMMUNITY CENTER

WASHINGTON AVE.

BISHOP AVE.

WESTERN DR.

GARRARD BLVD.

CUTTING BLVD.

STANDARD OIL PIER

CYPRESS POINT

RICHMOND AVE.

MUNICIPAL PLUNGE

TUNNEL

KELLER'S BEACH

Miller-Knox Regional Shoreline

POINT RICHMOND

Richmond-San Rafael Bridge. The Point Richmond turnoff is left from Cutting Boulevard at Garrard, and watch for it, because you don't get much of a crack at it in traffic. As landmarks, keep an eye peeled for the Point Orient restaurant, the big Richmond Municipal Plunge, or for the tunnels near it. Not much more than sixty years ago, 1,200 acres of this sprawling industrial slurb was blue bay water surrounding Ellis Landing. Point Richmond itself was an island until land-grabber Jacob Tewksbury dammed it to start the shoaling and fill. To another pioneer, A.S. Macdonald, goes the credit or blame for enticing the Santa Fe Railroad to build its terminal yards here. Pullman cars were also built nearby in the heyday of railroading.

At the outset, park near the triangle defined by Washington Park and Richmond Avenues, in whose core are two recent municipal buildings, one housing fire trucks, the other a community center and library. Then browse the periphery, a colorful conglomeration that includes the Santa Fe Market, a name that bespeaks the origin of the town; Masquer's Playhouse; Judges and Spares, a restaurant taking its name from a poem by George Hitchcock: "The clock on the kitchen shelf neither judges nor spares . . ."; the Famous Original Hotel Mac, known for its good food and racy past; a remodeled Old Firehouse accommodating a variety of offices; the L.L. Boone shop of unusual gifts; and the Baltic Bar, with its stained glass windows which keep their promise with rich mahogany and classical saloon nudes within. The Cantonese Point Orient, the Mexican Inn and Jumbo's Burgers all have more than county-wide following. Look uphill to spot four nearby churches.

Then, for unexpected contrast to the sophisticated little outpost, walk on Richmond Avenue to Garrard, the point at which the municipal tunnel goes under Nicholl Nob, just past the plunge. Observe as you enter the tunnel the faded letters that say this is the way to the San Francisco Ferry. Walk through to emerge at Keller's Beach, now part of Miller-Knox regional shoreline, a park complete with picnic tables, cliffside trees, a sandy sun trap and a rare chance to

dip a toe into bay water. Tarry a while in the sun.

A man-made lagoon, winding paths shaded by new trees, and more picnic tables attract visitors to the flat parklands along the bay. Across Dornau Drive, new grass and wildflowers cover lands that were cut up for years by motorcycles and that now form a natural amphitheater.

As the shadows lengthen, follow Western Avenue to Bishop; then start uphill on Washington, which will take you up over the ridge to return you to the shopping area. Mountain goats who would look both ways from the saddle of hills can digress a few blocks south on Crest for the view from Nicholl Nob, now a feature of the urban regional park. It should be renamed for Lucretia and Tom Edwards, the civic-minded citizens who dug into their own savings to buy Nicholl Nob until it could become a park.

Mount Diablo State Park

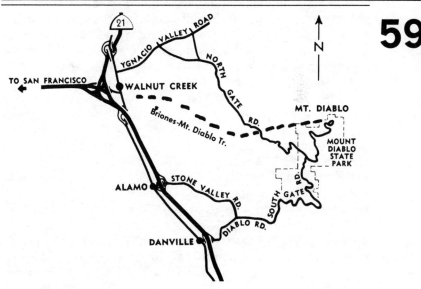

59

Almost every winter, there is a gloriously clear morning on which the Bay Area awakens to discover new snow glistening whitely on the double peaks of Mount Diablo, the jewel of Contra Costa County. Then, for San Franciscans who seldom see snow, and especially for nostalgic expatriate midwesterners, it is time for a walk around the south peak of Diablo.

At 4,336 feet above sea level, Diablo is the Bay Area's highest mountain. In 1862, William H. Brewer, a member of the official California Survey field party, estimated that from Diablo's summit it was possible to see "spread out in tolerably plain view—over 300 miles from north to south and 260 miles from east to west."

With today's ever-increasing smog, it is unlikely that the walker will see that far, yet given a scintillating day, the trip is worth the effort. To enjoy a well-planned summit-loop observation trail, begin this walk by driving to the parking lot at the summit, west of the lookout building.

Mount Diablo State Park seems discouragingly dedicated to the automobile and other mechanical devices, rather than to people, especially those on foot, so reconcile yourself to walking on the road uphill at an easy grade to the stone observation building. The building itself is worth a little inspection since it was built from fossiliferous Upper Miocene sandstone quarried near the south gate in 1931, shortly after Diablo became a state park. Space inside is devoted to a museum.

The devil that gave Diablo its name is not the ugly communications monster near the crest, but an Indian evil spirit, or *puy*, reputed to have helped the Bolgones Indians defeat a military expedition from the Spanish presidio in San Francisco in 1806.

North Peak, privately owned, obscures the view north. Look south and west to see San Ramon and Diablo Valleys, and southeast to see the Livermore Valley. Mount St. Helena and Mount Hamilton are sometimes visible.

In 1851, Diablo was chosen as the base point for U.S. surveys of California; a meridian line through the peak near the tower establishes other locations. Field party member William Brewer wrote:

The great features of the view lie to the east of the meridian passing through the peak. First, the great central valley of California, as level as the sea, stretches to the horizon both on the north and to the southeast . . . on the North are the Marysville Buttes, rising like black masses from the plain, over a hundred miles distant; while still beyond, rising in sharp clear outline against the sky, stand the snow-covered Lassen's Buttes, over two hundred miles in air line distant from us . . .

Rising from this great plain, and forming the horizon for three hundred miles in extent, possibly more, were the snowy crests of the Sierra Nevada. What a grand sight! The peaks of that mighty chain glittering in the purest white under the bright sun, their icy crests seeming a fitting helmet for their black and furrowed sides!

Closer at hand, the odd formation east of the tower is known as the Devil's Pulpit. According to the State Division of Mines *Geologic Guidebook of the Bay Area*, "Mount Diablo is a sort of geologic freak. The core of the twin-peaked mountain consists of jumbled massive rocks of the Franciscan Formation which literally have been punched through the once-overlying Cretaceous and Miocene Formations from below. Upturned edges of these ruptured formations flank the mountain on every side and a large fault zone can be followed around the base." Geologists interpret this to mean that Diablo, high as it is now, was once a sea bottom.

If you yearn to come back to explore the mountain more intimately, from the U.S. Geological Survey headquarters, obtain the Clayton and Diablo quadrangle 7½-minute series maps. These show the terrain with utmost accuracy. On park maps issued at the gate, many trails are unmarked, especially those in the recently purchased Mitchells Canyon. Bring your own first-aid kit. Rattlers are not uncommon on Diablo and in at least one recent episode, there wasn't a snakebite kit available in the park.

Alameda County

Lake Chabot

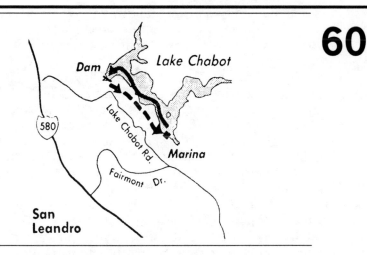

60

Lake Chabot, the fisherman's paradise in the heart of 4,935-acre Lake Chabot, has some open secrets on its shore that even its regular visitors may not know about.

One of them is Yema-Po, the recently discovered ghost of a Chinese village. Another is a 22-nest blue heron rookery visible only from the water.

There are more, including a miniature Roman temple, but one of interest to walkers is an unusual weekend ferry service. It is comparable to those often found in Europe, notable on the Binnen Alster in Hamburg, Lake Como in Italy and Lake Geneva in Switzerland.

For 25 cents, from April to October, it is possible to board the Lake Chabot Queen and be dropped off at several different landings around the lakeshore. This makes it possible to go ashore in a remote spot and amble back from semi-wilderness to urbanity.

To enjoy this unusual combination of boat ride and walk, plan to arrive in time to board the ferry at 9 a.m., noon or 4 p.m. Bring along lunch or supper in a daypack and, if you wish, license and tackle for freshwater fishing. You can leave your swimsuit at home, because Lake Chabot, for 90 years the primary water supply for Oakland, is still an East Bay Municipal Utility District standby reservoir and does not permit swimming. For this outing, leave Fido at home too. Dogs are welcome leashed in the park but are not allowed on the ferry.

From San Francisco, cross the Bay Bridge and head south on Highway 580. Past San Leandro take the Fairmont Drive exit east to Lake Chabot Road. (Don't confuse the City of San Leandro's little Chabot Park with the much larger Lake Chabot Regional Park farther south.) Drive in, pay your parking fee and look for a spot.

Once afoot, start near the big map of the park by the trailhead on the east side of the parking lot. Then follow the route that leads through Turtle Meadow, swinging north around Tadpole Pond.

On a fair day, this area shows the population pressures of the encroaching suburbs. (Fortunately, the park system has purchased the nearby hill formerly belonging to the Lutheran Church.) Sometimes the crowds are as colorful as the visiting waterfowl. I was standing near a steep slope where children on cardboard slides had eroded a channel into the soil and reading the plea, "Help Save These Hills. No Sliding Please," when I was distracted by a passing poodle. He wore a lime-green sweater and sported a punk-style hair clip. I didn't notice the owner's garb.

Turn left when you reach the bridge, cross it and walk uphill, to the right. Past the restrooms, turn right again to reach the Lake Chabot Marina. If you plan to fish, stop at the snack bar-bait shop to purchase an East Bay Regional Park District daily fishing permit for $1.50. You'll need it in addition to your California fishing license.

The boats for hire here—canoes, pedal boats, rowboats

and electric-powered motorboats—have been chosen both for their silence and their nonpolluting qualities. Rowboats and canoes rent for $4.50 per hour, pedal boats for $5 an hour and electric boats for $7 an hour. There is a $10 deposit on all boats.

"Until 1966, fishermen used to look longingly over the fences around Lake Chabot," Park Superintendent John Maciel told me. "There were legends circulated about the size and number of the fish in the lake, how you could see six or eight big ones jumping at a time . . . The day it opened, 30,000 fishermen rushed in and a lot of them caught whoppers. They still do. Any catch above 8 pounds qualifies the fisherman for the Whopper Club. The biggest wide-mouth bass taken from the lake weighed 17 pounds 14 ounces. The record catfish, caught in 1981, was 39 inches long and weighed 35 pounds."

Board the canopied little ferry and you may have Ranger Jackie Kurtz-Boggs, whose specialty is park history, piloting you, as my party did.

"Lake Chabot covers 315 acres, has 8½ miles of shoreline and is the oldest working reservoir in the United States," she told us. "When it is full, it holds 3.37 billion gallons of water. It was EBMUD's first reservoir and could be taken off standby anytime it is needed. The drought of 1976 was the last time it was put back into service."

On her advice, we planned to be dropped off at Alder Point as close as possible to the earthwork dam Anthony Chabot built in 1874, using 200 wild mustangs to trample the ground. After inspecting the dam, we would walk back, as you may wish to do, to the marina via the West Shore Trail.

The boat trip out across the serene lake is a fine mood-setter. Here and there along the quiet shore, boats pull into little coves, each looking like a painted still life as fishermen await a fishy nibble. Once past Live Oak Island, off limits except to nesting waterfowl, one could be miles away, instead of being in the heart of Oakland, San Leandro and Castro Valley. If you are observant, you may see a great blue heron, skimming the water heading toward Bass Cove, on whose south side the heron rookery is located.

"That's Leroy," Kurtz-Boggs told us pointing to a lone great blue. "He seems to be the front-runner. The other great blues arrive soon after Lerov shows up here."

Looking northeast across the water, we could see Chabot's little tower with its classical columns, looking like a Maxfield Parrish painting, and also the prototype for the two "water temples" at San Francisco's reservoirs at Sunol and Crystal Springs. "Chabot greatly admired the aqueduct-building Romans," Kurtz-Boggs said, "and in tribute to them, he had his Chinese laborers hand-lay the tower in Italian stone."

Once ashore, walk north to examine the dam and spillway. Yema-Po, which means "Wild Horse Slope" in Cantonese, is the site where the Chinese workmen lived during the construction of the dam and for 20 ensuing years. As many as 800 were employed on the dam. The village was located on the southern bank of San Leandro Creek, west of the original spillway.

When anthropologist George R. Miller and his students from California State University at Hayward sifted the soil of Yema-Po, they found several hundred artifacts documenting the village. Cooking utensils, hand-forged iron tools, locks and latches, opium bottles and other treasures, all the property of EBMUD, are on loan to Hayward State. Don't be tempted to seek out the excavation sites. They have been carefully covered, and poison oak abounds in the area.

Go as far as the dam and look over both sides to discover that it is 100 feet above the waterline, then try to imagine a band concert being held on top of it. Such concerts were held here in the 1920's.

As you start back, look near the two monuments on the natural overlook on your left for historical markers. This is also a good place to view the water temple and to picnic.

If you have a strong feeling of Indian presence nearby, your sensibilities are acute. During the late 1700's, the tiny tribe of 100 Indians called the Jalquins (for their leader) who lived along the shore of San Leandro Creek were removed to Mission San Jose to be converted to Christianity.

Keep the lake on your left as you walk back and you

can't get lost. Joggers, dog walkers, bicyclists and strollers will pass by. "What brings you here?" I asked Anne and Don Cawood of San Leandro, who told me they are regulars on this trail. "It's such a quick getaway to nature," Anne said. "Just walking a short way, you can get away from people, right in the densest part of the East Bay."

The Heart of Oakland

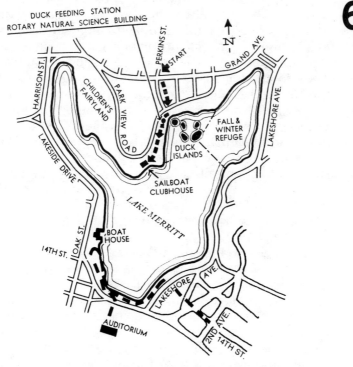

Oakland's Lake Merritt, the 150-acre tidal slough that was transformed 110 years ago from a smelly tidetime marsh into the city's greatest asset, offers without doubt the most urbane walking in the East Bay. One could stage the

New York musical comedy "Up in Central Park" there any time without having to import a single prop. Indeed, Oakland could provide some diversions that Manhattan's park lacks.

Originally the north arm of San Antonio Creek, as the Oakland Estuary was originally known, it was dammed in 1869 thanks to Dr. Samuel Merritt, then mayor, who personally funded the project and named it Lake Peralta. When it was renamed, a local daily called it "A most Merrittorious project." Ten years later Lake Merritt became the first state game refuge on the North American continent; more than 4,000 migratory birds still check in annually for a visit. There are also bandstands, bicyclers, boathouses, benches, civic buildings, a college, colonnades, churches, a children's Fairyland, excursion boats, fishing piers, gardens, lawn-bowling greens, hotels, private homes, statuary and trees, to mention just a handful of the diversions visible in the almost 3.2 mile circumambulation of the lake.

Walkers familiar with my newspaper column or my book about walks in the East Bay, *There, There,* will have been introduced to the first two of these, but Walk III, which begins near El Embarcadero and goes along the east shore with a sidetrip into a nearby neighborhood rich in architectural styles, may be a new experience. For the benefit of those dependent on public transportation, I recommend doing it in reverse of the Camron-Stanford pamphlet.

From San Francisco, the Lake Merritt stop via BART is the handiest. AC Transit's transbay Line A to 12th and Fallon is another way to go. From the East Bay, Lines 14, 15, 18, 40, 43, 82, or 83 all stop at Oakland Auditorium. Once at the auditorium, look on the side facing the lake parallel to the big arched door which has the word "Intellectual" carved over it, for a tunnel that goes under the roadways between the auditorium and the lake.

Once through the tunnel, if it is between 1 and 5 P.M. on a Sunday (or 11 and 4 on a Wednesday), bear left toward the big Italianate Victorian house in the trees visible on the lakeshore lawn. This is Camron-Stanford house, locally known as "The Lady of the Lake," nicely rehabilitated within the last few years and furnished in the period of its heyday, the late 1800s. Go in to visit it, admire its parlors and pick up a copy of the booklet.

When you have enjoyed pretending that you are President Rutherford B. Hayes or his wife, "Lemonade Lucy," visiting for a weekend on the lake, retrace your steps to the tunnel and, pamphlet in hand, walk past it to Adams Point. The sculpture on the point is painted steel, done in 1974 by Jan Evans. The pamphlet's Point 54 is a Christian Science church whose classic architecture mirrors the Scottish Rite Temple (Point 16) visible across the lake. Both of these buildings were built after the "City Beautiful" concept was adopted by Oakland for the lake's perimeter.

Although the temptation may be to head for the boat landing at the East 18th Street, size it up as a landmark and make an architectural sidetrip instead. From the church, leave the lake and take 14th Street to 2nd Avenue. An eastern shingle cottage, a larger "brownie," the Lakeside Baptist church designed in the Mission Revival style of Julia Morgan, a Craftsman style bungalow, a classic box or Colonial Revival home and a Queen Ann cottage are all within a short distance of one another on this digression.

When you have scoped them out, return to the shoreside path, with that beautiful boatlanding as your landmark. It's a great place to laze a while in the sun, watching the crews as they pass in their sculls or the ladies rowing club in its whaleboat.

When you are ready to continue, bear right on the lakeside path again, noting number 145 Athol Avenue, built in 1890, a Victorian in the Queen Anne style despite its later shingles. Fronting the gray and white building with the red tile roof (built in 1916 and one of the oldest apartment buildings on the east shore), Athol Circle was once water. It was filled when the rock wall was built in 1893. Concrete stairs were once a boat dock. As you continue walking toward those classical columns of the pergola, try to imagine sailing craft coming along this way from the sea. When this area was part of the big Peralta land grant, Rancho San Antonio, a small wharf called Castro's Landing stood at El Embarcadero. It was here that hide droghers from new England came to trade their "Boston goods" for tallow, lumber and cowhides. Many a rancher ordered his own hides returned in the form of boots and shoes.

Pine Knoll Park is the two-acre greensward that you soon reach. A city park since 1908, it has restrooms for the small walkers in your party. California bungalows, Provincial style homes and farmhouse style box homes are all ranged along the shore behind the Park. The next large expanse of land is point 43, Cleveland Cascade Park, a strip of open land connecting Lakeshore and Merritt Avenues to provide access for residents of the Park Boulevard area. At one time, a seventeen-tier waterfall ran the full length to give the park its name. Now dry, the Cascade offers a great view of the lake at its acme, for those game to climb it.

Beginning point for Walk III in the pamphlet is Our Lady of Lourdes church, 2808 Lakeshore, where a plaque commemorates Father Juan Crespi of the Fages expedition for celebrating the first mass in Alameda County in 1772. The church and school, which have humorous lions, elephants and sheep in the stone archways between them, date from 1961.

My choice for a place to end this walk is the pergola. Here one can linger to watch the birds come and go between the little islands reserved for nesting. During winter, when the bird population is greatest, the log boom to prevent boat access to this part of the lake may expand to Hanover Street. It contracts when the birds are fewer. Birders can always count on adding the double-crested cormorant to their life-lists at Lake Merritt.

If you are up to more walking, continue on around the lake, which has Lakeside Park, the biggest on the shore, between this point and the Oakland 19th Street BART Station. It is about the same distance back to Lake Merritt BART Station. You can enjoy the restored lamp posts along the route as you go.

A Birder's Walk

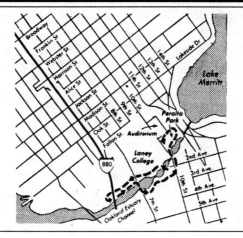

62

Birding, which is at its height in winter, usually conjures up the image of intrepid souls in galoshes and macintoshes, slogging through unfriendly terrain, binoculars at the ready, seeking a glimpse of rare wildfowl on the wing.

'Tain't necessarily so.

One of the best bird-walks in the Bay Area, the Charles Muckelroy Nature Trail, is so civilized one could walk it in golden slippers or high-heeled sneakers.

Located in Oakland's Lake Merritt Channel Park, the Charles Muckelroy Nature Trail, dedicated in 1982 to honor a school teacher who once taught nearby, has such an easy grade along paved walkways that even birders in wheel-chairs can negotiate it.

En route one might see 30 great egrets or a pair of little snowy egrets, as retired Oakland park naturalist Paul Covel and I did recently. Other migrant birds drop in to the park for a snack, a rest or a fresh water bath.

The park is so rich in wildlife that Covel, who intro-duced me to this trail, has made an avocation of conducting groups along it. To arrange the services of the East Bay's best-known and best-loved naturalist, call ahead to

273-3739 to set up a date for your group.

If you prefer to make the well-marked walk on your own, take the Nimitz Freeway (Routes 880) to Oakland. Follow signs for the Oakland Museum and Oakland Auditorium. Take the Broadway off-ramp, turn left onto Broadway and go under the freeway to Tenth Street. Turn right on Tenth and go past the Oakland Auditorium to Second Avenue. The closest BART station, if you prefer public transportation, is at Ninth and Oak streets.

Once at the site, walk to the big trail sign on the south side of Tenth Street across from Second Avenue. The three panels of the trailhead sign describe the park wildlife, give a history of the land and tell a little about Charles Edward Muckelroy's career as a special teacher in the public school across the street.

If there is a little yellow folder tucked into the wooden pocket of the sign, borrow one, then start down the ramp-like sidewalk toward the bridge.

A pair of female goldeneyes flew past us toward the channel as we descended. There were so many tall white egrets landing and standing on the far bank that I almost missed seeing the gaudy purple pylon, granite slab and Day-Glo pink sculptures left about on the nearby lawns after a sculpture fair held several years ago.

Pause mid-bridge to see, on the left handrail, a square Post No. 1. It calls your attention to the water below. Incoming tides bring in clean, green saltwater loaded with plankton and small fish to feed the denizens of the channel. Outgoing tides often carry muddy brown rainwater runoff from Oakland hills surrounding the lake.

Lake Merritt, which is two blocks north, and this flood control channel, along with the estuary beyond, once were all a single body of water. Called Lake Peralta, it was actually a large bay where the son of Don Luis Peralta shipped hides from the surrounding Rancho San Antonio, a land grant of 48,000 acres.

San Antonio Slough, as this part of the marshy shoreline was known, led to San Francisco Bay until 1869, when part of it was dammed by Dr. Samuel Merritt, then Oakland's mayor. Citizens renamed the lake for the mayor.

Turn left when you cross the channel to find Post No. 2 along the water's edge. It marks the fringe of the salt march. Mostly saltgrass at this season, the marsh is punctuated by the red leaves of sea lavender. There is also a post marked 2-A, suggesting that one look in the mud for footprints of sandpipers, killdeer and gulls.

If you had come this way 200 years ago, Covel told me, you might also have seen the prints of condors, grizzly bears, otters, raccoons and coyotes.

"In the days when the Ohlones were the only people living here" the guide pamphlet says, "there were so many shorebirds they darkened the sky when they took off. By filling in many of the estuaries along the Bay, we destroyed the habitat these birds needed to survive.

"Today you will be lucky if you see more than a dozen birds along this estuary where so many thousands of birds once flew only 200 years ago." You are not likely to see otter, either.

When you near the three sculptured figures on your right ("I call them the half-people," Covel says), take the trail to the left. You are now at the shoreline the Indians knew. From this point on, it was water until 1909, when filling began to make the land first known as Peralta Park.

At Seventh Street, you reach a $3 million pumping plant that moves water in and out of Lake Merritt. Look for Post No. 3 nearby, which points out the barnacles that cling to the concrete walls.

Pause a moment before you enter the tunnel under Seventh Street. Sometimes you can see smelt and bass swimming through the metal gates. Although a company has contracted to repair the plant, which leaks at high tide, there was an inch of water on the tunnel floor when we came by. If you're wearing golden slippers, go over the top.

Follow the water to Post No. 4, locating pickleweed, which is red during the winter months. It must have fresh rainwater to germinate.

All too soon, you arrive under Highway 880, where a forlorn little fenced lawn on the far side is a herald of the proposed greenway that will one day connect this portion of Channel Park with Estuary Park on the inner harbor shore beyond the Oakland Embarcadero.

Retrace your steps to the Seventh Street Bridge. Climb up to street level, cross the concrete bridge and go down the steps on the far shore. At the foot of the steps, turn right. Follow the estuary back on the east bank. Post #5, the final one in the guide, is in the bank of benches overlooking an old levee often used by fishermen.

As you near Tenth Street again, notice the casuarina trees on your right, an indicator of the warmth of the climate here. If you are still eager for more walking, the Oakland Museum, one block west, has a marvelous historic and natural walk across California.

Oakland's Chinatown

63

"The Chinese are coming," Lawrence Ferlinghetti has written. "It is time to prepare tea." As a demographer, the poet is right on. Throughout the United States, old Chinatowns are breaching every boundary and new satellite Chinatowns are springing up.

One of the most vital of the expanding old Chinatowns is in Oakland. It now covers 28 square blocks, has more than 30,000 residents and has become the richest commercial area in our stepsister city across the bay.

Walkers who explore the area east of Broadway, especially around Eighth and Webster streets, will find that Oakland's Chinatown has many things going for it, including wide sunlit streets. No chilling highrise looms over the area, and it is close to downtown and to parks, public buildings, libraries, a college, a museum and good public transportation.

In addition, there is a refreshing paucity of tourists, largely because the trinket shops are few. Oakland's Chinatown, which could well be called "Asiatown," exists to serve its own people. These now include Thais, Laotians, Cambodians, Hmongs, Meins, Vietnamese, Taiwanese, Koreans and Filipinos, in addition to the Chinese. Indeed, many of the Asians from other countries are of Chinese ancestry.

To make this walk, transport yourself to Oakland, preferably on public transit. Using BART, leave the train at the Lake Merritt stop at Ninth and Madison streets.

By car, cross the San Francisco-Oakland Bay Bridge and take the Nimitz Freeway (at this point it is the route of Highway 880) south. Leave the freeway on the Jackson Street off-ramp and begin looking for street parking around 10th Street. Nearby streets are largely one-way, so it may take some circling. There is public parking under the Oakland Museum, 11th and Oak streets, if you get desperate.

Walk west on either 10th or 11th street, to Alice Street. For the safety of children who attend Lincoln Elementary School or play in Lincoln Square, in this block Alice Street has been shut off to traffic with chainlink fencing. Walk through the gate on either side of the closed street.

Lincoln School, on the east, whose students are mostly Oriental, is open on Saturdays to teach young students calligraphy and other Chinese arts, including the basics of the complicated language.

Two-acre Lincoln Square, on the west, one of Oakland's seven original town squares, began as Oakland Square. On Abraham Lincoln's birthday, Feb. 12, 1898, it was renamed for the Great Emancipator.

Like the other town squares, it is shown on the Julius Kellersberger Survey of 1853 as a public park. Oakland's title to its squares wasn't formally cleared until 1869, when Dr. Samuel Merritt, then mayor of the city, had them fenced, after paying "Squatter" Horace Carpentiere $900 for quit-claim deeds to the seven parcels.

As you stand in the middle of Alice Street, safe from traffic, notice the Oriental motifs that cap the park fenceline beside the tiny tots, playground. Early architectural embellishments on nearby restrooms and the fieldhouse seem to reflect both Oriental and Latin American influences.

Go through the mid-block gate on the east side and walk into Lincoln Square. In a moment you are alongside a huge play structure in the form of a Chinese junk, currently under repair. As you enter the playfield between the fieldhouse and the Lincoln Square Neighborhood Center, look to your right for a fine unobstructed view of Oakland's downtown cityscape.

Bear left toward the big magnolia trees to find a remarkable wall of tiles on the neighborhood center. Each tile in the mural was handmade by young people in 1977 under the auspices of the Wa Sung service club. Individual tiles represent signs of the Chinese zodiac. My favorite is one entitled "Fat Rat."

When you are even with the Chinese-red mailbox labeled 250 10th Street, turn south and walk out of the playground. Pause at the 10th Street curb a moment to look across the street at the Yuk Yau Children's Center, a handsome new tile-roofed day-care building with three huge, round, eye-like windows. Then turn right toward Harrison Street, noting the bilingual street signs bench.

This corner is a stop for No. 14 AC Transit bus and BART bus connector 33A. Across the street, the tile-roofed red-and-green building is the Episcopal Church of Our Savior, tucked between a discount furniture store and the Happy

Season restaurant.

Cross both Harrison and 10th streets and walk south to discover Oakland Seafood Supermarket Number One. If it is open, go in to see the huge tanks of sea turtles and other live sea creatures for sale here.

Continue along Harrison to Ninth, then turn right. The handsome Chinese Community Center, with its recurved eaves, tiled roof and greenery, was built by the Joe Shoong Foundation. Philanthropist Shoong founded the National Dollar Store chain, reputedly with money he won on a 10-cent lottery ticket.

The large structure across the street is now the Asian Resource Center Building, housing social service agencies. Notice the A-Thai Meat-market just beyond it.

Most of the Thais, Laotians and Cambodians in the community are Buddhist. I and other walkers around nearby Lake Merritt one day not long ago were treated to the spectacle of seven boats in the Thai Floating Festival. Led by a golden dragon boat and drummers, the boats were full of colorfully costumed dancers and other celebrants making their way along the surface of the lake banishing evil spirits. Other ethnic parties, festivals, parades and dances seem to arise almost spontaneously in the Chinatown area.

Turn left on Webster Street. This block is restaurant row. For 30 years it has been a center of Cantonese cookery. Notice the Silver Dragon, the bamboo street trees at the Golden Peacock, the Royal Restaurant, the Bang Wan Club, the Lantern Restaurant and the Central Bakery.

For the best street show on the block, pause at No. 824, the Yuen Hop Noodle Factory, where as many as five skillful workers can often be seen in the window, creating wonton skins and spring-roll wrappers.

At the corner of Eighth and Webster, you are in the traditional heart of Oakland's old Chinatown. It was the third Oakland location in which the Chinese tried to settle. In the 1870s, this area came alive with Cantonese farmers, cannery workers, fishermen and railroad laborers after Oakland's first Chinese settlers had twice been displaced farther north—in Ocean View (now Berkeley) and

Emeryville. Turn left and four more restaurants are visible.

Walk to the left on Eighth Street. In a few steps you are at the Star Building, a warren of doctors, dentists and family associations.

At Harrison Street, notice the Oriental touches on the gas stations. Several more churches are visible farther west, but for the moment, cross Eighth Street and return along it to Webster. En route you will pass the Chinese United Methodist Church; which has a huge green-tiled cross set into its red brick wall. Its tile roof features dragons. A bazaar was under way when we passed the church's little garden.

Nan Yang Restaurant next door to the west is Burmese.

The signs of robust construction are everywhere as you continue toward Webster Street. Joy Luck Restaurant and the Orient Market are oldtimers in this block. Huge houseplants adorned with red and gold ribbons for good luck lined several of the establishments we passed— indicators of recent openings. At one shop we were greeted by a tremendous burst of firecrackers as the doors opened to the public for the first time.

When you reach Webster Street, which once had a railroad track running down its center, you are again at Chinatown's busiest corner. Explore as you will. Worth seeking out are Sam Yick Grocery, Kum Hay Tea House, Tin's Tea Shop and the Filipino Oriental Market, featuring live sea cucumbers and sea snails as well as lucky mirrors, altars and painted tin dishpans.

If you would like to see more of this community, plan to return next May when the municipal Oakland Tours Program (telephone 273-3234) opens its free guided walk series. By that time there will probably be double the number of new places to see, so fast is this old Chinatown growing.

Dimond Canyon

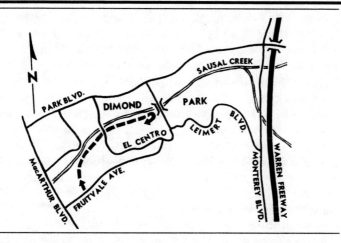

64

Old Oakland has its secret places of enchantment and one of them is a genuine hiking trail in the heart of the metropolis. A living stream burbles happily alongside it. Great bay trees bend and sway overhead, carpeting the trail with leaves. Blackberries bear their sweet jet jewels on the sunny streambanks. Birds dart through heavy brush on the canyon slope. Butterflies flit along the path. Frogs jump and the wild blue penstemon sways by the brookside. One could be a million miles away, instead of being surrounded, to give a modest estimate, by ten thousand homes within a mile.

This special trail runs beside Sausal Creek through Dimond Canyon. As Oakland's city planning department report number 277 says, "no stream is more loaded with opportunity than Sausal." To enjoy its woodland, pick some summer day when the weather forecast says "early morning fog along the coast." Nine times out of ten it will be sunny in Dimond Canyon by the time you reach it.

Transport yourself east from San Francisco, preferably via BART and AC Transit's Fruitvale line 53. If using your own wheels, take Interstate 580 east from the Bay Bridge to the Fruitvale offramp and east about five blocks on Fruitvale to

Lyman Road. Park where you can and walk into Dimond Park, whose entrance in summer is a king's ransom in marigolds.

In 1872, when Dimond Park was a private beer and deer garden, one of many in the Dimond district, the Highland Park and Fruitvale Electric Railroad line ran double-decker cars to this spot. One otherwise quiet Sunday morning, a car tipped over when a 200-pound woman flopped down in an outside seat as it rounded a curve. Although the car rolled to the bottom of the canyon, losing passengers as it went, no one was hurt.

Go up the red brick steps by the big sign which says "For a More Beautiful City." The happy luck-pluck sounds of rebounding tennis balls on the courts in the background will accompany you as you bear right to reach the avenue of tall pines that borders a big lawn and ball field. Shortly you reach Dimond Cottage, built in 1897 as a playhouse for the Dimond boys from adobe bricks that had been handmade in 1821 for the home of Don Antonio Peralta. Oakland purchased twelve acres of the land from the Dimond estate in 1917. By 1924, the cottage was headquarters for Troop Ten of the Boy Scouts.

Pause a moment to examine the big bell that sits on a carriage block used at the Dimond home until it was destroyed by fire in 1913. It rang first at an Oakland carbarn, then at the Dimond Fire Department. Walk around to the right to discover a 150-year-old oak whose surrounding free-form seat-wall is also built of the recycled Peralta adobe bricks. The new building was created in 1955 during Dimond Park's redevelopment.

Walk toward the outdoor swimming pool, a gift of the Lion's Club. Kids have been splashing in it happily since 1929. When you are beside it, turn your back to the pool and look at the lawn to discern the place where Sausal Creek disappears under it. Then walk over to it and bear right along the stream beside the murmuring water. It passes a children's playground in a sandpit ornamented by a happy dolphin, then issues from a woods.

Follow the creek upstream. Within fifty feet, it is a bucolic tree-shaded nook that soon leaves the happy shouts and hurly-burly of organized fun and games. If you yearn to "wander through the wildwood where the morning glories grow ...," this is almost a Hollywood version of it. As one walks, it grows increasingly remote until the appearance of El Centro Avenue seems an odd intrusion.

Persist. The best is yet to come. Cross El Centro, watching carefully for traffic. Go through the hiker's stile at the far end of the pedestrian crosswalk and there on your right will be a big brown trail-sign, incised with the words "Dimond Canyon Hiking Trail" and a map showing routes of both the Sausal Creek Trail and the Sausal View Trail. If you are young and spry and live nearby, memorize it.

Otherwise, simply stroll along the creek under the graceful arches of the big bay trees as tiger-butterflies and damselflies dance from malva to snapdragon beside you. A picker of blackberries offered us a taste from her colander as we passed. The day was young and she already had enough for a pie.

Soon you will be alongside a little waterfall studded with short upended lengths of railroad track, a barrier designed by the WPA long ago to keep the adventurous from driving up the creekbed. It is the first of several such small dams.

When Leimert bridge looms far overhead, look up to get some idea of the depth of this narrow canyon. Gradually the going gets rougher, and the path becomes indistinct. Although the trail goes all the way to Warren Freeway and crosses a footbridge, it is the better part of wisdom to save this steep upper end for another day unless you are a mountain goat.

Stroll back the way you came, remembering the barefoot summer days of childhood. If you find yourself blinking in astonishment to find the surrounding city so quickly, remember that is one of the joys of urban living—to turn a corner and find another world.

Knowland Park and Zoo

65

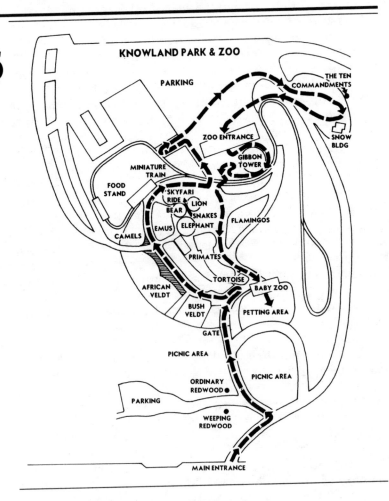

"Oh, I fed buns to the elephuns when I went down to the zoo . . . ," wrote A.A. Milne.

Instead of leftover buns, the Christopher Robins who visit Knowland Park and Zoo feed the animals cones of well-balanced zoo food. They are the same papery cones used for ice cream. Cones may seem extravagant at first flash, but the progressive East Bay Zoological Society, which is in the process of taking over the zoo from the city of Oakland, saves on litter pickup by putting its money into the many mouths to be fed. If he wants to get a refill on the cone, the feeder has to be quick, for the llamas, burros, and goats will crunch the cone down sooner than you can say hippopotamus.

A hippopotamus named Muggs, incidentally, is one of the great reasons for visiting Knowland Park and Zoo. So is the baby camel, the shaggy Highland cattle, the trained African elephant, the gibbon penthouse, the fine collection of primates (monkeys to anyone younger than ten), the sky tram, the miniature train, the frozen bananas and the view. Walking around this 453-acre oasis in the Oakland hills is pleasant indeed.

To make this walk, take yourself and a picnic to Oakland, preferably via BART and AC Transit bus line 56 to Mountain Boulevard and Golf Links Road. There is no park entrance fee for those who arrive on foot. On your own wheels, transport yourself east via the San Francisco-Oakland Bay Bridge and Interstate 580 to the 98th Avenue offramp. A left turn under the freeway on Golf Links Road (at the bottleshop called, appropriately, The Bottleneck) and then a right turn south onto Mountain Boulevard will bring you to the main entrance after about half a mile. Drive in, pay your parking fee, bear left at the sign indicating the picnic area road, and park as soon as you can.

Walkers enter the same way, and should pause just after making the left turn to examine the remarkable weeping redwood tree, which looks like a short-necked giraffe or oversized fiddleneck fern. A *Sequoia gigantea*, it is one of only two such weeping specimens known to exist, according to William Penn Mott Jr., formerly general manager of the park and now director of the National Park Service. It recently bore cones for the first time. Look across the drive to locate a specimen of the typical sequoia for comparison. Both trees were planted around 1888 by lumber tycoon Fred Talbot, whose front yard this once was. Title for the property later passed to Cliff Durant, manufacturer of the Durant automobile, who lived here until his mansion burned in 1921. A picnic grove directly ahead now stands on the site.

Follow the one-way arrow and stroll uphill until you are parallel to the children's playground. Head uphill abreast of the pink elephant. In a trice, you will be at a junction marked by the tortoise pen. If you pause to examine the California native tortoise, you may not learn "ambition, distraction, uglification, and derision," as Alice in Wonderland learned from the Mock Turtle, but you will discover that tortoises have broad feet like elephants. Then bear left into the veldt. Aviaries will be on your right, animals of the bush on your left. At the viewing pit, sit awhile and discover the variability of zebra stripes before you come to the water hole where ostrich, elands, giraffes, Thompson's gazelles, vultures and cranes strut and browse.

By now you will be aware of the bucket-seated tram swinging its passengers up over the hills in the background above the animal paddocks. Continue past the camels and emus if you yearn to make this "skyfari" ride. It takes you up over the animal "biomes." Under the Knowland Park master plan, which is gradually becoming a reality, there will also be a coniferous forest, a tropical rainforest, grasslands, a farm, a lumbercamp and an educational center created among the biome section of the park, now largely open land. Presently the ride overlooks a remarkably quiet transitional zone in which bison and deer feed below, and it reveals some unexpected terrain. There is, of course, a modest fee, but where else can you see San Francisco, Tamalpais, the bay, Oakland Coliseum, a tumbling waterfall, and wild animals and tame all at once in an unfolding panorama.

When you disembark, walk toward the gibbon tower (unless the kids persuade you they must also ride the Skyline Daylight, a miniature train. It, too, is worth the trip for the novelty of the terrain and the view). Like the other concessions, the amusement park rides nearby were purchased not long ago by the zoological society, a nonprofit organization which plows everthing back into the park.

When you have played carnival long enough, go up the path in front of the formal zoo entrance with its two gilded iron couchant lions. Between 1880 and 1963, they guarded the Alameda Hall of Records. Skip the building for the moment and walk uphill toward the Snow Building, headquarters for the zoological society, to discover a fine auditorium and, fronting it, a stone tablet bearing the Ten Commandments. Then swing back to the Gibbon Tower (the frozen bananas are for sale alongside that spacious sidewalk cafe) and climb the whirligig ramp before heading down to see the lions, bears, elephant, parrots and flamingos. Until Smokey, the African elephant here, responded to the efforts of trainer Val de Leon, African elephants were considered untrainable. Smokey usually performs around 1 P.M. on weekends. The raccoon dogs were donated by Oakland's sister city, Fukuoka, Japan. If you hear a great roaring thunder as you approach the apes, it will be the siamang, the noisiest animal in the zoo. After you have admired his neighbor, the colorful mandrill, continue downhill to the Children's Zoo where there are animals to mingle with and pet.

Eleanor Lyons was celebrating her twenty-fifth year as a volunteer at the Handicapped Children's Picnic for Children's Hospital of Oakland when Bill Mott and I made this walk. She can remember when the zoo, which grew out of a small private collection of animals collected by Sid Snow's father, a big-game photographer, was housed in Joaquin Miller Park. Subsequently owned by the state, the shift to administration by the zoological society will bring the park, named for William Knowland, a Park Commissioner, full circle.

Mission San Jose

66

Near the base of 2517-foot Mission Peak, in Fremont at the southeastern most finger of San Francisco Bay, nestles La Mision del Gloriosisimo Patriarca Senor San Jose, 14th in the chain of 21 pioneer Spanish missions.

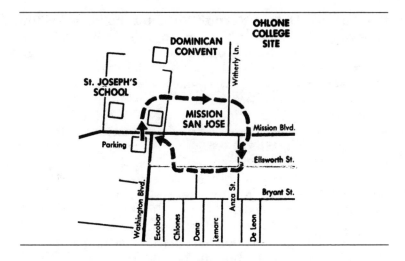

Via El Camino Real, the King's Highway, an Indian footpath that became the first California long-distance road, the missions linked San Diego with Sonoma. Each mission was located a distance that was regarded then as "a comfortable one-day's walk" from the next. The padres walked it barefoot or in sandals.

Although the King's Highway has been widened repeatedly, renamed in some places, paved over in others and rerouted occasionally, short unspoiled lengths of it still remain. One unchanged length of it, nine feet wide, and a block long, unpaved and sheltered by olive trees, still runs through the Mission San Jose section of Fremont.

Appropriately enough, it parallels Mission Boulevard, not far from the mission itself, which has just been reopened after completion of a reconstruction project called "The Bells Shall Ring Again." For the historically minded, the walk around it is pleasant indeed.

To make this walk, transport yourself from San Francisco across the San Francisco-Oakland Bay Bridge. Take Highway 17 south to Washington Boulevard, then follow Washington to its end at Mission Boulevard. Like the peak beyond, it takes its name from the mission. Turn left and park at the Olive-Hyde Community Center public parking lot. Via public transportation, the handy way to go is via BART to the last stop, which is in Fremont. AC Transit bus service, line 28, goes from the BART station to the mission.

Once parked, carefully cross busy Mission Boulevard. Then walk up to the restored adobe church of Saint Joseph, first rebuilt in 1869. The original was built in 1809.

Once the wealthiest of all the missions, it has been the last to be restored. Its restoration is also the most authentic.

First, look at the church cornerstone with its re-dedication plaque. The stone came from the grave of Padre Fermin Lasuen, buried at Carmel Mission, who was the founder of Mission San Jose. Appropriately enough, the rededication was made on June 11, 1985, exactly 188 years after Lasuen raised the first cross.

The old simple adobe building was one of the few missions to be decorated professionally and the reconstruction may surprise you with its neoclassical interior. Tours of the mission and the adjoining museum are held daily from 10 a.m. to 5 p.m. by volunteers. There is no charge.

If you are lucky, you may draw as a guide, as I did, the Rev. Mike Norkett, who showed me the grave of pioneer Robert Livermore, for whom the valley is named, or architect Gil Sanchez, who pointed out the broken buttress walls outside the church. These walls too are scheduled for rebuilding. Another surprise is the rebuilt priests' quarters, which house a well organized musuem and museum shop.

When you have savored the cool ambiance of this historical site sufficiently, return to Mission Boulevard and walk north past the adjoining mission cemetery to the parking lot just beyond. Walk to the right into this lot. Go uphill between St. Joseph's School chapel and the cemetery. Just as you reach the uphill corner of the cemetery, turn right into the olive tree-bordered lane. It divides the mission cemetery and a Dominican convent cemetery. On your right in a small grove of trees is where Lasuen first planted the cross and chanted the litanies that began the settlement of this piece of land. Until that day in 1797, Mission San Jose had been an Ohlone Indian village called Orysom.

As you walk through the olive grove, you are in a remnant of a once magnificent orchard of olive, fig and other fruit trees. They were planted in the early days by padre Ysidro Barcenilla and Augustine Merino, who also laid the foundations of the mission. The work of building took 10 years. Earthquakes in 1812 and 1822 damaged the old church, but the bigger quake in 1868 tumbled it completely, not surprisingly since Mission Boulevard follows the Hayward Fault.

When you are parallel to the rear of the church building, turn left and continue under the shady trees for one block. Turn right at the next corner, part of the entrance road built long ago for the Josephineum Orphanage, now the Dominican Convent.

As you walk south on it, Ohlone College is visible uphill with the open fields below Mission Peak, giving one the illusion of what this lovely land was like in the Alta California times. Alta California is the old Spanish name for California.

At the next corner, tempting as it is, do not turn on Witherly Lane, which is temporarily closed off at the western end, but continue instead on the road with the yellow line down the middle. It soon curves around to bring you out beside an apricot orchard on the lower grounds of Ohlone College. The original mission orchard had only one apricot tree, which the padres labeled the "forbidden fruit" to teach the Indians the story of Adam and Eve.

When you reach Mission Boulevard again, you are also at the unchanged blocklong section of El Camino Real. Olive trees separate it from the apricot orchard. Bear right on it a while, then walk to Anza Street.

On the east side of the street, the old Mission San Jose grammar school and some Victorian homes hint at the vintage of the historical shopping district of Mission San Jose. Cross Mission Boulevard with the stoplight at Anza and walk west to find, midblock, the old mission rectory, another attractive Victorian, in a reincarnation at this site. It was moved to facilitate the reconstruction of the church. A wooden church building that stood for many years adjacent to it on the mission grounds has migrated even farther west to San Mateo County.

When you reach the firehouse, turn right and follow Ellsworth Street past the shopping center. Streetlights in the shopping center parking lot imitate the Mission Trail bells that once traced El Camino Real from end to end.

A few steps beyond the shops, one reaches an old-fashioned neighborhood of modest white cottages, rambling

roses and orange trees. They stand on yesterday's side of the street. Tomorrow's side has tried to approximate the mission style of architecture, but its scale belies the little town.

When you reach the vacant lot, turn right and go through the parking lot, following the fence. This is Sunderer's Lane, named for the early resident. It was in this area that the street would be roped off as far as the mission itself for bull and bear fights "before the *gringo* came."

Soon the lane pops the walker out again at Mission Boulevard, where the shops on either side are trying to stay true to their historic origins.

In places the goal breaks down, especially on names. As charming as Lord Bradley's Bed and Breakfast Inn, just across the street, may be, there was never a historical personage by that name there. Instead it was originally the Washington Hotel. Next door was Brown's Barbershop.

Similarly, Helium Happie's Party House, which purveys balloons, may be a great favorite with the kids, but it was never a great favorite with the pioneers, who enjoyed neither the luxury of balloons nor helium in the original mission heyday.

Despite these historical solecisms, Mission San Jose has its own charms to discover. The discoveries you make yourself are the best.

To return to your wheels, walk north on Mission Boulevard to the Hyde-Olive art center. If you are game for a longer walk, pick up Mill Creek Road about three blocks north and follow it uphill toward Mission Peak Regional Preserve, which has several long trails. On the other hand, if it is too warm for sunny climbing, say, "Vaya con dios, amigo," and save that climb for another time.

Dry Creek Pioneer Park

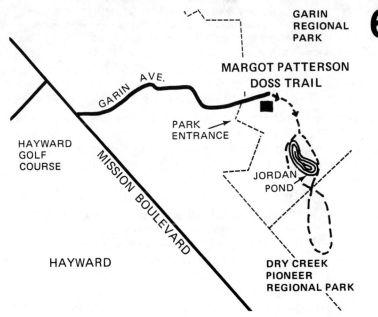

67

GARIN
REGIONAL
PARK

MARGOT PATTERSON
DOSS TRAIL

GARIN AVE.

PARK
ENTRANCE

HAYWARD
GOLF
COURSE

MISSION BOULEVARD

JORDAN
POND

HAYWARD

DRY CREEK
PIONEER
REGIONAL PARK

"Tra la! It's May, that gorgeous holiday . . ."
Alan Jay Lerner, in *Camelot*

When May Day was a holiday and not a distress call, the transplanted citizens of this lovely land did as their European forebears had done for hundreds of years. They would "a-maying go." Light of heart and sometimes equally light of head, with baskets, bonnets, ribbons and viands they went out like pagans to sniff the flowers, dance in the fields and enjoy the springtime.

The place to do it in the Bay Area was at the pioneer picnic grounds of Dry Creek in Decoto. There, according to *The History of Washington Township,*

> May Day was considered the great holiday and was looked forward to with the liveliest pleasure from one season to

another. Elaborate preparations were made in the way of dress and entertainment. Refreshments were planned many weeks in advance.

As the years advanced and the county became more thickly settled, one day was not enough to satisfy the ardor of the pleasure seekers and for several years the festivities of the May season were kept up for three days. A good floor was laid and excellent music was in attendance, dancing being the principal amusement.

The tradition had started in 1854 when the grounds of Dry Creek ranch were first opened as a pleasure resort. By the 1870s, people were coming by ferry, train and on horseback from as far away as San Francisco. The resort closed after August May, Sr., bought the property in 1884.

Now, thanks to the generosity of his granddaughters, Mildred, Jeannette, and the late Dr. Edith Meyers, the 1,200 acres of Dry Creek Pioneer Park have become the fortieth property in the East Bay Regional Park System. It had its formal opening May 12, 1979 when, to my delight, I found there was a trail named for me.

The walk around Dry Creek, or Segunda Creek as it was known when this property was part of the four square leagues of land in Jose de Jesus Vallejo's Arroyo del Alameda rancho, is very pleasant. To explore the Margot Patterson Doss Trail, transport yourself southeasterly from San Francisco via the Bay Bridge and Interstate 580 to Hayward. There swing onto California Highway 238 south, to Mission Boulevard. At Garin Avenue (opposite Hayward Golf Course), make a left turn and continue on it uphill to the end of the road. AC Transit bus line 21 also stops at Garin Avenue and Mission Boulevard, about two miles downhill from the park entrance.

At the outset, look into the old barn near the park entrance. It has been reinforced to meet earthquake codes, and has become an interpretive center, housing among other displays, an exhibit of barbed wire and ranch equipment. Old photos and slide shows are part of the ongoing program offered by Park Supervisor Ron Muller and Coyote Hills naturalists. Notice that new water faucets and restrooms have been designed for convenient use by those in wheelchairs, as well as for the rest of us.

From the barn, walk away from the bridge toward the bare hills with the creek on your right. When the road forks, bear right, walking past the picnic area toward Jordan Pond, first dammed by Hanibul Jordan. His son Lowell built the home visible uphill beyond the creek, now occupied by park personnel.

Once round the bend in the trail, the ring of hills in Walpert Ridge gives one the illusion of being a hundred miles from civilization. Birders can watch for tree, barn, and violet green swallows. Northern or Bullock's orioles have been spotted in the cattails you soon pass, along with the redwing blackbirds. (They're the ones whose song sounds like a melodic but squeaky hinge.) Occasionally a golden eagle will swoop on one of the many Beechey ground-squirrels in the park, if there are not too many walkers on the trail.

Follow the line of Lombardy poplars as the pioneers did on May Day and you will reach a tree-encircling bench, built by "Bud" Jordan. Picnic tables, barbecue pits and the old stone retaining walls attest longtime use. Park volunteers and Alameda County probationers in the "weekend academy" have built the old boat dock to make it easier for fishermen to catch channel cat, largemouth and black bass and bluegills in the pond.

Follow the trail as it swings around the farthest end of the pond. En route, you will pass both wild and cultivated flowers in rich profusion. When you reach the dam, ford it and bear left uphill on the fire road that curves away from the pond and climbs through buckeye and oak to emerge in open grassland. At the next fork, follow the trail to the right and prepare yourself for a jolt. When you reach the top of the ridge, the wide fantastic view of the South Bay is spread below like a patchwork quilt. In the foreground are the proliferating suburbs of Hayward, Alvarado, Newark, Decoto, Union City and Fremont. Coyote Hills Regional Park is easily discernible as the low ridge near the water with Moffett Field and Los Gatos behind it. Looking north from the hills, one can pick out hikers, horsemen and bicyclists on the Alameda Creek Regional Trail following the Alameda Flood Control Canal. Mount Tamalpais, the pyramidal Transamerica Building, and San Bruno Mountain lie beyond the bay.

When you have wearied of the evidence of ever-encroaching development below, take a few steps south along the trail and escape once again into this backyard wilderness. Bear left along the fence line to see the lone tree on the central horizon, which marks a "gossip rock," site of a Costanoan Indian village where squaws once ground acorns and chatted with their tribal sisters as they worked. In another of the canyons visible below, the embryo movie industry that once inhabited nearby Niles also filmed early Westerns.

Park naturalists Jan Southworth and Norman Kidder, with whom I made this walk, identified white-throated swifts, the lark sparrow, and horned larks as we neared the gap in the next fence. Go through and follow the cowpath at a slight downhill grade. According to rancher Paul Santos, whose family has lived nearby for five generations, Dry Creek seldom dries before September. He also told me that a hermit, a Russian immigrant, lived in the canyon below around 1910.

As you skirt the great live oaks, diverge from the path enough to step under one. Temperature under the oaks may be 30° cooler than in the sunshine ten feet away. When a big live oak with a salt lick under it is visible on your left, walk past it to a big sycamore where stepping stones cross Dry Creek. On the far side of the creek, bear slightly left again, leaving the creek to go through a meadow. At the next fence, step over the pipe-and-beam hiker's stile, then follow the path toward the spillway. Soon you will be back again at the end of Jordan Pond.

Instead of retracing your steps along the nearest bank, ford the spillway once more to take the trail along the opposite shore of the pond; then, once past the tule rushes, loop it a second time to complete this figure-eight trail near the bridge. If you are eager for more walking, the 1,000 acres of Garin Park adjoin Dry Creek on the north.

All of the canyons of Dry Creek are open for your

pleasure as well. "This is Dry Creek and we bid you welcome," said the sign Dr. Edith Meyers used to have up over her doorway; "We pray you to maintain with us the holiday spirit; leave care and worry behind you; enjoy the beauties of nature here in your midst, and pause for a moment in your rush through life to give thanks to the Great Artist who painted this ever-changing picture of the hills and fields and stream."

Coyote Hills

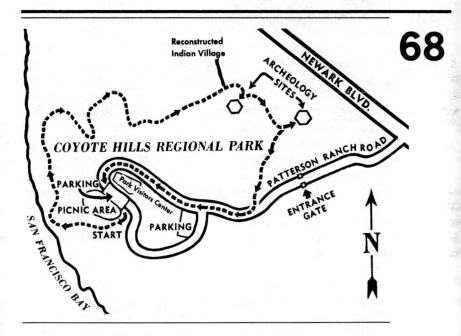

68

"All day," Fr. Pedro Font wrote in his diary in April, 1776, "the commander and I have been in doubt as to whether the island at the end of the estuary which I mapped yesterday is really an island or not."

The supposed island that puzzled Capt. Juan Bautista de Anza's party was Coyote Hills. Many a motorist driving across the Dumbarton Bridge must also have puzzled on this one elevated area in miles of flat terrain, wondered "What do you suppose is up there?" and resolved to go someday to find out.

What is up there today is 1,000 acres of public playground, the Coyote Hills Regional Park. There are shallow bays where fish spawn. Intertidal mudflats host small invertebrates, the little crawly things on which shorebirds, terns, ducks and gulls feed. Salt marshes and natural bay shores here support the plants essential to many birds and small mammals. There are also wooden board-walks, accessible by wheelchair. And then there are Indian mounds and a rebuilt Ohlone Indian village, open Sunday afternoons for talks by park naturalists. Trails meander along the shoreline above salt flats and ramble up the hillcrest, overlooking a rare portion of San Francisco Bay that Fr. Font would recognize if he came this way again. There is also a twelve-mile trail for hikers, bikers and horsemen from the shores of San Francisco Bay to the mouth of Niles Canyon, a unit in the projected 500-mile chain of trails through the hills that form the eastern flank of the bay.

To make an exploratory excursion from San Francisco, head south on the Bayshore Freeway (U.S. Route 101) to the Dumbarton Bridge and cross the bay there. The park lies on the Alameda County shoreline between the San Mateo Bridge and the Dumbarton Bridge. Access is via Patterson Ranch Road, a paved lane that turns west from Union City— at Paseo Padre Parkway. California Highway 84 or 880 are the easy routes to Coyote Hills from elsewhere in the East Bay.

After paying the parking fee at the entrance gate, follow the road uphill around a curve to the Visitors Center and a parking lot adjacent to a picnic area snuggled in trees against the eastern slope of the center hill. Elevation is about 200 feet. Then park and walk south along the upper road to find a trail on your right that goes west over the crest of the hill for a sensational view of the bay. The J.P. Munro-Fraser *History of Alameda County* credits John Quigley and F.A. Plummer as the early pioneers in salt-making at Union City. The *Second Report of the State Mineralogist of California, 1880* indicates that as early as 1848 that native

Californians were gathering salt from natural reservoirs that filled at high tide and became sun-dried later. Indians may have taught them, for the Indian kitchen middens on these shores, according to an estimate by the late archeologist Dr. Adan Treganza, may be as old as 4,000 years.

To see one of the excavated mounds, follow the trail north, then up over the hill and down across the flat near the flood control channel. Two of the sites, in which arche-ologists worked for twenty years, thanks to the scientific interest and good will of the Patterson family who owned this land as well as Ardenwood the farm—park just to the east, are open Sunday afternoons for the public to inspect. (Use the clumps of trees in the flatlands for your landmark as you walk.) When you have marveled at the vanished primitive culture, walk south to pick up the road and make a loop back to the picnic area. The round trip is about three miles. Walking boots and jeans are recommended; and it is advisable to take a thermos, for there are no concessions in the park.

San Francisco Bay National Wildlife Refuge

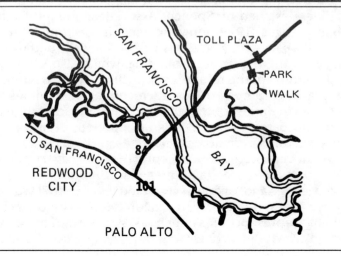

69

A whole wonderful world unfolds when you walk along the marshy shorelines of the 21,662-acre San Francisco Bay National Wildlife Refuge in the South Bay. Here life ebbs and flows with the tides, changing subtly as the seasons change. Sandpipers and dunlins flit along the sandy flats at low tide like mechanical toys. A parade of mallard ducklings may follow Mama Duck into a tidal pond. The rare red-bellied harvest mouse rustles in the pickleweed. A clapper rail, as disproportionately shaped as a Siamese hand-puppet, may appear suddenly out of the fat-hen clumps. From a graying heap of driftwood, the lilting song of the salt-marsh song sparrow may ripple melodic as a nightingale. The day-to-day rhythms are those of eternity, a grand anodyne for the rat-race pace of modern man's metropolitan life.

To enjoy this great boon to the Bay Area, transport yourself south from San Francisco via U.S. Route 101 (Bayshore Freeway) to Redwood City. There swing east with California Highway 84 across Dumbarton Bridge. Toward the east end of the bridge, edge over to the extreme right lane as you approach the tollbooth (which you will see about 1,000 feet beyond you), turning into the parking area of the handsome new U.S. Fish and Wildlife Interpretive Center, instead of proceeding onto Thornton Avenue.

Park and go up the steps. That massive post-and-beam building, designed by Spencer Associates, opened to the public in August 1979, and welcomes visitors from 10 A.M. until 5 P.M. everyday. Walkers will find a well-routed trail that loops the big wooden building, which also serves as headquarters for the refuge, and the hill it nestles under. It offers a fine sample of the recreational possibilities of another thirty miles of trail that will become accessible as additional parcels of tidelands are opened, bringing the refuge up to its ultimate 23,000 acres.

At the outset, go into the Center to see the displays, and scope out the book sales area and auditorium where movies, slides and talks are scheduled. As you stroll around its airy spaces, reflect, if you will, on the shift in focus this building represents, inasmuch as game wardens have learned to say "welcome" instead of "stay out," a little miracle that accompanied passage of bill H.R. 12143, enacted into law in 1972 with help from Congressman Don Edwards.

When you have enjoyed the building sufficiently, go out on the middle level to find, just across the driveway, an overlook with a good view of Newark Slough, the Dumbarton Bridge, and the new construction. "The drawbridge has been taken out of the center section of the old bridge visible off to the left," assistant manager Mike Bitsko, who showed me around, said. "And it has become two fishing piers, each with parking areas." Other access points to the vast refuge are scattered all round the South Bay, with two located in Coyote Hills, others at Alviso, Fremont, Menlo Park, and East Palo Alto. An environmental education center, primarily for school classes and organized groups, is accessible through Alviso at 1751 Grand Boulevard.

Look across Newark Slouth at the little red building visible in the marsh. Formerly a hunter's cabin, it has been restored as a mini-museum, with exhibits of the salt refining industry, hunting history, the marsh itself, and the scows and schooners that once carried freight on the bay. When you have pondered the amazing vastness of the mudflats between this point and the blue water, start up the hill on the road immediately behind you. Once past the building and over the crest, you feel remote from all the hurly-burly of traffic on the bridge. Sage bends along the path, sending its pungent aroma into the air. Poppies sway in the grasses on either hand. Jack-rabbits and cottontails may spurt ahead of you. A swallowtail butterfly drifts lazily overhead.

Mission Peak is the mountain you see ahead. Both the Hetch-Hetchy Aqueduct and the Southern Pacific railway tracks across Dumbarton Point, visible across the marsh toward Palo Alto. The big Moffett Field hangar makes a great landmark off at the bay border between Mountain View and Sunnyvale. Watch your step on the scree as you come down the hill. When the road forks, look to the left to spot some old agaves, which may date from the 1780s, indicators of the long-time use man has made of this land, however wild it may seem to the uninitiated. Fix this focal fork in your mind for a later, longer walk when migrating birds are moving in thousands along the Pacific flyway.

For now, bear right to find another attractive wooden overlook at just the right place to spot red-winged blackbirds, swallows, pintails, avocets, or stilts. Bicyclists will be pleased to find the handy parking racks. If you thought to bring your binoculars, pause here for a little quiet marsh-watching. Wildlife that hides at the sound of footfalls or human voices on the path will often emerge if one sits silent for a while. Do it and you discover this is a magical place. The grasses seem to move like water in the wind. Jets out of hearing overhead left trails of white wool as we watched, apron strings to the clouds. A graceful tern wrote in shorthand on the sky.

"San Francisco Bay covered 700 square miles of the earth's surface in 1850," Mike Bitsko had told us. "Sixty-seven percent of the marshes are gone and a third of the water is filled or dredged. Today there are only 435 square miles of bay left." Take a few deep breaths as you walk. One of many great services the marsh does is to replenish oxygen in the air. Indeed, naturalists sometimes demonstrate the function of a swamp in smoggy areas by capturing pure oxygen in a plastic bag as it bubbles up out of the digesting ooze.

As you round the hill below the building, another overlook is revealed in the eucalyptus grove. Pause here for a different view of the tidal flatlands to prepare yourself for a return to the world of gasoline, motorcars, drivers, and the driven . . . It will come as a jolt.

Peninsula

San Mateo County

Pacifica Pier

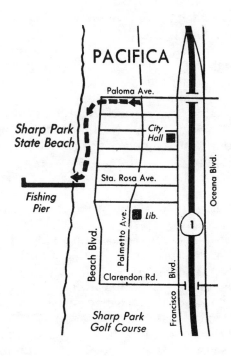

70

PACIFICA

Paloma Ave.

Sharp Park
State Beach

City
Hall

Sta. Rosa Ave.

Fishing
Pier

Lib.

Palmetto Ave.

Oceana Blvd.

1

Beach Blvd.

Clarendon Rd.

Francisco Blvd.

Sharp Park
Golf Course

"Where Are You Going Sunday?" was the bold headline on a large display ad that appeared in The Chronicle 80 years ago.

Under photos of Ocean Shore Railway Company's steam locomotive and coaches filled with smiling passengers, readers were invited to "appreciate the beauties of Edgemar . . . Come prepared to be convinced and Edgemar will win you!" it promised.

Edgemar is still a great place to go. If you don't recognize the name, Edgemar is part of Pacifica, which also includes the old Ocean Shore Railway stops of Pacific Manor, Vallemar, Rockaway Beach, Linda Mar and Sharp Park. This blanket also covers what used to be Salada and Brighton Beach, which combined themselves into Sharp Park in the 1930's after Honoria Sharp donated 480 acres for a park to the city of San Francisco.

Recently, Pacifica has been creating a beachfront promenade leading to the Rev. Herschell Harkins Memorial Pier, a free municipal pier better known as the Sharp Park Pier or Pacifica Pier. During the gray whales' annual migrations, is a great time to walk out on this 1300-foot-long fishing pier. Fishermen have reported seeing the great grays swim past so close "you could smell their fishy breath."

Plankton, which thrives on the clean water from the 1100-foot-long outfall pipe of Pacifica's elegant tile-roofed sewage treatment plant, attract the whales. It also attracts small food fish that bring Dungeness crab, *cancer magister*, salmon and sometimes bonita.

So take along your fishing tackle or crab traps if you are a fisherman. Wear your warmest jacket, gloves and hat, but leave your dog at home. Dogs aren't allowed on the pier. Then head south from San Francisco about 5 miles along State Highway 1.

Take the Francisco Boulevard off-ramp, turn right on Paloma Avenue and look for a place to park. Since 1957, this has been Pacifica. Before that it was Salada, with Edgemar immediately to the north. Salada took its name from Laguna Salada, the saltwater lagoon which is surrounded today by Sharp Park Golf Course.

Walk west on Paloma toward the beach. Pacifica

Planning Commissioner John Lucia, who conducted me on this walk, says a fresh breeze is blowing through Pacifica since nearby Sweeney Ridge has come into the Golden Gate National Recreation Area.

"We're trying to make our community and waterfront attractive for users of the national park as well as ourselves," Lucia said, and pointed out that Paloma Avenue is the actual start of the Pacifica Promenade.

The fine old cypress trees, which were planted along the street in 1907, are now protected. In the past, property owners or street pavers tore out trees indiscriminately. Today they must apply for a permit and undergo a hearing on each tree.

At Palmetto Avenue, you are on an old county road, now Pacifica's main shopping street. When it was built in 1900, the County Road Market, one of Pacifica's earliest commercial endeavors, was called the Seaside Inn.

Notice the Wavecrest Apartment building, which Commissioner Lucia describes as "a remnant of the poor planning of the 1960s."

"There was a time," he said, "when the City Council was about to allow all of Pacifica to be covered with such stark and unimaginative cracker boxes." Today, Pacifica cherishes its more historic single-family homes, such as No. 15 Paloma, which was an old farmhouse.

Pacifica planners would like to see the Veterans of Foreign Wars Hall, now for sale, become a hostel, bed-and-breakfast inn or restaurant. When you reach the southeast corner of Paloma Avenue and Beach Boulevard, notice the classic collection of flotsam and jetsam adorning the garden.

Cross Beach Boulevard and you are at Sharp Park State Beach. According to the local Coastal Land Use Plan submitted by Pacifica to the California Coastal Commission in 1979, the seaside trail ultimately will link all of Pacifica's communities and reach a string of well-planned coastal access points.

Last November, the trail took on greater importance when the California Recreational Trails Committee officially registered its support to the State Coastal Conservancy for the border-to-border California Coastal Trail, in which the Pacific Promenade would be a link in the designated San Mateo County North-South Trail Corridor.

As you walk, if you can take your eyes from the spectacular off-shore show the winter ocean often provides, observe the architectural mix of old farmhouses, late 1920s beach cottages, 1960s apartments and new houses under construction.

At Santa Maria Avenue, look east to locate a flag on its standard at 170 Santa Maria Avenue. Built in 1914 as the San Pedro School House, it later became the Pacifica City Hall.

When you reach Salada Avenue, look uphill to the east to see "McCloskey's Castle" on the slopes of Milagra Ridge. Built in 1906 by H.H. McCloskey, attorney for the Ocean Shore Railroad, it became infamous as "Chateau Lafayette," a Prohibition-era speakeasy.

During World War II, it became a Coast Guard Station. Now it is again a private residence.

Look about you as you walk. Sharp Park's 18-hole municipal golf course, which has been described as "The Poor Man's Pebble Beach," lies ahead. On your right, the broad bay is loosely defined by Mussel Rock at the end of Thornton Beach two miles north and by Mori Point, about a mile to the south.

When you reach Santa Rosa Avenue, you are at the Pacifica Fishing pier and at a convenient bait and coffee shop with public restrooms on its south side. Stroll out on the pier for a look back at the beach and a different view of the crashing waves.

Whales like the south side of the pier, possibly because the water may be a little warmer where the plankton feed. Spanish arches identify the sewage treatment plant on shore whose long outfall pipe divides at its western end like the fingers on a hand. The treated effluent is reputedly clean enough to drink.

Linger as long as you like, enjoying the Pacific at play. The pier is open 24 hours a day, every day, and when you are ready to call it a day, you are sure to come back refreshed by the wind, waves, sunlight and passing clouds.

You may have watched a fisherman haul in his catch, hauled in some crabs yourself, or, if you've been lucky, you may even have seen a whale "sky hop" in a dramatic leap.

Sneath Lane

71

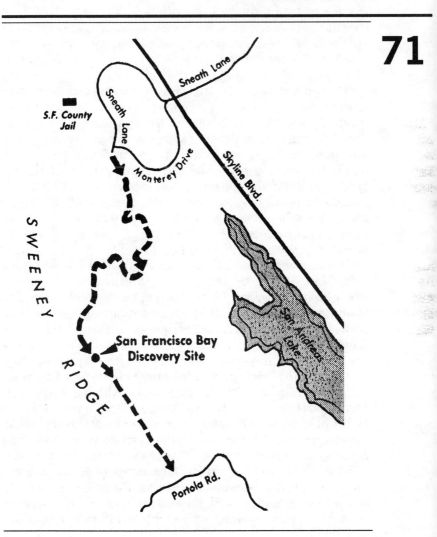

Sneath Lane has a sneaky, snaky sound to it, like a name Charles Dickens might have invented for a sinister Limehouse alley. Don't be misled by the sound of it. The western end of Sneath Lane (named for an 18th century San Mateo County dairy farmer) is one of the most expansive, heartlifting of trails. On a fair day, the views from it are spectacular.

Best of all, Sneath Lane offers a convenient east, or bayside, approach to lofty Sweeney Ridge, the spine of northern San Mateo County and part of the Golden Gate National Recreation Area.

If you have been wondering how to get onto Sweeney Ridge without going to the coast side, here is one good answer.

Pack a picnic and canteen for this walk. There is no concessionaire, nor is there likely to be, on Sweeney Ridge. The park policy for the ridge is "to maintain its natural qualities important to the preservation of the historic setting . . . and the Discovery Site. Most use of Sweeney Ridge will continue to be dispersed use of trails and open space by people seeking quiet enjoyment of the setting and the spectacular views. The character of the area will remain essentially the same."

Hiking boots and a windbreaker are advised—although I did see runners on the Sneath Land trail in Nikes and singlets. Once your gear is stowed, head south from San Francisco on Highway 280, then continue south on Highway 1. Beyond Serramonte, swing over to Skyline Boulevard (Highway 35), and continue south.

Sneath Lane is well marked, the fifth major road that intersects the highway from the time you get on it. Turn right on Sneath Lane into Portola Highlands, which is within San Bruno's city limits. Drive one block to the point where it meets Monterey Drive and turn right, continuing on Sneath Lane, until you reach an automotive drawn toward the San Andreas Reservoir, one of the chain of sag ponds that sparkle along the San Andreas fault zone. Farther south are the two Crystal Springs reservoirs. Pilarcitos Reservoir, famous for its luxury cabin for entertaining politicoes, is out of sight from this trail, hidden by surrounding folds of Montara Mountain.

Follow paved Sneath Lane uphill, disregarding the graveled San Andreas Road that soon goes off to the left. Like Sneath Lane, San Andreas goes through San Francisco watershed lands. Although the GGNRA and San Mateo County park plans call for low-key hiking use of this extension of the well-known San Andreas Trail along the east side of the San Andreas Reservoir, arrangements are not yet complete.

Stick to the center of the trail. Spring Valley rose, the watershed workers' nickname for poison oak, grows here and there among the coyote bushes, so don't be tempted to step off the trail. Fortunately, Sneath Lane is wide enough that one need not touch California's most noxious chaparral plant.

As you climb uphill, the view broadens out, revealing, at one turn, the prospect east toward the airport and the bay. At another turn, the view is south toward Burlingame and Hillsborough. Ancient rivalries between these little cities reached a furor around 1929 when Burlingame tried to annex its neighbors. This municipal tug-of-war finally ended in 1946, when Millbrea, another of Burlingame's antagonists, became San Mateo County's 13th city.

An incredibly wide firebreak bulldozed across the hillsides by the San Francisco Water Department comes into view at another turn. There is also a house, occupied by water department personnel, that becomes visible on an eminence at the north end of the San Andreas Reservoir.

Lizard's tail, Indian paintbrush, the pearly everlasting and sticky monkeyflower were growing near the edges of Sneath Lane when last I came this way.

When you have climbed high enough to see San Bruno Mountain, there will be a yellow line painted mid-road. No need to divide the traffic—it's a fog line to keep you on the trail if the fog comes in, as it tends to do early and often in this area.

By the time you reach fog-line elevation, you may see redtail hawks, marshhawks and turkey vultures almost at eye level. Ranger Kevin Cochary, who made this walk with me, says a white-tailed kite also frequents this part of the ridge occasionally.

Cochary has also startled brush-rabbits, foxes, coyotes, bobcats and deer. As if to corroborate him on the richness of wildlife here, a little parade of quail ran across Sneath Lane as we climbed.

When you reach the crest of Sweeney Ridge, you will find yourself stunned by the vastness of its views, given a clear day. Pause to look about you. Both San Francisco Bay and the ocean are visible at once from this height, as well as Marin County and Mount Diablo.

To explore Sweeney Ridge a little more, turn left on the old ranch road that is the Sweeney Ridge Trail along the ridge itself. Within 100 yards, you are abreast of the knoll where Don Gaspar de Portola and his party became the first Europeans to espy San Francisco Bay. They arrived in November 1768, a party of 60 men who thought they had found Monterey Bay, never realizing that their discovery was infinitely more important to history.

Pause for your picnic near the Discovery Site, nick-named "The Plymouth Rock of the West." Commemorative markers herald Portola's visit as well as historian Carl McCarthy's effort to preserve this National Historic Site.

Linger as long as the weather is fair. The Sweeney Ridge Trail, if you are game for more walking, can take you south to two beautiful meadows. The closest, less than a quarter-mile away, is defined on its west side by a pair of lonely eucalyptus trees silhouetted against the sky, a mute reminder that a farmhouse once stood nearby. No one seems to know today if it belonged to Sweeney, an early pioneer on the ridge.

The second clearing, South Meadow, is somewhat lower in elevation. Beyond it, the trail stops at the fenced-off Portola Road, also within San Francisco's watershed. It is to be hoped that this too will one day be open to walkers, who might want to reach the McNee Ranch state park just beyond.

When fog or weariness says it is time for you to go, the way back to your wheels is the way you came.

Walkers who arrived via SamTrans have a second choice. One can follow Sweeney Ridge Trail north and descend toward the Shelldance Nursery, easily identifiable by its greenhouses on a shelf of land above Highway 1. SamTrans buses stop just south of Shelldance in Vallemar, at the junction of Reina del Mar and Highway 1.

Shelldance

72

The "tulip-mania" that swept through Holland and western Europe in the seventeenth century has nothing on the "bromeliad fever" surging across the United States today. Bromeliads are survivors—beautiful, uncommon, exotic, remarkable South American plants that know how to make it in jungles, deserts, mountains, or barren sea-coasts when the going gets rough. This may be part of their appeal today. Some of them live almost rootless in air, clinging to treebark, rocks, or tiles. Some contain their own storage receptacles that not only nourish the plant itself but sustain a whole symbiotic ecosystem of fish, frogs, and bugs. Some are as gorgeous as orchids, as fragrant as frangipani, as bold as a target. Almost all of them like the same kind of warmth man likes and so do well in overheated apartments, or get by with the ministrations of chronic under-or over-waterers. Small wonder that the plant buff who has blown it with his philodendron or aspidistra looks on the magic pink wand that grows its own silver vase as the answer to an apartment dweller's dream.

Much of the impetus for the new bromeliad fever originates, as so many trends do, right here in California where the two biggest wholesale nurseries devoted to the species are located. One of them, Shelldance, lies in plain sight in Pacifica. Normally accessible only to the trade, Shelldance opens its doors to walkers twice a year, Mother's Day and the weekend before Christmas, and on weekends. If your only experience of bromeliads thus far has been a glass of pineapple juice, watch for this open house at Shelldance and be amazed by the variety and the lush tropical man-made jungle within.

To make this walk, transport yourself south from San Francisco via Interstate 280 to the Cabrillo highway, U.S. Route 1. Go south past the three Pacifica exits to overshoot 2000 Cabrillo, which lies between the Sharp Park and Vallemar districts of Pacifica opposite Mori Point. You will see the Shelldance sign about a quarter of a mile past the spot where the freeway ends. Do *not* turn there. Instead, drive on past and make a U-turn at Vallemar, returning to approach from the east side of the highway.

"I should see the garden far better," said Alice to herself, "if I could get to the top of the hill, and here's a path that leads straight to it . . . But how curiously it twists! It's more like a corkscrew than a path!" In *Through the Looking Glass*, Lewis Carroll might have been describing the route up to Shelldance after you cross the highway. Nevertheless, persist past layers of greenhouses at each hairpin turn until you are at the top of the hill. Park there in the lee of Sweeney Ridge and look for an entrance in the middle of one glass house, at right angles to an unusual blip, blister, or bulge on the adjoining one.

"A jungle," Darwin wrote, "is one great wild untidy luxuriant hothouse, made by nature for herself," and he likened it to the scenery of another planet. This jungle, man-made or not, is no exception. From the moment you step into the growing room, you are instantly in a different world. Unlikely plants hang from overhead pipes, are tucked into pockets in great screens, surge in waves, and drift over wire-mesh-topped benches. One area, where the leaves of neoregelia are all finely striped in white and green, is a "British pin-striped jungle" to co-founder Bruce Rothenberg. "I guess the pink, green, and white striped leaves would do for a Cecil Beaton jungle extravaganza."

From the growing room, the route leads to the collection or specimen room, pride of owner Michael, who is also founder of the National Consortium for Plant Conservation. Thousands of plants crowd every inch of space. There are great candlelabralike vresias, operatic and overpowering. There is modest Spanish moss whose green flower is only a "silly millimeter" in size. Near them are striped blushers so sexy a mandrill monkey would feel envious; shy earthstars that look like little red-brown jewels; bold tillandsias that resemble mustachios whirled, twirled and convoluted; formal aechmeas rigid as parade marshals waving purple batons.

The aviary with its finches is next on the route. Once you've seen it, you'll understand that bulge in the exterior wall designed by Dan Smith. The birds are the enthusiasm of Nancy Davis, who is usually on hand to answer questions of the interrelationship of birds and bromeliads. It may not be tidy, but it is certainly energy-efficient.

As you stroll from one complex area to the other, you'll pass through a display room, growing house, greenhouse, work room and the shell hall. Here, bromeliads that seem to be dancing up out of shells reveal the origin of the nursery's name. Keep your eyes open and you may also discover the *Glovula rubberri*, a botanist's joke. It is a gray rubber glove inflated and potted, looking no more unlikely than many of the plants surrounding it.

When you have browsed to your heart's desire, try tuning in on one of the question-and-answer sessions sure to be under way. The lore of bromeliads comes out with wit and humor through the eyes of Michael Rothenburg, a scholarly man with several degrees in English literature who wrote a chapter on bromeliads for a Rodale Press encyclopedia. He tells, for example, how a plant collector pirated one tillandsia from another and will pay the penalty in its botanical nomenclature ever after, or how the 35-foot-tall flowerstalk of the *Pya raimonda* is annually set on fire in a Bolivian festival. My own favorite bromeliad story dates from rum-running days when a pineapple, always a symbol of hospitality, would be displayed in the window of any coastal house boasting a friendly pier, as an indicator that this was a safe haven for contraband.

Wander back to your wheels by way of the long alley between glass houses and you may find yourself tempted into a new enthusiasm for these stranger-than-fiction plants. On the other hand, if more hiking suits your fancy, the Portola Trail is just uphill and any local resident can direct you to the handy route.

San Pedro Creek in Linda Mar

73

To longtime Californians who remember Pedro Valley with bittersweet nostalgia for its unspoiled beauty, Linda Mar, as it became known in its developing days, sounds like the ill-advised name of a stagestruck starlet. Both names have since been swallowed up by Pacifica, the 12-square-mile megapolis which merged nine villages into one small atypical city a few years ago.

By whatever names, the land still has the rugged terrain that the followers of Capt. Gaspar de Portola found when

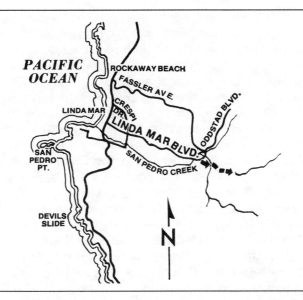

they camped near San Pedro Creek in November, 1774. Fortunately, some of this splendid land, including a steep waterfall, is being reserved for a park. The exploring walker can understand some of the hardships the Portola discovery party underwent.

To make this walk, transport yourself fifteen miles south from San Francisco on the Cabrillo Highway, U.S. Route 1, to its junction with Linda Mar Boulevard (just before San Pedro Road). Follow Linda Mar uphill to its end. En route you will pass the Sanchez Adobe, now a museum surrounded by a five-acre park. An Indian village stood at this location when the Portola party camped downhill. Tempting as it may be to stop immediately and enjoy this fine example of early California architecture, once the headquarters for the 8,928-acre Rancho San Pedro, hold it in reserve for the return trip. When you reach Oddstad Road, which passes the end of Linda Mar Avenue like a T, turn right, away from St. Peter's Roman Catholic church with its unusual outward-supported roof. Mario Ciampi was the architect.

Right of the T, the road subtly becomes Rosita. Go

about 100 feet on it and turn uphill on the dirt road. At the first fork in the road bear right. On the second, swing left downhill and park. The church roof then will be visible at eye level. Put on your stoutest lug-soled hiking boots, wellingtons, or grip-soled sneakers, for part of this walk may include bushwacking up the creek or creek fording. During winter or spring, you may also want gloves. Look for the sign indicating San Pedro Valley County Park. The road near it that goes uphill between the arroyo willows was an old ranch road that long served as the first creekside trail. A shorter one, The Oak Glen nature trail is described in free park leaflets.

When botanist John Kippig, an expert in the Indian uses of native plants, led me up this canyon, we saw steelhead in San Pedro Creek, gooseberries and hazelnuts on the banks, and the delicious shaggy-mane mushrooms growing on either side of the trail. John pointed out that year-old shoots on the willow were just the right size for Indian basketry. When the road forks, go right and look for coyote mint and pitcher sage. At the seven big eucalyptuses, go left and take the small path by the creek uphill. The giant horsetail reed and the scouring rush, used by Indians to file their nails and polish arrowpoints, both grew along this section of the trail. The agile can ford the creek on stepping stones, working uphill until they are in sight of the waterfall that cascades off Fifield Ridge uphill on the left. The less spry should return to the trail when the going gets strenuous.

For the observant, changing light will reveal new wilderness treasures on the return trip. Look for the long red roots of the willow in the stream, John Kipping suggests, or the duckweed, *Lemna*, floating on the surface of the water, or monkey-flower pods which can blow up and float downstream. Archeologists can discover traces of truck farms that stood here not long ago, or even, with luck, an arrowhead in the water. But best of all is the slant of sunlight on the moving stream, the play of shadows in the gorge, and freshness of pungent winter woodland odors.

Sanchez Adobe in Pacifica

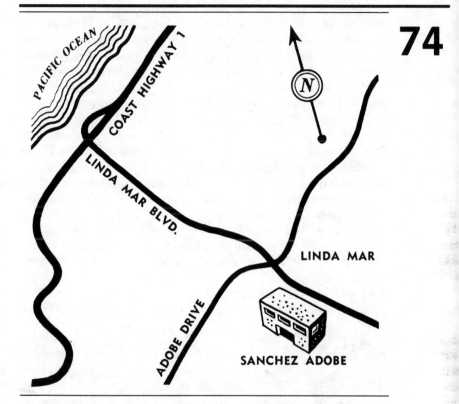

"At every step we came to paths well-beaten by heathen," wrote Fr. Francisco Palou in his journal of his exploratory peninsula expedition conducted in 1774 by Capt. Fernando Rivera, an officer of Capt. Gaspar de Portola's intrepid band.

"Boylike, he longed to follow one of them," historian Frank Stanger, author of *South from San Francisco* says about Palou's journal entry, "to see what there was on the shore." Rivera didn't let him, alas.

If he had, there might be a good description existing of the Indian village that once stood uphill from Portola's two-day camp on Pedro Point, at what is now the junction of

Linda Mar Boulevard and Adobe Drive in the growing megapolis called Pacifica.

Historians, and newcomers to the Bay Area who may wonder that so little of the early Indian-Spanish-Mexican vestiges remain on the land, will find a walk around this area rewarding. Here, half forgotten, is the well-preserved Sanchez Adobe, once the home of Francisco Sanchez, seat of the 8,928-acre Rancho San Pedro, and coincidentally, a fine example of authentic Monterey architecture.

To make this walk, transport yourself south eleven miles to the Pedro Valley section of Pacifica via coastal U.S. Route 1. Take the Linda Mar turnoff uphill to Adobe Drive (or walk it if you have come by bus). The Sanchez Adobe, which during its 130-odd years' existence has been used for a hunting lodge, a bootleg saloon and, at low points, a shed for packing artichokes, is now a museum operated by the San Mateo County Parks and Recreation Commission.

It is open to the public on Tuesdays and Thursdays from 10 A.M. to 4 P.M., Saturdays and Sundays from 1 P.M. to 5 P.M. with an hour's closing at noon so the ranger can have his lunch. If you arrive by miscalculation at 12 noon, the grounds will still be open. Sit down against a wall, pull your

hat over your eyes, *amigo*, and take a short *siesta*. The adobe backdrop is exactly right for that scene.

As you stroll about the five-acre park on which the building is located, try to envision the dancing, music, horsemanship displays, and color that existed here when prominent visitors came to see Francisco Sanchez, one time commander of the Spanish presidio in San Francisco. If fifteen miles from the Presidio seems a long way for a man to issue commands, consider that the first white-man's building to stand on this site was a rancho outpost of Mission Dolores, whose cattle ranged this far. In 1837, the adobe replaced an earlier house built in 1817 with materials salvaged from a ship wrecked on San Pedro Point. In its heyday as Mission Farm, there were thirty-six acres of wheat, eight acres of corn, an orchard, and a vineyard planted just west of the adobe on what is now the Whites Field playground. Traces of the earlier Costanoan Indian village disappeared around 1794 when an epidemic of missionary-introduced bugs annihilated the native inhabitants.

For the highpoint of your walk, enter the museum to examine artifacts found nearby, to enjoy the coolness of the thick adobe walls if the day is warm, and to stroll the wide upstairs veranda. Gov. Juan B. Alvarado, William Sharon, John C. Fremont, Henry Meiggs, W.C. Ralston and Hall McAllister are only a few of the history-makers of early California who have surveyed the world from this vantage. (They didn't see the park department workshop building you'll see at the end of the parking lot, however. The routed-wooden signs that are made here supply all Pacifica parks.)

Picnicking is permitted on the lawn beside the house, following an old tradition here. The last big *merienda*, or Mexican style picnic to be held on the grounds was given by the San Mateo County Historical Society on October 12, 1946, the centennial of the adobe. County supervisors bought the historical building and began its restoration the following year.

Historically minded San Mateo citizens who are working for a national park with rest-stops at Portola expedition sites, and especially the discovery site, had an ideal reason to hold another *merienda* in 1969. Two hundred years earlier, on November 4, 1769, Don Gaspar de Portola had stood on Sweeney Ridge uphill a few miles and first beheld the world's largest natural harbor.

Spanishtown

75

Spanishtown, one of the most pleasant anachronisms in the Bay Area, has all the deicious small-town flavor, the easy pace, the unspoiled creek banks, the general stores, the picket fences, vegetable gardens and grace that the pushy tracts have lost.

Although the post office has been called Half Moon Bay since 1872, oldtimers know that Spanishtown, centered around Kelly, Main and Miramontes streets, is the town proper, the nucleus of the settlement that may well be the oldest community in San Mateo County.

It began when two neighboring ranch owners, Candelario Miramontes and Tiburcio Vasquez, built their homes near the creek that was their joint property line. Authorities differ on the founding date of the village, which was platted in 1863 in the southwest angle formed by Arroyo Leon and Pilarcitos Creek, largely because Don Candelario had been granted the land before 1820 and regranted it in 1841.

The village life really began when San Benito, as it was first known, became a refuge for unhappy Spanish and Mexican families who fled San Francisco in 1846 "when the Gringo came." Today, Spanishtown is the oldest part of Half Moon Bay, 25 miles south of San Francisco on Highway One.

To make this walk, turn west off the highway on Kelly Street and drive to Francis Beach, the main beach access and headquarters of the San Mateo County Beaches State Park. The all-day parking fee is $2. Barbecue pits, picnic tables, restrooms and miles of beach good for surf fishing and sunbathing are at hand here. Because there are dangerous sleeper waves, swimming is discouraged, but shore breezes often make for great kite-flying.

Once you have parked, save the beach exploration for later and walk east on Kelly Street to discover the 150-year-old barn, from which the produce of the Andreotti Family Farm is sold. The 60 acres surrounding the barn has been farmed by Dino Andreotti since 1926.

After enjoying its authentic redwood architecture, walk east again noting, beyond the vacant lots as you near Highway 1, a huge sign announcing condos for sale. It tells the tale of a long-dormant community, now becoming a "Yuppieville."

Cross Highway 1 with the stoplight and continue east, and note how the ambiance changes as soon as you are parallel to the blue-trimmed white Victorian house that now shelters Ocean View Properties, a real estate firm.

The Church of Our Lady of the Pillar, at the corner of Church Street, is the third structure to bear the name. The original church, built in Pilarcitos Cemetery, was destroyed by fire in the 1870's and had no pews. Manuel Chunha Intermediate School stands on the opposite side of the street.

When you reach Main Street, you are at Index Corner, a name that appeared at a time when Half Moon Bay housed its own telephone company—with its own index, or directory—in the Debenedetti Building. Later, a saloon called the Index occupied this site. Since 1924, it has been Cunha's Country Store, a classic that still sells general merchandise in the old country way.

Across from it is little "Mac" Dutra Park, with a bell tower, benches, picnic tables and restrooms. Named in honor of Antone P. "Mac" Dutra, it was built in 1929 to honor a native son. Pause here to get your bearings. Kelly Street runs east to the brook and canyon called Arroyo Leon. Main Street runs north to Pilarcitos Creek and south through Spanishtown.

Once, hitching posts lined what is now the curbside. Walk south on Main Street. George's Toggery on the east side of the street was once Bortano's Saloon, one of eleven that lined Main Street. The Half Moon Bay Bakery, which announces "spring-water coffee," has a 19th century brick oven. Attractive pansies in bloom in front of the dentists' office are a reminder that flower growing was long the principal industry of Half Moon Bay.

At Miramontes Street, turn east to reach the blue-and-white United Methodist Church, built in 1872. A wing of the church was once an Ocean Shore Railroad station.

Equally unusual is the Sunday service schedule. Each week, two Methodist services are held early by the Rev. Tom McArthur, and a later service is offered by the Holy Family Episcopal vicar, the Rev. Ann L. Smith.

Continue on Miramontes Street to Arroyo Leon Creek, where some of the bankside trees have been cut, unfortunately, to accommodate a new concrete bridge replacing the quaint old wooden one. It has no pedestrian lane, so cross carefully; then, about 50 feet along the road, turn right and cross a tributary of the creek on another older bridge that leads to a cemetery.

The gurgle of water over stones, the rustle of leaves on the trees and possibly bird song will accompany you as you climb the cemetery hill. Although this is not the oldest cemetery in Half Moon Bay, it is worth the climb to see the sturdy old hand-hewn stone crosses that mark many of the graves, the Debenedetti family crypt, the crosses marked on graves covered in cement and the great view westward overlooking the Pacific Ocean. All of the graves face the setting sun.

Retrace your steps back to Miramontes and turn right on San Benito Street. Houses along here all back on the creek, and at each dead end, one can overlook the Arroyo Leon. Individual cottages, little Victorians, Greek Revival types and farmhouse-style homes make a tidy and interesting vista as one walks past their gardens and lawns.

When you reach Kelly Street, turn west. Number 751 Kelly was built by Adam Simmons, a pioneer undertaker, and still has its unusual double scallop of shingles bordering the roof. At Johnston Street, named for James Johnston, an Ohioan who brought the first wagon down the coast and later subdivided Spanishtown a little further south, bear right to No. 423, the home of Robert Knapp, inventor of the side-hill plow.

Mill Street takes its name from a water-powered grist mill that stood beside the creek. Later, a slaughterhouse stood at the end of Mill Street. Turn left to reach Main Street and then turn left again on Main. The bridge visible on your right was built in 1900 and is the first reinforced-concrete bridge in California. It has a pedestrian lane. Tiburcio Vasquez, one of the original landowners, lived on the far side of the creek.

At 356 Main stands the San Benito House, which began as the Hotel Mosconi. Often the natural-food store in this block and the old fashioned soda fountain at the Half Moon Bay Drugstore are aswarm with bicyclists, who find Spanishtown a convenient place for a coffee break between the Point Montara and Pigeon Point youth hostels. Good coffeehouses and restaurants abound along Main Street.

At Kelly Street, turn right and walk west to return to the state park beaches. En route you will pass Shoreline Station, a shopping center where a little red caboose houses the chamber of commerce. If you are eager to know more about the architecture of the town, call them at (415) 726-5202 for a map and architectural walking tour brochure.

Then plan to return during the last week in June and the first week in July, when the Coastside County Fair is held, complete with a Fourth of July parade, a rodeo and cattle judging, or in May, when the Portuguese community celebrates the festival called the Chamarita.

San Bruno Mountain

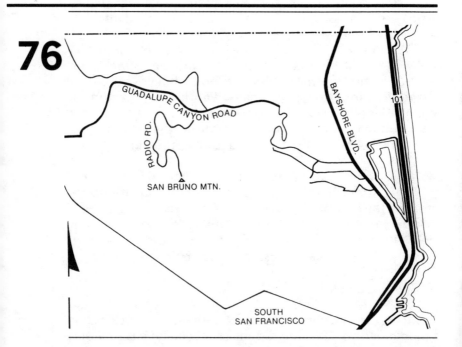

San Bruno Mountain, which ecologists call the "last Franciscan wilderness," looms out of the urban jungle south of San Francisco like a giant whale, mysteriously stranded. As yet largely unchanged from a time when it was part of Rancho Guadalupe La Vistacion y Rodeo Viejo, it is the last refuge of ecosystems that flourished for thousands of years around what is now San Francisco. Six rare and endangered species of plant, the coast rock cress, the Montara manzanita, the San Bruno Mountain manzanita, the Franciscan wallflower, and two plants so little known they have no common names, the *Chaetopappa alsinoides* and the *Helianthella castanes* live on its slopes. For how much longer is anyone's guess.

San Mateo County long ago designated San Bruno Mountain a potential regional park. Subsequently, San Francisco's Board of Supervisors in unanimous resolution questioned any development of the mountain and requested a study be made by the Association of Bay Area Governments (ABAG). And like young Lochinvar riding out of Sacramento, the State legislature passed a bill that would provide $4 million for land acquisition of San Bruno for park purposes.

To understand possible consequences if the mountain were to be developed for housing instead, consider a walk on threatened San Bruno Mountain, and then make up your own mind about the issue. To make this walk, drive south from San Francisco on the Bayshore Freeway (U.S. Route 101) to the Cow Palace/Brisbane exit. Follow the old Bayshore Highway (Bayshore Boulevard) past Geneva Avenue to Guadalupe Road and turn right, up the mountain's saddle. At Radio Road, turn left and park on the shoulder.

Once up on the mountain's saddle, you will find that freightyards, freeways and industrial ticky-tack have fallen away, along with the nerve-bending sixty-cycle growl of the city. Silence of the wild land, like a living thing, seems tangible here. As poet David Schooley, who has devoted his life to the 1,314-foot-high mountain, has written, "only the hawk is still here, guarding its nest with high wounded cries, forever circling ridges and valleys, even in the heat and stillness of noon."

From the Radio Road shoulder parking, walk to Guadalupe Parkway and cross it to the chuckholed old country road. Follow this through the unaccustomed quiet of the Great Meadow until you enter what aficionados of the ridge call the "fog forest," a beautiful, sometimes eerie area made up of introduced plants intermingled with wild ones. As the road leaves the sunlit stillness of the forest, it continues, crowded with acacias, alive with darting birds. The Great Meadow on the left slopes down to a gathering of ground waters into the last natural Franciscan marsh on earth, habitat for three endangered species and a mecca for science classes from Bay Area schools and colleges. It is here that developers proposed a terraced concrete platform for shopping center, parking garage, and a series of twenty-storied skyscrapers to house 18,000 people.

Just past a clump of pampas grass, go right on a dirt road to the top of the knoll ahead for a glimpse of the Pacific Ocean. If you had glanced that way in 1853, you might have seen twenty-one settlers and their families barricaded with a four-pounder brass cannon and Kentucky rifles behind sacks of potatoes, prepared to fight a "Battle of Colma" against a large land speculator. In a dispute that went on for years, the U.S. Supreme Court finally decided in favor of the small holders, the North San Mateo County Settlers Union.

Move on to the right, bayward, keeping always to the widest path for a leisurely walk through the hollows. It is this area that thousands of North Peninsula residents have petitioned for a park.

Just before the two lone pines at the end of the hollows, turn right on a trail that slants up to the highest southerly knoll to offer final vantage for an unfamiliar back view of the city, the bay, and one of the area's best kept secrets, the hidden valleys of the mountain which harbor the only undisturbed village sites of the Awashtes tribelet of the Costanoan Indians. According to Miley Holman, assistant curator of the Treganza Museum at San Francisco State University, the Book of Baptisms and Book of Deaths at Mission Dolores chronicle the disappearance of this now vanished people, and await scholarly archeological correlation with the sites.

To return to your wheels, descend in the direction toward the mountain's summit, again following the widest trail through a break in the trees in sight of your car.

Coyote Point Museum

77

Imagine yourself as a drop of water, rained down into the Santa Cruz mountains and launched on a journey to the sea. If the possibilities sound exciting, the new Coyote Point Museum, in San Mateo County's wonderful oasis, the Coyote Point Park, is for you.

To make this walk, go seventeen miles south from San Francisco via the Bayshore Freeway, Highway 101. Take the Peninsula Avenue exit at Burlingame and follow the park signs east. Approaching from the south, Poplar Avenue offramp is the key that unlocks this treasure trove. Be prepared to pay a $3 parking fee per car and, unless you go on Friday which is free, another $1 per adult or 50¢ per child for 6 through 17 year olds and seniors over 60, at the museum door.

Park and walk uphill toward the handsome new Douglas fir building designed by Palo Alto architect John W. Stypula. It is so sensitively placed among the tall eucalyptus, planted long ago by John McLaren, that it looks as though it had been there forever, or conversely, had popped up overnight like a mushroom. Actually it had been twelve years in the planning and building and cost $1.9 million in federal, state, county and private money.

You enter to a broad corridor with classrooms and auditorium on one side, a museum shop on the left. Tempting as it is to head up immediately on the stairway to the left, stop for a moment to look out the window toward the upper right to see the big bee-tube. This is a transparent entrance to the museum for a resident hive whose honey will be harvested and ultimately offered for sale in the museum.

At the upper landing on the stairway walk straight ahead before entering the exhibit hall for another look into the honey bee-tube. As you approach the showroom, be prepared for a surprise.

The big airy room, clean as a shaker meetinghouse, is the point at which you turn into that drop of water, for you arrive, cloud-high at the uppermost of four descending levels. Bare oak floors treated like a basketball court to withstand abuse are connected by ramps leading downward. Overhead poet Gary Snyder's voice is caught on paper "Air, Fire, Water and Earth is our dancing place now" he says on the story board. Black Elk speaks too: "To the center of the world you have taken me and showed the goodness and the beauty and the strangeness of the greening earth, the only mother . . ."

To one side is a biosphere, a slice of the earth created in decoupage by volunteers, members of the museum association or of the Junior League, which has long contributed its support. "Nature to be commanded must be obeyed" enjoins Francis Bacon near the rock which depicts earth, under a lotus form which represents the sun by the introductory exhibit "A Place called Earth." To get more local, go around behind the next panel for "A Place Called San Mateo."

Next level down, the scene-stealers are sculptured oak trees and redwood trees, whose startling dimensions look as though they were conceived in a giant kaleidoscope, rather than a seed. When you stand under the conifers, look up for a great illusion. Under the wagon-wheel oaks, walk toward the wall on your left to discover live bees and termites in the display on communities and ecosystems.

Ease on down the ramps as you will. By the time you reach the lowest level you will have passed through designer Gordon Ashby's interpretation of the coniferous forest and grassland on your way to the coastal scrub on one side of the gallery and through broadleaf forest, chaparral and finally baylands on the other. You'll also have a new understanding of man's place in the natural world. "Human Impact" cases, financed by a grant from the National Endowment for the Humanities, are displayed with each of the six biotic communities to demonstrate historical use, environmental concerns and future possibilities.

Level three has another scene-stealer, the food-chain pyramid, an arresting tower done in soft sculpture which depicts the diet of a red-tailed hawk for one year—1069 mice, 98 small birds, 20 gophers, 18 rabbits, 15 squirrels, 15 shrews, 9 game birds, 7 snakes, 4 rats and two weasels to be exact. It is as graphic a biosystem as one could envision. Be sure to walk to the opposite wall and take the steps down for the thrill of walking over "the marsh" on the lowest level. Then cross to find the tule pond and walk through the aquarium behind it.

"It is my hope that the exhibit will provoke people to do something in their own lives that moves them closer to an accord with nature ... make changes that allow them to live in harmony with natural process" Gordon Ashby said of his aim for the museum. Whether they do or not, the message is so subtle, they'll enjoy the walk.

The San Andreas Fault Trail in Los Trancos Open Space Preserve

78

280

LOS ALTOS

PORTOLA VALLEY

PAGE MILL RD.

LOS TRANCOS OPEN SPACE PRESERVE

SKYLINE BLVD.

As a tribute to the U.S. Geological Survey, walkers grateful for those beautifully detailed topographical maps we all depend on might consider a walk along the San Andreas Fault Trail in the Los Trancos Open Space Preserve.

It is a geologist's *tour de force*. The joint project of Foothill College and the Midpeninsula Regional Open

Space District, the trail itself is an outdoor laboratory or classroom in which one can see more earthquake-related phenomena within one kilometer or .6 of a mile than almost anywhere else on the world's longest and most active fault. In frequent use for students, it is also open to the public at no cost; on Sundays at 2 P.M., there are docent-led walks along the trail open to all comers. A docent is also available at any time to any group of five or more. The phone there is (415) 949-5500.

Scenically, the trail is one of the more spectacular in the Bay Area, with vast distant vistas visible. The day I was introduced to the trail by geologists Tim Hall of Foothill College and Mary Hill of USGS, we could see the snowcaps of the Sierra beyond Mission Peak and Mount Diablo. It is also so well-sited and so rich and varied in the terrain it traverses that even nongeologists who complete its short, irregular loop, using self-guided tour pamphlets, will feel they have been miles away.

To make this paragon of walks, pack your lunch and a canteen, for there are no concessionaires or water faucets in Open Space District lands. Bring along your hiking boots, but not your dog, for it is also a wildlife preserve. From San Francisco, head south on the Junipero Serra Freeway (Interstate 280) toward Palo Alto. Take the Page Mill Road offramp and stay on Page Mill Road, driving uphill westerly for seven miles. A parking lot on the north side of the road and a large sign announcing Los Trancos Open Space Preserve is the tipoff that you have arrived. Park, pick up a folder from the pockets beneath the sign and look at the map immediately.

Summing up the essence of plate tectonics in a paragraph, the pamphlet says, "the earth's outer skin is a jigsaw puzzle of 60-mile-(100-kilometer-) thick plates of solid rock floating on a sea of plastic rock. When two of these plates move against each other, the rock breaks, forming an area of weakness called a 'fault zone.' On the preserve, the San Andreas Fault zone is a 3/10-mile-(½-kilometer-) wide belt where the Pacific Plate is grinding northwestward past the American Plate."

Resist the impulse to take the trail at the foot of the

sign. Instead, go back to the parking lot and through the stile on the west side. Like the bear that goes over the mountain to see what he can see, geologists like an overview to begin any walk. This is exactly what Station 1 is. Cross the little erosion gulley and climb up to the yellow-topped 4-inch by 4-inch stake. You are west of the fault, and some pieces of the big jigsaw become evident immediately.

First of all, look at the boulders of marine conglomerate lying about at your feet. Then look south along the San Andreas Fault through fold after fold of hills. Tim Hall pointed out Loma Prieta Mountain on the American Plate south and east by thirty-eight kilometers (twenty-three miles). Mount Humunum is on its flank, over near Gilroy. The boulders at your feet were on the slopes of Mount Humunum between one and two billion years ago. Movements along the fault shifted them here a little at a time.

When you have absorbed all of the view you can encompass, go back to the big entry sign and you will be en route to Station 2, another lookout point. From it, look north to see Mount San Bruno and Mount Tamalpais, San Francisco and, in the foreground, San Andreas Lake and Crystal Springs Reservoir, both created by damming the fault to supply water to the city.

Station 3, deep in the woods, shows where a fence was rent by the 1906 jiggle. At Station 4, in a meadow, you are near a big poison oak clump from which a Stanford student photographed a long furrow ruptured in that classic quake. Copies in the Stanford library can even match the big tree and the poison oak clump when held up for comparison. Only the furrow itself has been healed by surface erosion. Incidentally, poison oak pushes its branches up so straight and true, they were used for arrows by the Indians. If there are no deep trilobed leaves or bright red buds to warn you that the clump is poison oak you can recognize it for the candelabralike spread of its bare branches.

Head back toward the woods and you are soon at an offset fence, reconstructed by Tim's father, Nick Hall, and volunteer Foothill students from old wood found on the grounds. Once it contained a paddock for a famous race horse; now it continues a fence whose original sections still stand farther down the canyon toward Los Trancos Creek, Sag ponds, trees both topped and toppled by past earth movement, rock lines and terracing are other lessons on the land.

All too soon, you find yourself back in the parking lot after completing this fascinating circle. If you are eager for more walking, there is a 3½-mile trail through the preserve that takes off just below Station 2. Another peels off from Station 4. Either one will lead to a sunny spot for your picnic. While you are enjoying it, lift a glass to toast the USGS. Without its maps, topos, transections and such, not even geologists would know as much about the land as they do. Neither would you and I, fellow walker.

Sam McDonald Park in San Mateo County

79

It was a jubilant occasion for walkers of the Bay Area when a hiker's hostel imported from Denmark to San Mateo County's Sam McDonald Park was dedicated with a celebration, a walk, fun, fanfare, feasting, songs and skits.

To Woodside City Councilwoman Olive Mayer, a lifetime hiker, and a handful of likeminded friends who saw the prefabricated hut arrive at customs complete with fittings and furniture tucked rather like a Chinese puzzle into a single ship's container, it was a little miracle to see the finished product standing on Towne Ridge, all airy lines and light clean Scandinavian wood. The hostel welcomes hundreds of fanciers of "the long traverse," as walking tours are known in Europe, who have been frustrated on the West Coast for lack of shelter in making such outings. Walkers can reserve a space at the hostel and for a modest fee, weekend in the wilderness as easily as though the Santa Cruz Mountains were the Alps or, for that matter, the Appalachians.

In most mountainous places, hostels are traditional. Since Sam McDonald, a walk-in park dedicated a scant ten years ago, is linked by trails to Memorial County Park, Pescadero Creek County Park, and Portola State Park, this hostel has opened for walkers infinitely more possibilities than just the adjacent 850 acres. Indeed, under the county trails plan being funded by the Murphy bill, ultimately it will be possible for a walker to begin in Santa Cruz's Cowell Redwoods and walk in unspoiled country along San Mateo County ridges all the way to Thornton Beach in Daly City. Castle Rock, Big Basin, Hoover Ranch and Ano Nuevo parks are all links in the chain. Lest this seem a long journey to children of the automotive age, it is pleasant to recall that when author Bayard Taylor made his walking tour from San Francisco to Monterey in 1850, it took him three days.

The Towne Ridge trail is a fine appetizer for such a prospect. To make the mile-and-a-half walk from Sam McDonald park headquarters to the new hostel, transport yourself south from San Francisco to Woodside via Interstate 280, complete with hiking boots and knapsack lunch. Take the offramp with a right turn onto California Highway 84 and go through the town of Woodside. It gets tricky in the woods as you climb. At Skylonda—where Skyline Boulevard and La Honda Road come together—make a left to stay on 84 so you don't find yourself continuing on Skyline by mistake. Three-fourths of a mile beyond the town of La Honda turn left on Pescadero Road at the junction with Alpine, then right to the park entrance.

Sam McDonald, for whom the park is named, was the son of slaves, and lived from 1884 to 1957, working as a janitor at Stanford University. Here he became such a favorite with students and faculty alike that he became superintendent of grounds. President David Starr Jordan is reputed to have doubted he could get elected if he had had to run against Sam. During World War II, children at Stanford Convalescent Home named a "Sam McDonald Day" for him, celebrating both the vegetable gardens he planted for them and the barbecues he cooked. He left his property to Stanford, specifically asking that the land he had owned be used as a park for the benefit of young people. Go inside the headquarters to see a display that tells more about him. In 1958, San Mateo County bought the 417 acres he left Stanford for this purpose; an adjoining 450 acres were later acquired from rancher Kendal B. Towne to bring the park to its present size.

When you have perused the park history, cross the parking lot to the southwesterly curve to pick up the trail to the hostel. Bear left by the big burned redwood after passing two picnic tables and a barbecue grill in the redwood grove. In a trice, you reach Pescadero Road. Watch your step as you cross. Then go through the hiker's stile alongside a vehicle barrier. At this point, ignore the trail sign (it is for Big Tree Loop Trail) and go straight up the left-hand fork, which is the old wagon road long used to bring milk and cream from the Towne dairy to San Francisco. Don't be alarmed if you reach a big redwood that is down. A storm, not loggers, felled it: the thrifty San Mateo park department makes its own fenceposts from wood obtained this way.

At the next fork, continue uphill unless you want a rest. The trail arrow here points to an overlook with benches about 150 yards into the trees.

Hew to the road and soon you pass a big tank on the left, the water supply for the park. Landowners below would like to usurp this supply for denser tract development. When you reach the gate, the old Ridgeway Rawlings ranch will be on your left. A county maintained horseman's camp now stands there. Bear left at the next fork in the road (the right fork goes to the San Francisco and Oakland YMCA camps). Now you leave the redwoods and go into open meadowland with the horsebarn visible uphill on your left. As you go through the gates on the main road, close each after you. They keep George Bordi's cows from straying. Grazing rights are rented to keep fire danger minimal during dry times. After the second gate, continue left uphill at the next fork (the right fork here goes to Portola State park). From this vantage, the view to the right is Pescadero Ridge. Everything you see to the west is parkland.

Soon you approach the hostel, an architectural triumph of simplicity which gives the illusion of having sprouted among the trees as spontaneously as a mushroom. Everything in it—from coffee cups to cushions, walls, windows, and water taps, as well as the kitchen stove—came in that one box from Denmark. Only the deck is a California afterthought, an additional especially designed for our snowless indoor-outdoor climate.

Loma Prieta chapter of the Sierra Club paid for this hostel with cash, helped by private gifts from the San Mateo, the Packard, and the Hewlett Foundations; the modest fees go to pay the resident caretaker.

A Walk to see the Jepson Laurel

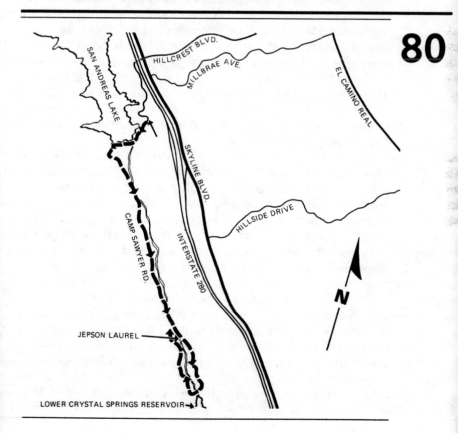

Because redwoods and bristlecone pines—the biggest, tallest, and oldest growing trees—grace California, we sometimes ignore our other spectacular trees. One of these is the California bay or laurel, *Umbellularia californica*, which in a northern coastal state is claimed exclusively, uniquely and incorrectly as the Oregon myrtle. Given the chance, the California bay tree grows big enough to live under.

One that has had the chance is the Jepson Laurel, named in honor of Dr. Willis Lynn Jepson of the University of California. When the California Botanical Society dedicated it in 1923, it was marked in bronze as "the second largest laurel in California." The only larger laurel then known grew near Cloverdale in the alluvial bench of the Russian River. It has since come down. Unless some larger unreported tree has since been discovered, this leaves the Jepson Laurel as the largest. Whether it is or not, it is a beautiful tree to see. Walkers who would like to stand under the great canopy of the huge tree can do so at the end of a pleasant two-mile walk along Sawyer Camp Road, which links San Andreas Lake with Lower Crystal Springs Reservoir in the long rift valley of the San Andreas Fault just southwest of Millbrae.

To make this walk, transport yourself south from San Francisco via Skyline Boulevard or the Junipero Serra Freeway (Interstate 280). Go off the freeway at Hillcrest Boulevard (or from Skyline make a right turn under the freeway) to Sawyer Camp Road. San Andreas Lake, created in 1860, will be at your right as you drive into the watershed land. Park at the widest point of the road a few hundred yards along, in what was once a quarry. Then lock your car, take your bird and bottle in a knapsack, and start off downhill along the public county road that skirts the south end of the lake. As you walk, try to envision the band of explorers under the command of Capt. Gaspar de Portola, Governor of the Californias, coming over Sweeney Ridge, the horizon line on your right. It's a tough climb for able men, let alone the expedition's scurvy victims who were carried on improvised stretchers slung between mules. The campsite where they rested in November 1769 is now beneath the waters of San Andreas Lake.

When you reach the fountain ahead, a monument to the dam built at the time of the dam's centennial by underprivileged children,there is the welcome opportunity to enjoy a drink of the sparkling water you have been passing. Along the road to the right about half a mile, another monument commemorates the late, much-loved John O'Marie, longtime superintendent of the Peninsula watershed land. Forbear it at this time, however, and take the road on the left. It swings along through willow trees, embodying all the intimate roadside charm our grandparents enjoyed in the horse and buggy days. Oxen drew lumber to the sawmill along this road. Hayracks of happy children came along here singing under the harvest moon. Fashionable broughams with matched hackney pony pairs came this way to the inn that once stood in Sawyer Camp.

When you reach the Jepson Laurel, which stands a little off the road to the right, you will know it by the vast spread of its crown. In some places it has rooted to look like several trees where the boughs touch down to earth. Go up close to find the 1923 plaque that lists the circumference as 22 feet 4 inches and the height at fifty-five feet. Today it is certainly bigger around, though no one has measured it lately. I'd estimate the height close to eighty feet.

To amateurs of archeology, irregularities in the land nearby are clues to the buildings that stood here when Sawyer Camp offered food and lodging to horsemen. Walk a few yards south of the laurel to find, near the road, evidence of the offset caused by the 1906 quake. Lower Crystal Springs Reservoir has its northern terminus just beyond. When you have located it, loop back to retrace your steps on Sawyer Camp Road. The mountainous land along Sawyer Ridge, uphill on the west above, like the lakes, is part of the 19,000 acre wilderness area in the San Francisco Public Utilities Commission master plan. Thus far, the hiking trails, alas, are few indeed.

Filoli

81

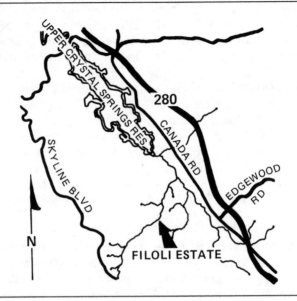

FILOLI ESTATE

Filoli. Roll the name on your tongue and it sounds like an Irish lullaby. Glimpse its tantalizing red roofs from Interstate 280, surrounded by the green woodland watershed south of Crystal Springs Reservoir, where Sleeping Beauty could be in a trance, awaiting her prince. Or perhaps your imagination runs more to seven weekend guests down to hunt quail, marshalled in the morning room while the Inspector decides whether The Butler did it.

However romantic the fantasies about Filoli, the reality of this forty-three room, 125-acre Peninsula estate is even better. It well may boast the most sumptuous house and distinguished gardens in the Bay Area. So private for the last sixty years only a select few people saw it, Filoli, now in the hands of the National Trust for Historical Preservation, is open to the public five days a week February through November. May and June, when the roses are in full bloom, are the best of times to see it.

To make this walk, plan your excursion ahead by calling

the Friends of Filoli at (415) 364-2800 or writing Filoli Tours, Canada Road, Woodside 94062. It is closed Sunday and Monday. There is a fee to walk through the vast succession of gardens in small groups led by a volunteer docent. Touring the house is more, but for my money, to see the ballroom murals alone would be worth it. Fees all go toward the upkeep of the grounds.

Once your reservation is made, head south form San Francisco on the prizewinning Junipero Serra Freeway (Interstate 280). Take the Edgewood Road offramp to Canada Road and bear right on Canada. One and one fourth miles north is the entrance gate at a sign which says Filoli Center.

Even entering the grounds has aspects of enchantment. Driving through the parklike approach can make you feel like a happy wayfarer en route to Glockamorra or a hobbit on the loose. When you sight the building, park and walk around to the entrance court of Filoli. The name is a contraction of Fight, Love, and Live, coined by William Bowers Bourn II. He was president of the Spring Valley Water Company when he built the Stuart style house designed by Willis Polk in 1916. Like Bourn, whose forebear Jared Bourn came to Massachusetts in 1630 with Governor Winthrop, the house's line of descent is impeccable. Inspiration to Polk was the home built for the Duke of Devonshire in Green Park, London, by Inigo Jones and Sir Christopher Wren after the great London fire of 1666. A tile roof was substituted for the prototypical slate as being more Californian. Filoli cost $109,308 when it was built with money from the Empire Gold Mine in Grass Valley. Today estimated replacement cost might be upward of $6 million.

If you go into the house, the ballroom paintings may remind you of the reservoirs that sparkle along the San Andreas Fault. Bourn chose the site because of the similarity. Actually the murals are of Muckross Abbey and the adjacent Killarney Lakes, which Bourn so loved that he bought the site as a wedding present for his daughter Maude, who left it to the Irish National Trust.

Docents usually pick up their dozen walkers in the

court and start off around the Ballroom Park, then come behind the house to the terrace. The William P. Roths, who occupied the house from 1937 to 1975, when Lurline Matson Roth made a gift of the estate to the National Trust, added the glassed-in sleeping porch that overlooks the garage court. The Roths preferred to think the first syllable of the name of the estate could stand for Fidelity, rather than Fight.

A sunken garden is next on the itinerary, followed by the Walled Garden, the Dutch Garden, the Wedding Place and the Wild Garden, all designed by Bruce Porter. In its heyday, there were sixteen to twenty gardeners living in a Spanish style mansion on the grounds. It's considered impolite to ask how many gardeners there are today. Historic derivations of the gardens begin with the Mughals of India, and pick up ideas from the Persians, from Mediterranean gardens and from classical European country gardens. Yew trees in the long double *allée* were brought from seed gathered at Muckross Abbey.

When you reach the Wedding Place, look down the long grassy steps through trees toward the tea house. Like the carriage house, which is usually full of horsey equipage lent by the San Mateo County Historical Museum (although many were used here originally), the tea house was designed by Arthur Brown, Jr. Gardner Dailey designed farm buildings, while Charles Porter and Alex Yuill-Thornton designed the swimming pool and its pavilion.

That Latino motto "Festina Lente" over the entrance to the Wild Garden means "Make Haste Slowly" and Renaissance scholars will recognize the doctrine of opposites in the crab and the butterfly, meant to instruct while entertaining. Rhododendrons by the north wall of the Wild Garden are a hybrid named 'Lurline.' Like the famous ship, they were named for the generous lady whose home this was for forty years.

The Rose Garden, the Greek Columns, the Knot Garden, and the Cutting Garden all have their charms, but quite possibly the most unusual is the Stained Glass Garden, whose beds represent a Chartres Cathedral rose window. A succession of plants in bloom, many of them in the deep rich colors of cineraria, pansies, begonias or peonies, represent the glass. Privet hedges stand in lieu of lead between the glass panes.

"Time Began in a Garden," says the sundial at Filoli, but it ends there, too. If you find yourself hungry for another chance to play the country squire vicariously, plan to come back another day. Next time there will be something different in bloom.

Santa Clara County

Villa Montalvo

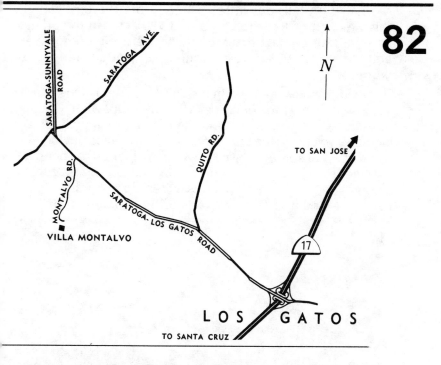

82

"Thither I sped o'er the King's Highway on a morning bathed in bliss," wrote Kate B. Palmer in 1926 on her way to spend the annual poet's "Day in the Hills" when prizes for the best local writing were awarded by Sen. James Duvall Phelan on "sheltering Montalvo's slope."

Nobody today could equate a trip down El Camino Real with a blissful bath, but culture is still an important consideration at Villa Montalvo, administered now by the Santa Clara County Parks and Recreation Department. In the Senator's day, a walk in the woods was an important part of the good life in the country, and was something the poets looked forward to when they came as the Senator's guests. Indeed, one of the earliest California watering places was nearby Congress Springs, where fashionable San Francisco went to drink the "lemon fizzes" and walk in the woods.

Many miles of hiking trails, well maintained, lie uphill of Montalvo on hillsides little changed from the time when this was part of Rancho Quito—13,590 acres in the Sierra Azul, as the Santa Cruz Mountains were once known— granted in 1841 to José Zenon Fernandez and José Noriega.

Traditionally, the "Day in the Hills" was held in the early autumn, a lovely time of year at Montalvo. A pavilion would be erected on the lawn to contain the luncheon fete, a memorial volume of the prizewinners work would be published, and each year some lucky poet would be invited to spend a few months or so in residence at one of the many guest cottages on the grounds, much as writers do today at Yaddo. Edward Markham, George Sterling, Ina Coolbrith, Helen

Wills, Gertrude Atherton, David Starr Jordan, Kathleen Norris and Robinson Jeffers were just a few of the honorees.

These days, the walker who goes to Montalvo is more apt to find a play, concert or an art opening in progress. In any case, it can add a charming note of contrast to a day "beneath a sky as blue as Parma's own," as Kathleen Norris described her day here.

To make this walk, from San Francisco head south on Interstate 280 to Saratoga (via Saratoga-Sunnyvale Road), rucksack packed. From Saratoga, take California Highway 9 (Saratoga-Los Gatos Road) southeast, or left, to Montalvo Road. Watch for the small sign that announced Villa Montalvo. Once, its large cat statues alerted the approaching visitor to the estate. Now contemporary ranch style houses cluster around it like baby chicks. Before you reach the Italianate villa, the creation of architects William and Alexander Curlett and C.E. Gottschalk, there is a small building on the edge of the grounds, which is the park headquarters. Trail maps and parking information are available here.

Unless a wedding or play is in progress, park to the right of the villa; otherwise gardeners may put you in an outlying lot.

Climb up past the building and the outdoor amphi-theater until you reach busts of two poets flanking the sidewalk. Joaquin Miller is the one on the right. Make a right turn by his statue across the walk from tea trees, or leptospermum, trained as standards. Continue uphill at each of the next two forks in the trail. This will bring you past the former tennis courts (marked by a picnic table) and past a platform where bleachers once stood. Helen Wills was one of the poets who also availed herself of the tennis courts.

Pass the reservoir to reach an important trail junction. If you are good for an easy two-mile nature trail, take off into the canyon of Wildcat Creek. If you want an easy half-mile view trail, bear left instead by the large burned redwood stump, near the unusual hidden seat, the third trunk of the three-trunked live oak. Across the path, a drinking fountain is concealed in another stump.

Notice the lover's bench as you walk along the hillside ledge. Phelan, a bachelor, was consistently romantic. He put his benches where they would take in the sweeping panorama of Mount Hamilton, San Jose and the Santa Clara Valley. A prudent man, he also installed a siren to summon his private physician, Dr. Louis Mendelsohn, when he needed him to come for a house call.

Bear left downhill at the next fork. (The other fork climbs into Redwood Canyon.) The octagonal roof visible below was Phelan's carriage house, whose floor revolved. Now a theater-in-the-round, the carriage turnaround has become a revolving stage.

Soon the trail returns to the villa at Parking Lot 1. Go into the villa to see the galleries, then to the back garden where a tablet explains that Montalvo was a Spanish sixteenth century novelist who first used the word California. It is found in his book *Las Sergas de Esplandian*. Then return through the villa to the front steps and look through the long formal lawn and its *allee* of trees to discover the Temple of Love.

Young lovers play guitars under the great deodars. Mourning doves coo. Bird watchers and plant fanciers wander among the lemon trees and on the grass, small children often roll in merry oblivion. It could be a pointillist painting entitled "Afternoon in the Park."

Fitzgerald Marine Reserve (Moss Beach)

83

Tidepooling, as any veteran slosher of the rocky reefs can tell you, must be done at the lowest of tides. Even then it can be an adventure.

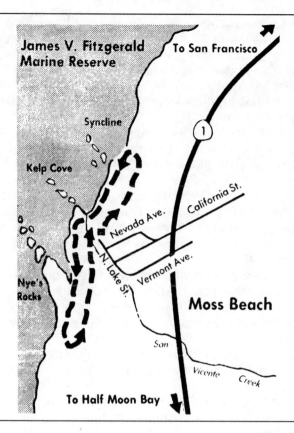

As Don Graeme Kelley described it in "Edge of a Continent":

"To follow the receding tide by a random progress from one slippery rock to another, sloshing through seaweed, poising for a jump across a swift ebb-stream, making it to a more engaging vantage—is to build excitement and wonder at the vitality and variety of living things. The wonderment is roused most by the growing sense that here, between the splash zone and low water, there are greater numbers and more kinds of things alive than one has ever seen before in a small area."

Every tidepool has its little resident miracles, but quite possibly the best tidepooling in the Bay Area is to be found about 15 miles south of San Francisco at Moss Beach. Richer in species than Point Reyes, equal in complexity to Point Lobos, the rocky strip between Point Montara and Pillar Point in San Mateo County ranks as one of the most diverse intertidal regions in California.

Dozens of master's and doctoral theses had their source in the abundant life on Frenchmans' Reef and the Moss Beach Syncline, an unusual geologic formation. Indeed, for almost 70 years, the richness of Moss Beach tidepools was a well-kept secret of scientists and a handful of divers and fishermen.

Since 1969—when the sensitive oceanside strip of the Pillar Point headland gained some county protection as the James V. Fitzgerald Marine Reserve—word has been seeping out to the public that Moss Beach is a little water wonderland.

The period of any new moon or full moon is a good time for walking Moss Beach. The lowest of low tides for daylight walking come in the fall and winter. For tidepooling, consult your calendar and tide-book before you embark on this excursion.

If you miss the lowest tidal time, Fitzgerald Marine Reserve also has a pleasant trail through trees on the headland cliffs.

Plan to leave your dog at home for this walk. Wear your oldest tennis shoes and dungarees, and take a windbreaker. Pack a picnic if you wish, then head south from San Francisco on Route 1, the Cabrillo Highway.

After you pass Montara Light, which now has a youth hostel in the old Coast Guard barracks, look for a sign on your right for the Fitzgerald Marine Reserve. Turn west on California Street and follow it to North Lake Street. Turn right on North Lake and right again into the parking lot just before you reach Nevada Avenue.

The San Mateo County Parks and Recreation Division has constructed picnic tables, restrooms and a small ranger station-museum in the woods surrounding the parking lot. Friends of Fitzgerald Marine Life Refuge are hoping to raise enough money to build an interpretive center to better display the scientific information the reserve has yielded.

Look on the bulletin board outside the ranger station for a fine geologic interpretation of the reefs. Naturalist Bob Breen and his staff daily post locally corrected times of the low tides nearby. Wise walkers doublecheck their own tide-book calculations against the posted local figures.

If the station is open, go in to pick up a copy of an inexpensive guide to the intertidal zone. if you are lucky, you may also get to tag along with a ranger-led tidepool expedition. Early birds who arrive before the station is open can check into the little museum on their return.

Cross at the junction of Nevada and North Lake streets to reach the trailhead. It leads into the canyon San Vicente Creek has cut on its way to the sea. On your left, a log across a path crossing the head of the canyon marks the access point for the headland trail.

For the beach walk, continue downhill toward the bayside exhibit. This display will give you some idea of the crabs, limpets, chitons, sea anemones, kelps, barnacles, sea stars and other small creatures that inhabit the tidepools. There isn't room on it to list all 26 kinds of nudibranchs that have been found here, much less the 125 species of shelled gastropods. Three kinds of tidepool life found here—a shrimp, a worm and a seaweed—exist nowhere else in the world.

Not surprisingly, collecting is forbidden, as a nearby sign warns.

The path curves down to the shore, past seaside flowers. When you reach the beach, turn to the right and walk as far as you can, to see the unusual semicircular formation of the offshore rocks beyond Kelp Cove. This is visual evidence of the Moss Beach Syncline explained on the ranger station bulletin board.

Then make your way back through Kelp Cove. When I walked here last, big coils of the bullwhip kelp lay on the beach. Entwined with them were other pink, white, maroon and mottled seaweeds, some slick and smooth, some warty, some as harshly crisp as Brillo. It looked as though a giant flower arranger had decorated for a party.

Although I spotted only 30 kinds, there have been 129 species of seaweed identified in Kelp Cove.

When you have explored it, walk south along the beach toward Nye's Rocks, a reef that comes in to the coastline at a slant. It was named for Charlie Nye, whose seaside dining room, The Reefs, stood on pilings here until 1931. Luther Burbank and Jack London were among the notables who dined here before the sea carried away The Reefs in a storm.

As you walk south, look up at the chimney-like formation eroded by wind and wave beyond the creek. Farther along, fencing indicates where the big storms of 1982 and 1983 brought down trees from the cliff.

The groves of cypress trees that remain, as well as those that came down in the storms, were planted by J.F. Wienke, who came to be know as the "mayor of Moss Beach" after he built his Moss Beach Hotel and resort here in 1882. San Francisco socialites made the long and arduous trip by horse and carriage over the mountain to stay with Wienke and his wife, Nee Meta Paulson, a cousin of sugar magnate Claus Spreckles.

One of the more unusual guests at the resort was Captain George C. Lovdal, who came by sea after his ship the lumber schooner Argonaut, crashed on Point Montara one foggy morning in 1890.

The hotel attracted the *bon ton* until a fire destroyed it not long after the 1906 earthquake. A later owner of the cypress cliffs above the beach was Arthur Smith, a doctor of divinity.

The white building visible beyond the next little cove is the Moss Beach Distillery, a restaurant whose parking lot was once the site of another hotel and tavern, the Marine View.

Explore the tidepools as you go, but remember, never turn your back on the sea.

Better still, when you have strolled this strand, find a warm place on the sand to sit and enjoy the beach. When I came this way, gull tracks in the sand looked as though the whole flock had had six lessons in the conga from Madame Lazonga.

There is also, for the walker who pauses awhile, the mesmerizing experience of wave watching. As Elna Bakker wrote in "An Island Called California":

"Where headlands drop into the sea, there is a glorious pageantry of color and motion as wave follows wave, confronting the terrestrial outposts in endless procession. First comes the subtle shift in blue or green as the breaker is born. Then the infant swell slides toward land increasing in height until it crests and spills down upon itself in a white cascade. Now, when it is almost spent, traclets of foam break away and eddy gracefully around the rocks and reefs at the foot of the cliff face, slipping seaward in the pull of the back surge."

Moss Beach is one of the greatest places to watch this pageant.

Rodin Sculpture Garden

84

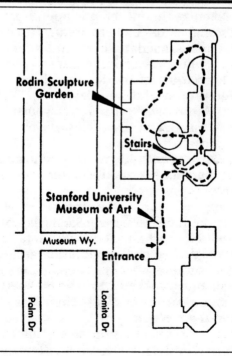

Have you ever stood entranced in the courtyard of the Palace of the Legion of Honor in Lincoln Park, wondering what "The Thinker" was thinking?

If you have, then there is a new perambulation in Palo Alto you must do, at least once in a lifetime. This is through the B. Gerald Cantor Rodin Sculpture Garden at Stanford University, one of the most remarkable walks in the Bay Area.

Don't put if off on the pretext that you know little of art. Anyone who has walked through a crowd is ready to enjoy the key piece in the Sculpture Garden, Rodin's "The Gates of Hell," commissioned in 1881.

Since the Rodin Sculpture Garden is outdoors, and soon to be lighted at night, one can enjoy the works in it at any time. It is better to go when the Stanford University Museum of Art is open, however. There are two floors more of the works of Auguste René Rodin on display within an octagonal gallery that adjoins the garden.

On weekends, the museum is open from 1 to 5 p.m. Tuesdays through Fridays, the hours are 10 a.m. to 5 p.m. It is closed Mondays, major holidays and during August and September, when students leave the campus.

Docent-led tours of the Rodin collection begin at 2 p.m. on Wednesdays and Saturdays.

To make this walk, transport yourself from San Francisco to Palo Alto. One can go by train, with a connecting bus to the campus from the station, or by SamTrans. On campus, there is a university-operated shuttle bus named Marguerite, after one of Governor Leland Stanford's horses.

Using your own wheels, the scenic route is via Highway 280. Go east from the freeway on Sand Hill Road. Sand Hill becomes Willow Road after crossing Santa Cruz Avenue. Turn south off Willow on Arboretum Road, west on Palm Drive, the main entrance to "The Farm" as Stanford Campus is still known, then turn right on Museum Way. On Sundays, parking is good near the end of Willow, close to the huge, pillared museum building.

Once inside, you can stop at the information desk. From there, go into the side gallery. Beyond this is the

Native American Indian Gallery. From there, turn right, and you're in the foyer of the Rodin Gallery.

The first statues you meet are busts of the benefactors, Mr. and Mrs. Cantor, who began collecting the work of Rodin in the 1940s. These statues are realistic likenesses done by sculptor Enzo Plazzota.

Take a few more steps. The first glimpse of Rodin's work is of busts of people important to him, including two of his mistresses, Camille Claudel and Rose Beuret, who became his wife. Continue into the center of the rotunda, where "The Age of Bronze" stands. "This was the first Rodin work ever publicly displayed," said docent Judith Amsbaugh, chairman of the Rodin Art Lecture Group, who conducted me on this walk. "When it appeared at The Salon in Paris, it had such an illusion of a living body, the sculptor was accused of taking casts from a live person."

Figures on the west side of the Rotunda are from "The Burghers of Calais," although the work is not the final version. The figure on the north side that looks like a very approachable Silenus is the writer Honore de Balzac.

Notice the anguished faces on figures near "The Kiss," one of Rodin's best-loved works. Except for the figure of Dante, which is by Jean Paul Aube, these are troubled figures included in "The Gates of Hell." Dante's "Inferno" was Rodin's inspiration for his monumental work.

Resist the temptation to go immediately into the garden, looking instead at the upper level of the Rotunda to see Rose Beuret in two aspects—one as the furious Goddess of War, the other as the tranquil Bellona.

Also interesting here are the little figures Rodin called his "snakes." Made from tubes of clay, they are quick studies done from life to catch movement and were not exhibited in his lifetime, except to other sculptors who came to his studio. Albert Elson, professor of art history at Stanford and curator of the Rodin collection, writes: "By the time he was 30, Rodin's hands were famous among his fellow workers, not only for their speed and dexterity, but for their ability to fashion work in a variety of styles." Continue past the nearby portraits of leading figures of his era to find a likeness of one of those hands holding a model in its fingers.

Pause now at the model of the museum building. Built in 1894, the building was larger before the earthquake of 1906. Iron reinforcing rods saved the rotunda, although some parts of the building were reduced from two stories to one.

Go down the stairs and out the side door near "The Three Shades," pausing at the nearby desk to pick up an explanatory brochure on "The Gates of Hell." Go down more steps and turn left past Adam to find "La Porte de l'Enfer," the name of the original commission.

Since the French museum the doors were to have enhanced was never built, "The Gates of Hell" remained in Rodin's studio all his life, "constantly changing in both physical aspect and philosophical meaning."

There is a bench fronting the work to let the spectator linger at the monumental piece. It is needed. More than 150 figures have been discerned in "The Gates." At a quick glance, one can spot the Three Shades and the Thinker. (Now you know what he was contemplating.)

As one looks, more and more figures emerge from what may be a maelstrom or a stormy cloud.

When the agony of the many faces at last sends you away, walk down off the circle, past Eve, and turn right. The architect of the garden was Robert Mittelstadt. Nursery expert Albert Wilson plans the seasonal replacement of annual flowers that surround "Spirit of Repose," who is leaning on air here just as he did in Rodin's own garden.

Consult the tables near the two outside entrances to the garden if you want to find a name, but don't expect to find titles of pieces on the works themselves. Elson, the moving figure behind the garden, felt it was more important for people to study the works, rather than get hung up on titles.

You may want to return to "The Gates of Hell for the fun of overhearing comments other spectators make about the stupendous piece.

"It reminds me of Breughel's Mad Maggie," an erudite young woman said.

"Nah," scoffed her male companion. "It's the White House basement."

Baylands in Palo Alto

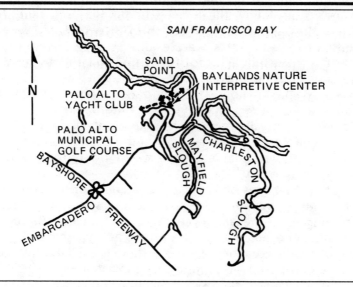

85

Magical is the word for estuaries, which change with every changing tide. But so is muddy—a simple fact of life that keeps the average walker from enjoying many mysterious marshes and their elusive wildlife on the fringes of the bay.

One exception is Baylands, in Palo Alto, where a catwalk and observation platform over the salt-marsh surrounding San Francisquito Creek's estuary makes squishing through the muck in hipboots unnecessary.

To enjoy this unusual walk, head south from San Francisco on U.S. Route 101 (Bayshore Freeway). Take the Embarcadero Road turnoff northeast, past Ming's restaurant, the Palo Alto Municipal Golf Course, the duck pond and the Palo Alto Yacht Club. Park by the yacht harbor on Sand Point near the confluence of Mayfield and Charleston Sloughs.

There on stilts in the marsh will be a handsome contemporary building faintly suggestive of docks and duck blinds, with the sign "Baylands Nature Interpretive Center." Designed by architect Jan Stypula of Spencer, Lee and

Busse, this unusual civic building won an American Institute of Architects award not long after it opened in December, 1969. Go through the maze of pier pilings that comprise the hiker's stile, follow the levee about a hundred feet and enter the center. Here, near the office of Larry White, director of Palo Alto's Nature and Science Department, surely unique among civic offices, one will find a saltwater aquarium, changing exhibits in a small museum, and possibly a film in progress or a guided tour taking off. Stop in the office to pick up a copy of the blue booklet for a self-guided boardwalk tour with its map, oddly like a steelyard scale. Then go out the rear door of the Center to reach the railed boardwalk that leads off toward the southern end of San Francisco Bay.

Small wedges on the map represent not the concrete PG&E pilings visible in the distance, but stations of natural life. Station 1, for example, centers on pickleweed, *Salicornia virginica*, the succulent and edible plant which dominates the intertidal zone of the salt-marsh. In the fall it turns from pale green to rich red. Station 2 is a place to look for the rare and endangered clapper rail, which looks chubby as a chicken from the side, thin as a stringbean head-on. Come out at twilight or dusk and you may hear his call, which sounds like a Zen priest clapping two boards together.

Halfway out on either side, one reaches an unrailed catwalk under the PG&E powerpoles, warning that one heads out on it at one's own risk. Unless you are agile, stay on the railed boardwalk. Along this route, one soon reaches Station 3 and the Pacific cordgrass *Spartina foliosa* which looks like minature corn and actually gives a higher food yield than any midwestern cornfield. Spartina is the number one food plant for the life chain of the marsh. As it decays, microscopic protozoa eat the nutrients, later to be eaten themselves by shellfish and worms who are then digested by fish and water birds, which in turn feed larger birds, seals, you and me, and our fellow consumers.

From Station 5, the observation platform at the end, the views are spectacular. Dumbarton Bridge lies to the northeast. The two white spots across the bay are Mount

Hamilton's Lick Observatory. Moffet Field's hangar, home of the old blimps, is the unmistakable shape to the south. Sometimes the wind caresses the grasses, making it look like waves except where the orange patches of dodder have rusted down to the mud below.

To enjoy the sweet serenity of this wilderness, sit awhile before heading back. If you have time, a companion levee walk takes off in another direction from the Center, and along that walk one may also spot another endangered species, the red-bellied harvest mouse.

Index